Obvious Murder

The March From Abortion to Infanticide

Kenneth Paul Fye, Ph.D.

ISBN-13: 978-1523820122
ISBN-10: 1523820128

"What hast thou done? the voice of thy brother's blood crieth unto me from the ground."

Genesis 4:10

Cover Image: Leonard da Vinci *Study of the Fetus in the Womb*

Contents

Introduction

In the years since Philadelphia doctor Kermit Gosnell and his colleagues were charged with eight counts of murder including the death of his patient Karnamaya Mongar, and seven unnamed newborn infants. Gosnell was convicted of murdering three of the infants and sentenced to life in prison without parole. Despite the sensational nature of the serial killings of newborn babies, the actual number of which were estimated as being in the hundreds, the trial gained little notoriety. It's been suggested that the lack of media interest stemmed from the fact that an abortionist was on trial for performing what were understood by him (and others) to be abortions. This is plausible speculation. The fact remains that Gosnell and his clinic staff failed to recognize that killing a child once outside the womb no longer constitutes abortion. That act is homicide, and punishable as such. Gosnell called his post birth procedures "ensuring fetal demise".

From the standpoint of the law once a child has exited the birth canal, it is born, and no longer "eligible" for an abortion. Nothing in the 1973 Roe decision withdrew the protection of homicide laws from children who are outside the womb. This was, after all, the sole reason for the legal fiction of "partial birth abortion". If you leave the head in, then it's *technically* still an abortion, not child murder. Gosnell assumed incorrectly that skipping this seemingly absurd step still entitled him to ensure the demise of a human being.

Onc can see how confusing this can be. Babies born prematurely look exactly like babies, only smaller. Pennsylvania's abortion law prohibits abortions after 24 weeks, and many times with proper neonatal care a baby can survive at that early stage of development. A 23 week old fetus looks exactly like a 24 week old baby, and with improvements in medical technology will likely have about as good a chance at surviving, assuming it has its mother's permission to live.

Gosnell wasn't just performing abortions on pre-24 week babies; many were well past that stage. Curiously, he listed many of

5

these as being 24½ weeks development, apparently assuming he wouldn't get in trouble over a mere three and a half days. That was just for the official paperwork. His actual fudge factor was a good deal longer that half a week. Gosnell noted and commented on this occasionally observing that one was "big enough to walk me to the bus stop." An individual that well developed and outside the womb is clearly a legal person even by the standards of the Roe Court, and everyone in Gosnell's clinic should have known that. What clouded their minds and consciences was the ideology of abortion.

This is the ideology that allows activists to imagine that the "Born Alive Infants Protection Act" was a violation of abortion rights. The same ideology allows them to complain that requiring abortion clinics to have the same standards of medical cleanliness and safety as any other medical facility is all about harming women's health instead of protecting it.

When Texas, reacting to the news of the Gosnell clinic, tried to enact safety standards that would have at least prevented the grotesque conditions found in the Gosnell case, hordes of out of state feminists took over the Senate galleries and rioted causing Senate business to be delayed until after the session deadline, and preventing the bill's passage. The Texas Senate reconvened a few weeks later and passed the measure handily.

The purpose of the abortion ideology and the abortion law it supports is to allow individuals (not just women) to freely engage in sexual activity without consequence. Since pregnancy is a sometime result of sexual activity, the guarantee of legal abortion provides a last minute stopgap to the consequences free love. A willingness to avoid sexual activity, or to raise any children conceived would eliminate the need for a Supreme Court ruling guaranteeing a "right" to abortion. In other words, it's all about having fun without responsibility.

The premise of this book is that as a *child* is created at conception, there can be no such right. The child is distinct from the mother. One can die while the other lives; each is a separate life, a different person. An abortion kills an innocent person. We have a

6

word for this. The word is murder. No one can have a right to murder any more than anyone can have a right to own slaves.

This is something everyone really knows. The life of a human being begins at the beginning: at conception. If it doesn't begin there, it doesn't begin anywhere and none of us are human.

Prologue
Zygote, Embryo, Fetus

"Is the babe young? When I behold it, it seems more venerable than the oldest man."
Henry David Thoreau

In April 1999, photographer Michael Clancy created a sensation with a photograph of a 21 week old baby named Samuel Armas. Little Samuel was born 4 months later. Many pro-choice advocates called the picture a fake. The only real question is whether Samuel grabbed the doctor's finger or whether it was the other way around. The image itself is real enough. The physician in question is Dr. Joseph Bruner who was performing surgery on Samuel to correct his spina bifida while Samuel was still in his mother's womb. Since babies as early as 21 weeks development (and likely earlier) are perfectly capable of feeling pain they are routinely anesthetized along with their mothers for surgery. Some doctors who perform this kind of intrauterine surgery also do abortions sometimes on the same day, one in the morning, one in the afternoon.

One can imagine the disconnect. What must be in the doctor's mind as he walks down the hall form one operating theater to another is something that must be hard to grasp. Consider another case.

Robert P. George and Christopher Tollefsen began their book *Embryo: A Defense of Human Life,*[1] with a story. During 2005's Hurricane Katrina, ten Illinois and Louisiana officers risked their lives in flat-bottomed boats to rescue Noah Benton Markham from a flooded New Orleans hospital where he and others were stranded. What made this particular heroic rescue stand out from all the others

---

[1] Robert P. George and Christopher Tollefsen, *Embryo: A Defense of Human Life,* (New York, NY: Doubleday, 2008).

was the nature of the individuals they saved. Noah and 1400 others were at the time embryos frozen in liquid nitrogen waiting implantation in their mothers' wombs. Noah was subsequently implanted and was born on January 16, 2007.[2]

Indeed, the authors note, the only thing that makes Noah different from many other children is the unusual circumstance of the rescue that saved him very early in his life. They also note that later in life, when Noah is asked (as he certainly will be) who was saved that day, his only possible answer will be "I was". That embryo *was* Noah Markham, even though his parents hadn't named him yet; he was the same human being that he now is, and will continue to be until he dies.

There is near universal agreement among embryologists that every human life begins at conception. It is at that moment of fertilization that the sperm and the egg unite and change radically from two separate entities into a completely new one, a new human being. This new entity then begins to grow and develop under its own internal set of rules along a predetermined path that will not end until it dies, in an abortion, as a toddler or teenager in a tragic accident, or as an octogenarian from old age. Throughout that time, it will be the same human person.

The new embryo is a new being, one which may die while its mother lives, or whose mother may die while it survives. It is a separate life, a separate being, even though contained within the mother's body. This new being is the product of the natural human reproductive process; it's how humans propagate their species. It has its own separate DNA profile, derived from its parents, but

---

[2] Ibid. p. 1.

nevertheless uniquely its own. As we will have reason to repeat, more than once, *"any being that is human, is a human being."* [3]

While there are many who will claim (without thinking about it much) that no one knows when a human life beings, it's closer to the truth to note that just about everybody knows when a human life begins. Nearly every embryology textbook that has a page on the subject will reaffirm that fact.

In 1981 United States Senate judiciary subcommittee took the following testimony from medical experts (Subcommittee on Separation of Powers to Senate Judiciary Committee S-158, Report, 97th Congress, 1st Session, 1981):

> *"It is incorrect to say that biological data cannot be decisive...It is scientifically correct to say that an individual human life begins at conception."* [4]

> *"I have learned from my earliest medical education that human life begins at the time of conception."* [5]

> *"After fertilization has taken place a new human being has come into being. [It] is no longer a matter of taste or opinion...it is plain experimental evidence. Each individual has a very neat beginning, at conception."* [6]

---

[3] Hadley Arkes et al, "The Inhuman Use of Human Beings" A Statement on Embryo Research by the Ramsey Colloquium, *First Things,* (January 1995).
[4] Professor Micheline Matthews-Roth, Harvard University Medical School.
[5] Dr. Alfred M. Bongioanni, Professor of Pediatrics and Obstetrics, University of Pennsylvania.
[6] Dr. Jerome LeJeune, Professor of Genetics, University of Descartes.

"By all the criteria of modern molecular biology, life is present from the moment of conception."[7]

"The beginning of a single human life is from a biological point of view a simple and straightforward matter – the beginning is conception."[8]

If it is true (and it demonstrably is true) that the zygote/embryo/fetus is a human being, then it follows that an abortion, any and *every* abortion, kills a human being; an *innocent* human being, if we may speculate.

Despite all claims to the contrary, this is not a matter of factual or scientific doubt. It hasn't been for a very long time. In 1859 the AMA published a position paper opposing abortion and calling for its universal criminalization. The reasoning was largely based on "the independent and actual existence of the child before birth, as a living being." The report described abortion as "the slaughter of countless children", and an "unnecessary and unjustifiable destruction of human life."[9]

More recently, but prior to Roe (so there can be no excuse for the Roe Court not to have known about it) is a 1970 editorial in *California Medicine*, stating plainly that "The result has been a curious avoidance of the scientific fact, which everyone really knows, that human life begins at conception and is continuous whether intra- or extra-uterine until death."[10]

---

[7] Professor Hymie Gordon, Mayo Clinic.

[8] Dr. Watson A. Bowes, University of Colorado Medical School.

[9] AMA Report on Criminal Abortion, 1859.

[10] "A New Ethic for Medicine and Society" *California Medicine: The Western Journal of Medicine*, (113, no. 3, 1970), pp. 67-68.

Curiously the Supreme Court itself in 2007 seemed to recognize what everyone else had by that time regarded as obvious that "...by common understanding and scientific terminology, a fetus is a living organism while within the womb, whether or not it is viable outside the womb."[11]

---

[11] US Supreme Court, Gonzales v. Carhart, 550 U.S. 124 (2007).

Preface
Inversion of Good and Evil

"And all the Arts of Life they changed into the Arts of Death."
William Blake[12]

Marxist ideology swept the world in the 20th century. While official communism has come and gone in several countries there is an intellectual remnant for the left everywhere in the desire to see all things in terms of power.[13] This is what we mean when we say that the personal is political. What the French called "deconstructionist" philosophy set out the intellectual framework for modern Marxist liberalism/progressivism in the 1960's. Oddly, this is a liberalism that is not about liberty, and a progressivism that makes no progress. Decades later, liberals who have never heard of deconstructionism have long since absorbed, as if by osmosis, the fundamental talking points. The result is a shameless refusal to engage the merits of any argument in preference for an attack on character. "Oh, you're just defending the rich white power structure" is the handy response to any and all comers regardless of content.

We call this "identity politics"; a politics that is skin color deep and no more; or perhaps skin color/gender deep. Even these identities are decided by questions of political power. Thus women who oppose abortion aren't really "women", African-Americans who oppose affirmative action aren't really "black", and Hispanics who oppose illegal immigration aren't really "Hispanic". On this reasoning Barack Obama isn't really the "first black president", Bill Clinton is.

---

[12] *"Jerusalem: The Emanation of the Giant Albion"* 1804.
[13] Roger Scruton, *Modern Culture*, (New York, NY: Continuum Press, 2006).

So we see words like "truth" and "love" are placed in ever-present scare quotes that have nothing to do with the old use-mention distinction. Scare quotes are a way of distancing us from the conventional meaning of words, as if to say "so-called 'truth'" or "so-called 'beauty'", or everyone's favorite, so called "reality".

While this might have been limited to the *written* word, the common habit of using finger quotes (first two fingers of both hands raised in a simultaneous scratching motion) has permitted the practice to become universal. All serious questions are now with a level of irony once only available to ignorant college sophomores, which was why those in the know viewed the attitude as *sophomoric*. Now, of course, we'd be obligated to view it as merely "sophomoric".

British philosopher Roger Scruton calls for a theological understanding of culture along the lines discussed by Alain Besançon in his *Century of Horrors*.[14] Besançon noted that both forms of socialism, National Socialism (Nazism) and Bolshevik Socialism (Leninist/Stalinist Communism) were equally criminal, perhaps because they were equally secular. Both the Nazis and the Communists regarded their own project as a form of philanthropy; each assumed they were providing humanity a service by exterminating large numbers of people.

Binding and Hoche began their theoretical justification for "permission to destroy life unworthy of life" as a medicinal and humanitarian enterprise. That the phrase in German "*lebensunwertes Leben*" became a Nazi designation for those individuals deemed to be non-persons devoid of the usual right to live doesn't mean that the idea was limited to Germany. It was as useful a concept to the rest of

---

[14] Alain Besançon, *A Century of Horrors*, (Wilmington, DE: Intercollegiate Studies Institute, 2007).

the left, particularly in Communist regimes as it was to National Socialism; much too useful a device to do without.

Numerically, it has garnered its greatest expression in the post-Nazi, world. 55 million non-persons have been killed in the United States alone since the 1970's. In Communist China the figure is closer to 400 million for the same time period.[15] Worldwide, one can only guess at the total. Over a billion is likely.

Such extraordinary numbers can only be achieved by reducing people to non-persons. Modern society is providing more evidence of this; as if more were needed. The "personhood" discussion so popular in academia, is not being conducted in full sight of the general populace. The average person is blissfully unaware of the judgment of experts in bioethics linking the "abortable" fetus with the equally abortable newborn. The PR apparatus of the university swings into full damage control mode when news of it is leaked to the outside world. Personhood theory hasn't been finessed enough for public consumption but it will be soon enough. As usual, the ideology divides humanity into two separate and unequal groups, persons and non-persons.

It is delusional to imagine that the class of "non-persons" can be limited to a small number. On the contrary, it will be an ever-expanding one, as centralized governments (the overwhelming norm for governments world-wide) seek ways to expand their influence. As Jefferson noted more that two centuries ago, the general tendency for government is always to expand its power, never to contract it. As the underclass of non-persons expands from the fetus to the newborn to the elderly and the handicapped, to the merely undesirable, the power of the state will also expand, as by its nature it must. It will eventually include the power of life and death over its

---

[15] National Population and Family Planning Commission of the Peoples Republic of China.

subjects (we can no longer call them citizens). The power of life and death is too useful a tool for any tyranny to do without. Ours will be no exception.

As intellectuals look for ways to expand *their* influence outside their own fields of expertise, they gravitate to bioethics studies departments where radical ideas for improving on 3000 years of ethical wisdom are encouraged and even required for admittance to the new social elites. Professional intellectuals are those whose only "product" is thinking. Under usual circumstances they can't expect to have much in the way of social or political influence. So the temptation of the intellectual is always to ally with a political creed and to borrow influence from the alliance. There is always interest on the loan.

Thus we get thinkers like Martin Heidegger, Carl Schmitt, or Ezra Pound who became Nazis or fascists, or Sartre and Marcuse who became communists. The seductions of power were too much for these all too ordinary people to resist, and they all found themselves defending mass murder.

In such a world, evil becomes good, and the reverse must also be true; good becomes evil. When the moral inversion is complete, Marxists and other liberals defend mass murder. Some even find themselves calling Beethoven's monumental description of Joy and the brotherhood of humankind in his final 9th Symphony as the "murderous rage of a rapist".[16]

---

[16] Susan McClary, *Minnesota Composers Forum Newsletter*, (January, 1987).

Born Alive Infant Destruction
The Mill

"And was Jerusalem builded here
Among these dark Satanic mills?"
William Blake

In January of 2011, Kermit Gosnell was indicted for multiple murders for the way he ran an abortion mill in Philadelphia, Pennsylvania. For years city and state officials looked the other way, no doubt claiming they had no knowledge of such things, oversight agencies repeatedly "stumbled upon and should have shut down" Gosnell's operation (known as the Women's Medical Society) but instead did nothing.

Pennsylvania Governor Ed Rendell said he was "flabbergasted to learn that the Department of Health did not think their authority to protect public health extended to clinics offering abortion services". In fact, by policy set up by his predecessor Tom Ridge, they didn't. It was the Republican Ridge administration that set a policy of no regular inspections of abortion clinics, and the state policy lasted until Gosnell's clinic was discovered (or re-discovered) by "accident" and at long last terminated.

The bill of Bill of Presentment and the Report issued by the grand jury makes for depressing reading. For the type of late term abortions that Gosnell specialized in, the preferred procedure is to induce labor. In many cases, this results in a live birth, i.e. a living human being, who, if the "abortion" is to be completed, would then have to be killed. This was accomplished by cutting the baby's spinal cord with scissors. The Report noted one employee played with the victim for 20 minutes while it thrashed about on the counter before killing it.

The grand jury made it plain that the "neglect" by public officials of this and other abortion facilities was not from laziness or by accident, but was a deliberately arrived at policy. The State knew perfectly well what was going on in the clinic but deliberately pretended not to know.

> *"Indeed, the department has shown an utter disregard both for the safety of women who seek treatment at abortion clinics and for the health of fetuses after they have become viable. State health officials have also shown a disregard for the laws the department is supposed to enforce. Most appalling of all, the Department of Health's neglect of abortion patients' safety and of Pennsylvania laws is clearly not inadvertent:* It is by design."[17]

The clinic was in fact inspected at highly irregular intervals, in 1989 and 1992. The clinic's certificate of approval had long since expired in 1980. Reports of abortions filed by the staff left many sections unchecked including things like "post-operative care" and "anesthesia". Even so, state inspectors noted that there were "no deficiencies" at the clinic. In the mean time babies bodies were discovered to have been collected in jars (along with severed feet) for no imaginable reason.

There were complaints delivered to the Pennsylvania Department of Health by various attorneys for patients and the families of patients, including several women who died. The complaints were buried. Nothing was done.

Pennsylvania law does provide for oversight of abortion clinics as well as all other types of medical facilities. Only in the

---

[17] Report of County Investigating grand jury XXIII, First Judicial District Of Pennsylvania Criminal Trial Division, pp. 137-138. Emphasis in original.

case of abortion mills, however, was the law routinely ignored. The title for Section VI of the grand jury report was "How Did This Go On So Long?" The answer was obvious. The grand jury expressed its astonishment at the longevity of the problem. State connivance in the practices of the clinic were precisely *because* it was an abortion provider rather than providing another type of medical procedure, like, say mammograms, pap tests, electrocardiograms, cat scans, urine analysis, or colonoscopy.

The report of the grand jury opens as follows:

> *"This case is about a doctor who killed babies and endangered women. What we mean is that he regularly and illegally delivered live, viable, babies in the third trimester of pregnancy – and then murdered these newborns by severing their spinal cords with scissors. The medical practice by which he carried out this business was a filthy fraud in which he overdosed his patients with dangerous drugs, spread venereal disease among them with infected instruments, perforated their wombs and bowels – and, on at least two occasions, caused their deaths. Over the years, many people came to know that something was going on here. But no one put a stop to it."*[18]

In a section the grand jury called "Murder in plain sight" the report describes the "regulatory framework" that abortion clinics are supposed to adhere to, including parental consent for minors, a twenty-four hour waiting period, ultrasound to determine the age of the fetus (Pennsylvania law regulates abortions after twenty-four weeks), and so forth. The grand jury notes that ultrasounds in particular were regularly falsified to show a fetus at the legal limit when it was generally well beyond the legal age at which it could be killed. This presents a general technical problem in that babies as

---

[18] Ibid., Overview, p 1.

late as twenty-four weeks gestation are large and difficult to kill in the womb. The report describes the solution to the problem.

> *"Gosnell's approach, whenever possible, was to force full labor and delivery of premature infants on ill-informed women. The women would check in during the day, make payment, and take labor-inducing drugs. The doctor wouldn't appear until evening, often 8:00, 9:00, or 10:00 p.m., and only then deal with any of the women who were ready to deliver. Many of them gave birth before he even got there."*[19]

This procedure results in a live baby, a human being even under abortion law, which the grand jury says would then be summarily murdered. The report notes that Gosnell developed a euphemism for the practice; "ensuring fetal demise".

> *"The way he ensured fetal demise was by sticking scissors into the back of the baby's neck and cutting the spinal cord. He called that 'snipping.'"*[20]

The report's harshest language is not for the defendant, but for the State regulatory apparatus that was supposed to prevent this sort of thing.

> *"Pennsylvania is not a third-world country. There were several oversight agencies that stumbled upon and should have shut down Kermit Gosnell long ago. But none of them did...In the end, Gosnell was only caught by accident...Once law enforcement agents went in, they couldn't help noticing the disgusting conditions, the dazed patients, the discarded fetuses. That is why the complete regulatory collapse that*

---

[19] Ibid., p. 4.
[20] Ibid.

occurred here is so inexcusable. It should have taken only one look."[21]

The report was also clear as to the motivation for the "collapse". A collapse is generally an inadvertent event. We usually talk about the collapse of a building as an accident. This "collapse" of regulation was not an accident. It was deliberate.

"Instead, the Pennsylvania Department of Health abruptly decided, for political reasons, to stop inspecting abortion clinics at all. The politics in question were not anti-abortion, but pro. With the change of administration from Governor Casey to Governor Ridge, officials concluded that inspections would be "putting a barrier up to women" seeking abortions."[22]

It was only after the police and federal authorities went in looking not for abortions but for drugs, did the scandal compel limited press attention and thereafter, action by the state. The Pennsylvania Department of Health and the Department of State, as well as the City of Philadelphia Municipal Department of Public Health went out of their way to avoid erecting "barriers" to abortion. Both had known about the problem for years but chose to do nothing, lest action produce a "chilling effect" on women's "choice". This extended to ignoring reports that fetal remains were being stored in the "lunch refrigerator".

Even two local hospitals failed to report the complications from abortions at the clinic that they treated, and the National Abortion Federation inspector failed to report her findings.

The grand jury report makes it clear that the reason for the lack of oversight that lead to the deaths of countless babies without name

---

[21] Ibid., p. 9.
[22] Ibid.

or number as well as the death of at least two of their mothers was this. The facility that needed the oversight was an abortion mill and that creating any difficulties for it whatsoever would be "politically incorrect". The report overview noted is its recommendations section that the State Department of Health had created a loophole for all abortion clinics and that the hole needed to be plugged. Indeed, they said it would have been an improvement had the department paid as much attention to the storage of fetal remains and other "waste" as it did to "swimming pools and beauty parlors."[23] There are, of course, no Supreme Court declared constitutional rights to swimming pools and beauty parlors.

The report supplies a paper trail to other suspect abortion facilities by means of the testimony of employees regarding their previous places of employment, including the Delta Women's Clinic of Baton Rouge Louisiana. Delta had its own list of stories in the press, including allegations of "ties" to Dr. Kermit Gosnell. They have since stopped performing abortions, at least temporarily. The trail also lead to Atlantic Women's Services in Wilmington Delaware, where the Philadelphia grand jury report places Gosnell one day a week. Delaware had no routine inspection of abortion clinics.[24]

No grand jury investigations have materialized yet for either facility, but the National Abortion Federation suspended the memberships of both clinics on advice of the district attorney.

The grand jury report also mentions what some call the "Mother's Day Massacre". This was a 1972 (and therefore pre-Roe v. Wade) "experiment, which seriously and permanently maimed

---

[23] Ibid., p. 17

[24] Wendy Saltzman "Delaware abortion clinic facing charges of unsafe and unsanitary conditions" 6ABC Action News Philadelphia, PA. April 10, 2013.

several women".[25] It involved an invention by one Harvey Karman that Karman called a "super coil", in reality a ball of sharp spring loaded plastic blades and balsa wood inserted into a woman's uterus for the purposes of shredding the fetus. In practice, several such coils would be inserted. Before the Supreme Court's 1973 ruling that legalized abortion nationwide, the search for a simple "do-it-yourself" procedure that women could do on their own in the second trimester was something of a quest for feminists looking for ways to subvert the law in the privacy of their own homes.

Karman (the inventor of the Karman cannula, an abortion curette still in use) ran an illegal abortion ring in the 1950's, and was an icon of the "self help" abortion movement; he spent two years in prison after a woman died in 1955 from one of his procedures performed in a California hotel room. The tool of choice in that procedure was a nutcracker. Governor Jerry Brown pardoned Karman upon taking office. Karman was also a 1970's activist and participated in the First West Coast Abortion Conference of 1973.

Karman had tested his coil on several hundred Bangladeshi rape victims at the invitation of the Bangladesh Government and the International Planned Parenthood Federation. Most of the patients were between the ages of 10 and 16. "Those women suffered a high rate of complications."[26]

Karman also trained illegal abortionists in the illegal "Jane" abortion ring (also known as the *Abortion Counseling Service of Women's Liberation*) in Chicago. In 1972 the Jane offices were raided by police, and Jane activists (those who hadn't been arrested) needed a place for Karman to perform further tests of his coil method of abortion. Kermit Gosnell volunteered his services in Philadelphia and a group of 15 of Jane's clients were bussed to

---

[25] Grand Jury Report, p. 98.
[26] Ibid. p. 97.

Gosnell's clinic, which even then was providing illegal abortions. None of the women had been told of the highly experimental nature of the procedure they were about to be subjected to. At Karman's invitation a public television station sent a crew to film the procedures for a documentary to be shown on a New York public television station.

At least nine of the women experience complications from the experiment, three were hospitalized, one required a hysterectomy.

Karman who passed away in 2008, is now remembered mostly as a "reproductive health pioneer". The Jane Collective has been remembered in a hagiography, *The Story of Jane* by Laura Kaplan.[27] Gosnell himself left the country for a period and was never charged in the incident. After Roe v. Wade made abortion legal he returned to his practice.

> *"The Pennsylvania Board of Medicine ignored his role in this grotesquely unsuccessful experiment, which seriously and permanently maimed several women. The Board overlooked Gosnell's unprofessional conduct not only in the 1970s but for the next three decades, as he continued to employ unlicensed workers to practice medicine at his clinic, and as his patients continued to suffer serious injuries or worse during abortion procedures."[28]*

The chief counsel for the Pennsylvania Department of Health, Christine Dutton is quoted by the report as defending her agency's inaction with the phrase, "People die."

Yes, they do.

In at least one Philadelphia, Pennsylvania abortion mill they

---

[27] Laura Kaplan, *The Story of Jane: The Legendary Underground Feminist Abortion Service,* (New York, NY: Pantheon Books, 1995).
[28] Grand Jury Report, p. 98.

died as if Pennsylvania were a third world country.

The only real difference between "legendary abortion underground" activists, "reproductive health pioneers" and pre- Roe v. Wade back alley abortionists appears to be the difference between a nutcracker and a coat hanger; and a Supreme Court decision.

In Gosnell's case, there's no record of either instrument because most of his "abortions" weren't really abortions at all. The grand jury report describes murders of individuals who were even by Roe v. Wade legal standards human persons. As the report outlines it, the usual procedure was to have untrained unlicensed staff (including one teenager working evenings after high school) administering doses of heavy medication and labor inducing drugs. The patient would then remain for as long as nine hours semi-conscious during which time the labor inducing drugs caused their babies to be delivered into toilets (among other receptacles), which were cleaned about once a week. Gosnell termed these births, "precipitations".

Pennsylvania has its analogue to the federal Born-Alive Infants Protection Act as part of its Abortion Control Act. It is against the law to kill a baby that is outside the womb if it shows signs of life such as breathing, heartbeat, movement, pulsating umbilical cord. Killing these babies was such standard procedure in the Gosnell clinic that the grand jury couldn't estimate the number of them.

They are only remembered by such names as "Baby Boy A", whose neck was cut. After being stuffed in a shoebox, which was too small for him, the baby continued to move. According the report this is a sign of both life and extreme pain. The child was about at 32 weeks, which accounts for its large size when it was killed. Other babies who "precipitated" before the doctor showed up would lie in basins moving and crying until the doctor came to cut their spinal cords. Staff who questioned what they saw were told that the movements weren't signs of life but just muscle reactions.

The process that the staff usually called "snipping" the neck to sever the spinal cord isn't as simple as it sounds. A late term baby has a sizable vertebral column which is a hard bony structure ill suited to cutting with scissors or other snips. Usually extreme pressure would have to be applied to completely sever the vertebrae. As the spinal column is the central bundle of nerves conducting signals to the brain, cutting it in this difficult fashion can be expected to produce agony in the victim. All signs of heartbeat, breathing, and pulsation in babies before they were killed in this fashion were dismissed as "spontaneous movement".

Some staff (most of whom plead guilty) would also take over the process of killing the babies when Gosnell wasn't present to do it himself. One "Baby C" had been living moving and breathing for 20 minutes before Gosnell's colleague Lynda Williams (who plead guilty to third-degree murder)[29] played with the baby briefly before slitting its neck.

As Gosnell specialized in late term abortions beyond the legal limit of 24 weeks which predictably resulted in viable babies, who were precipitated from the wombs of their drugged out mothers and killed at the doctor's convenience. The standard operating procedure

> "...required the clinic's unequipped staff to manage a clinic full of sedated patients who were thrown into full labor, and then to 'deal' with whatever precipitated, including live babies – all while the doctor was at home, or jogging, or working at a clinic in Wilmington."[30]

---

[29] "Dr. Kermit Gosnell's employees saw few options, three have plead guilty to third-degree murder", Maryclaire Dale, Associated Press, WPTV 04/12/2013.
[30] Grand Jury Report. p. 105.

Since Gosnell would often use a suction device to evacuate and collapse the skull after severing the spinal cord, his procedure bore a similarity to the type of late term abortion known as partial birth abortion, which has been against federal law since 2007. In such a procedure a doctor will leave the baby's head inside the mother when he cuts the spinal cord and then suction the skull contents to collapse it, thus making it easier to remove. Gosnell's only modification was to remove the baby completely first, thereby destroying the legal fiction of partial birth abortion. This also produced not a "fetus", but a live legally human being with its own right to life (and, if we may speculate, liberty and the pursuit of happiness). One grand jury witness tried to pass off the standard procedure of delivering live viable babies and killing them outside the womb as just a form of partial birth abortion. One can understand the confusion. There was, of course, no particular reason to suction the skull *after* killing the baby, but then there was no reason to keep large numbers of fetal feet in the lunch refrigerator either.

The medical necessity for partial birth abortion has been questioned, but part of its rationale was to make access to the baby's head easier. Since so many of Gosnell's patients precipitated their babies onto the floor or a toilet, one has to conclude that they couldn't have been difficult to remove at that stage.

After eight or nine hours of promethazine, Demerol, nalbuphine, diazepam, (to alleviate pain or induce unconsciousness) and Cytotec (the clinic's drug of choice to induce labor) babies would fall out on their own to be killed by Gosnell or one of his colleagues. When asked how often they had seen this, witnesses repeatedly said "hundreds of times".

The report makes note of only two deaths of adult patients (it seems inconceivable that there weren't more) and names only one of them, Karnamaya Mongar. Mrs. Mongar was a refugee from Nepal who spoke no English. The grand jury describes the process of aborting her baby by the staff in Gosnell's employ. They administered extremely large doses of anesthetic, primarily Demerol, and left her unmonitored for a period of hours. Normally a level of general anesthetic would have to be administered by two doctors, one of them a specialist in anesthesiology; then the patient would have to have her vital signs continuously monitored. According to the report, the dose of drugs was well above what would have been required, and was administered by an untrained ill-equipped staff. The Demerol dose was itself fatal and Mrs. Mongar was dead before paramedics were even called, several hours too late. Pennsylvania law requires the approval and supervision of at least two physicians for all late term abortions. Gosnell worked alone.

All this was so studiously ignored by a cornucopia of state agencies over such a long period of time that it can only have been deliberate. As we've seen, the report notes that "it was by design". Since, as the report also noted, nail salons and swimming pools get better oversight the inevitable conclusion is that the design of the neglect was to protect the sacred cow of abortion. This was a clinic, which had been in operation since before abortion clinics were legal. Gosnell's participation in the Mother's Day 1972 publicity stunt, with Harvey Karman, the Jane Collective, and a New York Public Television station that went so horribly awry was a pre-Roe v. Wade event.

The Supreme Court's decision to legalize abortion was said to, in part, protect women from the depredations of "back alley" abortionists and their "coat hanger" methods. Abortion activists and their supporters in journalism have claimed that illegal abortions caused as many as 10,000 deaths a year before the Roe decision. This number has been so sufficiently debunked that few still take it seriously. Still, it was part of the lobbying campaign to get the courts to legalize what legislatures were unwilling to do. The CDC reported less than one hundred deaths from abortion in 1972.[31]

Prior to Roe, some states had legalized abortion on their own and in the rest, illegal abortions were usually done by a competent physician. In 1955 Planned Parenthood estimated that 90% of abortions were performed by doctors with about 2% being self performed and another 8% being done by non-professionals, like the Jane Collective or Harvey Karman. Well before Roe, abortion was a relatively safe procedure, unless you were unfortunate enough to be in the hands of radical abortion advocates who were more interested in propaganda than safe medical practice.

What no one has apparently considered is how many deaths of women were caused, not by back alley butchers, but by abortion activists, at least in one case, in front of TV cameras. No one is known to have died in Gosnell's clinic on Mother's Day 1972 (other than around 15 luckless babies) but Roe did nothing to improve the quality of care delivered by Gosnell, Karman, and the Jane collective. That remained unchanged in its back alley nature for 40 years, coat hangers and nutcrackers notwithstanding.

The grand jury report told one heartening story amid the chaos of brutality.

> *"We learned of another illegal, third-trimester abortion only because the mother changed her mind. In 2004, a 27-year-old woman went to Gosnell, pregnant with her first child. She testified that she was surprised when Gosnell told her she was 21 weeks pregnant. On the first day of what was to be a two-day procedure, Gosnell inserted dilators in the woman's cervix. After Gosnell had finished inserting the laminaria, the*

---

[31] Centers for Disease Control Abortion Surveillance Annual Summary 1972.

woman asked him what happened to the babies after they were aborted. She testified that Gosnell told her they were burned.

At home, thinking over how Gosnell disposed of the fetuses, the woman had a change of heart. She called her cousin and the cousin called Gosnell to tell him that they wanted him to take the laminaria out. Gosnell said that he could not do that once the procedure was started. And he did not want to return the $1,300 that the patient had already paid. The pregnant woman ended up going to the Hospital at the University of Pennsylvania to have the laminaria removed. It was determined at the hospital that she was 29 weeks pregnant. A few days later, the 27-year-old delivered a premature baby girl. She was treated at Children's Hospital of Philadelphia and is today a healthy kindergartener."[32]

This little girl was by mere chance given a chance at life that was systematically denied to hundreds of others. In the end, the dead, Baby Boy A, Baby C, bear witness to the living.

It took about a year for the trial to proceed to its conclusion. One of Gosnell's associates, not named in the press release, has finished the assigned prison term and changed sides in the abortion debate.

A priest, Father Frank Pavone of Priests for Life, has asked for the bodies of the remaining Gosnell babies so as to give them a proper burial and funeral.[33]

---

[32] Grand Jury Report, pp. 86-87.
[33] Steven Ertelt, "Medical Examiner Still Refuses Proper Burial for Babies Kermit Gosnell Killed", *Life News*, July 15, 2013.

In Texas a new law banning abortions after 20 weeks was enacted and signed by the governor, despite disturbances in the Texas late night legislative session (that are probably best described as a riot) prevented the first attempt to pass the law. The new statute also requires abortion clinics to abide by the same safety standards as other medical facilities. All this is in direct response to the Gosnell controversy. So, large numbers of abortion defenders are willing to be bussed to another state to disrupt the democratic process, by whatever means necessary[34], to maintain the right to keep Gosnell style clinics just as they are. At least in Texas they failed.

Post Gosnell

Kermit Gosnell's murder trial ended in May of 2013.[35] After about two weeks of deliberation, the jury in the case returned a verdict of guilty on three counts of first-degree murder and more than 200 other lesser counts including infanticide, involuntary manslaughter, and racketeering.[36] He has been sentenced to life in prison. There is continuing speculation about the degree to which the stories about the Gosnell clinic are typical of the abortion industry as a whole, specifically in the late term abortion industry.

Any abortion clinic that specializes, as Gosnell did, in late term abortions will be killing babies that are to one degree or another viable by modern medical standards. In a recent interview a Washington D.C. abortionist estimated that at his clinic a baby that

---

[34] "Texas State Troopers Confiscate Suspected Feces, Urine, Other Items Ahead Of Abortion Bill Vote", *The Huffington Post,* July 12, 2013.

[35] Also on trial was clinic employee Eileen O'Neill, charged with engaging in "corrupt practices". She was convicted of conspiracy and theft by deception.

[36] Joseph A. Slobodzian, "Gosnell guilty of three murder counts" *The Philadelphia Inquirer*, May 13, 2013.

survives an abortion attempt might have "only" a 20 or 30 percent chance of surviving, if it were transported immediately to a hospital.

On April 28, 2013 Live Action Films[37] published a "sting" undercover film of abortionist Dr. Cesare Santangelo describing his own clinic's policy of "not helping" a delivered baby survive. In local Virginia hospitals, he noted, their policy would be to abide by the terms of the "Born Alive Infants Protection Act" and give all life saving care available to enable any baby to survive as long as possible. The "Health and Science" section of the *Washington Post* published the story on April 29, the day after the video was released. Nothing in the videos showed anything illegal, according to the Post.[38]

Some states have enacted restrictions on late term abortions in the wake of Federal Laws that have prohibited partial birth abortion, as well as the "Born Alive Infants Protection Act". Most of this was made possible only after Casey v. Planned Parenthood, loosened up the ability of states to regulate abortions. Pennsylvania requires two physicians to sign off on a late term abortion with the cut off time being 24 weeks. Even so, prosecutions for just the crime of late term abortion are rare in Pennsylvania or elsewhere. Actual regulation of the great mass of the iceberg, of which Gosnell is the small tip, seems unlikely.

In other news, the State of Ohio ordered another similar abortion clinic to shut down, a clinic which had a substantial string of violations.[39] Ohio found the clinic in violation of state law which requires a transfer agreement between a clinic specializing in

---

[37] http://www.liveaction.org/
[38] Sandhya Somashekhar, Lena H. Sun, and Alice Crites, "Antiabortion group releases videos of clinic workers discussing live births", *Washington Post*, April 29, 2013.
[39] "Abortion provider in Cuyahoga Falls being shut down", *Akron Beacon Journal*, April 24, 2013.

medical and surgical abortions and a local hospital to cover "medical complications emergency situations, and other needs as they arise".[40] During this time of operation they performed over a thousand abortions.

The University of Toledo agreed in August of 2012 to take on the clinic's emergency cases, and the clinic's license was not revoked. In April of 2013, the University notified the clinic that they would not be renewing the relationship. Nothing in all this prevented abortion enthusiasts from protesting the University's decision on this and another clinic, asking to "keep abortion safe and legal".[41] They missed the word "rare".

None of these folks, nor anyone of similar beliefs, ever protested the conditions in the Gosnell clinic, so one is left to wonder what they and their allies in government and the media might have done, had Gosnell been shut down for mere regulatory violations, instead of being charged with first-degree murder. The main stream media made only the slightest effort to attend, much less report on the Gosnell trial.

Absent a serious investigation, there's no way to know if the Ohio clinics were in any way as egregious in their violations as the Philadelphia clinic. Absent serious media attention, there won't be any investigation of any clinic at all, until the next Gosnell is discovered. His Women's Medical Society had been in operation for decades; he had been involved with the abortion movement since before Roe v. Wade. The empty chairs in the media gallery of the Philadelphia Courtroom tell us that it will be decades before we hear of another such case.

---

[40] Notice from Ohio Department of Health to Capital Care Network re: license number 0763AS, April 4, 2012.
[41] Kelly McLendon "50 rally for reinstatement of UTMC transfer agreements with abortion clinics", *Toledo Blade*, April 19, 2013.

Meanwhile, Planned Parenthood of Delaware has been "threatened" with investigation after a series of 911 calls from the clinic, and allegations from former employees. As there were *no routine* inspections required of abortion clinics in Delaware, there's no record of how long any of the alleged conditions might have been in effect.[42] The State will step in after a complaint, or series of complaints, to make an investigation, but since "inspections" are almost by definition routine by some sort of schedule to be effective, it follows that there were no genuine inspections of abortion facilities in Delaware. As of this writing this Planned Parenthood of Delaware clinic is the last surgical abortion clinic in Delaware and has been shut down. Delaware, for now, has no surgical abortion provider.

Meanwhile, in Mississippi, the state legislature passed a law in 2012 requiring all abortion clinic doctors to have admitting privileges at a local hospital. The Jackson Women's Health Organization is currently the only operating abortion clinic in the state, and neither of its doctors have the required standing. As is so often the case, a judge has ordered the law be delayed in its full effect, thereby keeping the last abortion clinic in Mississippi open. U.S. District Judge Daniel P. Jordan III has ruled that the clinic must be allowed to stay open for the time being to prevent a "patchwork system where constitutional rights are available in some states but not others."[43]

Such a system would be no different from what the country does with the administration of Second Amendment rights. State licenses are sometimes recognized by other states, and sometimes not. This provision of state licensing has never been challenged in

---

[42] Wendy Saltzman "Delaware abortion clinic facing charges of unsafe and unsanitary conditions," Action News WPVI-TV/DT (6ABC.com), April 10, 2013.

[43] "Judge rules Mississippi's only abortion clinic stays open for now" UPI.com April 16, 2013.

court. The abortion law that Judge Jordan ruled on may well be allowed to take effect in the near future, thereby making Mississippi the first state to be without any abortion facilities whatever.

There are those, of course, who claim that poor women were "driven" to Gosnell by lack of alternatives. Their solution: keep Roe v. Wade. Somehow, the multiple services available for abortion isn't enough to prevent the (apparently still prevalent) back alley abortions that were invoked to get Roe enacted in the first place. Even in the years just before Roe, as we've seen, there were never thousands of women at risk from "back alley" abortionists. Most abortions were done secretively in doctor's offices.

The real numbers of death from abortion complications (both legal and illegal) in the years prior to Roe were generally under one hundred a year. Mary Calderone, Planned Parenthood's Medical Director in the 1950's noted that by then abortion was no longer particularly dangerous, since even illegal abortions were usually done not by Karmans and Gosnells in back alley abortion mills but in doctors offices. She cited 260 deaths in the U.S. in 1957 a rate she regarded as "low".[44]

The most dangerous places women could go for an abortion, were the activist clinics run by Gosnell, Harvey Karman, and the illegal Jane Collective, which ceased operations after Roe. The real and dangerous back alley abortionists were in the movement to make abortion legal, if not necessarily safe and rare. Those abortion mills, and many more like them, are still largely in operation due to the willingness of "journalists" to sweep the grisly details of the industry under the rug, and liberal politicians' reluctance to regulate abortion.

As for Pennsylvania, the state legislature there has begun to

---

[44] Mary Steichen Calderone. M.D., "Illegal Abortion as a Public Health Problem " *American Journal of Public Health*, (VOL. 50. NO. 7, 1960), p. 949.

require stricter medical standards for clinics. Planned Parenthood of Southeastern Pennsylvania remodeled two of its clinics at a cost of $450,000. Local Planned Parenthood CEO Dayle Steinberg claimed that the regulations were merely a ruse to increase the cost of abortion. [45]

As a taxpayer supported billion dollar a year business Planned Parenthood shouldn't have any trouble affording it, especially since rooms for sterilization of equipment, and clean floors aren't really luxuries for any modern medical facility.

In any case the Gosnell trial has gotten so little publicity that many regard it as an urban legend and at least one wag suggested to Snopes.com that it be debunked. The debunking went the other way. Snopes rated the status of the story as "TRUE" while noting that the mainstream media had unaccountably failed to cover it. [46]

Why indeed *would* the mainstream media fail to cover such a "horrific story"? One may well wonder. Other mass killers don't have that problem, Jared Lee Loughner, Jeffrey Dahmer, James Eagen Holmes, the Tsarnaev Boston Marathon bombers, Ted Kaczynski, the Unabomber, never had any problem getting publicity. Usually, if a serial killer wants to get famous, that's no problem; the media will be all over it. Unless, of course, we're talking about abortion, in which case the story disappears so deep, some folks think it must be one of those urban legends, like bigfoot, sasquatch, UFO's, ghosts, vampires, chupacabras and the Jersey devil.

The *Atlantic* asked the Women's Medical Fund Executive Director Susan Schewel if they had ever dealt with Gosnell. Director Schewel replied "We had no idea -- no idea -- of how horrible things

---

[45] Jeff Brady "Pennsylvania Tightens Abortion Rules Following Clinic Deaths" *NPR* "All Things Considered" March 28, 2013.
[46] Snopes.com, April 12, 2013.

were there."[47] It shouldn't have been that hard. The regulation that needed to take place *couldn't*, by order of the Supreme Court of the United States. The Justices of the Court have "hobbled public health officials" for decades.[48] Since Roe, any doctor can challenge any regulation as an "unconstitutional burden." [49]

Evidence exists of other reckless abortionists, although few have ever been brought to justice. Florida clinics in Miami, Hialeah, and Miramar were still in operation after Gosnell despite run-ins with regulators and prosecutors. In the absence of clearly written and strictly enforced laws, an artifact of the post-Roe world, bringing to justice fraudulent, incompetent and sometimes homicidal abortionists is nearly impossible.[50] Bungled medical practices, including botched abortions, are often resolved in lawsuits and out of court settlements, but like the O.J. trials, these are a poor substitute for real justice.

Jillian Melchior's investigation for *National Review* reveals a long pattern of incorporation, legal dissolution, and re-establishment under new names for a string of "shady" clinics run by apparently equally shady characters just outside the reach of the law. The few sentences handed out have amounted to little more than probationary slaps on the wrists. Were Florida laws written with stronger regulation in mind, prosecution might not be so elusive. Hialeah Deputy Chief of Police Mark Overton simply noted that even "horrific procedures" are supported by Florida law. [51]

---

[47] Garance Franke-Rutam, "Kermit Gosnell and Intelligence Failures," *The Atlantic*, April 17 2013.

[48] Clark Forsythe, "The Supreme Court's Back Alley Runs Through Philadelphia," *The Weekly Standard*, January 24, 2011.

[49] Ibid.

[50] Jillian Kay Melchior, "Abortion's Underside (Kermit Gosnell is not the only seedy backroom abortionist operating in the age of Roe v. Wade)," *National Review Online*, May 8, 2013.

[51] Ibid.

For this we can thank the Supreme Court and its Roe/Doe/Casey decisions for creating an abortion culture that prefers to look away from the unseemly views and disgusting images that this culture gives rise to, lest they place obstacles in the path of "choice". A way should be found to force them to look.

Meanwhile the country's most prominent abortionist, Leroy Carhart (of Stenberg v. Carhart and Gonzales v. Carhart, partial birth abortion cases, both reaching the Supreme Court) has yet to shed the spotlight of controversy. The Maryland Department of Health and Mental Hygiene investigated Carhart in the death of one of his patients, Jennifer Morbelli in February 2013. Carhart is one of a handful of abortionists who are currently willing to take on the kind of very late term abortions that he became famous for in his two cases before the Supreme Court. Carhart does his late term abortions in Maryland, which has a liberal lack of regulations for abortions after 24 weeks. Morbelli was reportedly 33 weeks along at the time of her death, which has been confirmed to have been caused by "complications" from the abortion procedure.[52]

We know that Gosnell had connections with abortion providers in Wilmington, Delaware where he worked one day a week, and that his colleague, Eileen O'Neill had previously worked at a clinic in Baton Rouge Louisiana. Both Gosnell and O'Neill were further connected via the single owner of both clinics.

Minnesota, like Delaware has no routine inspection of abortion clinics, and most of the charges against Gosnell in Pennsylvania are not crimes in Minnesota.

The Gosnell verdict may cause others to be smoked out of the woodwork. There are a dozen or so abortion providers around the country being investigated for being the "next Kermit Gosnell".

---

[52] Shawn Cohen, "Coroner: Woman bled to death after late-term abortion," The (Westchester County, N.Y.) *Journal News*, February 21, 2013.

This includes a squelched investigation in Texas despite the testimony accompanied by gruesome photographs of aborted babies (one with its eyes wide open) provided by former clinic workers.[53]

Most of the other investigations will likely be shut down as well. The legal and political environment of the post Roe/Doe/Casey era doesn't permit much else. Even with Casey's slightly more permissive view on regulating the abortion industry (without which Gosnell could never have been charged) prosecutions of an industry that operates far beyond the range of district attorneys will continue to be a rarity. Even in states with similar laws to those of Pennsylvania the political will to take on such a hot potato is nil. Not even the lives of over a million innocents a year is enough to motivate the ruling class to investigate and prosecute. Of course, in some states it's not legal to prosecute abortionists for much of anything, but elsewhere, as in Texas, an available legal apparatus is evidently not quite enough. In any case more clinic workers are coming forward in various parts of the country, perhaps to avoid the fate of Gosnell's colleagues, and partly, no doubt, because a human conscience can only be deadened to a limited degree before turning its owner into an automaton.

As for the abortion industry itself, they cling to the notion that dangerous abortionists are the product of regulation, not its absence. The grand jury report itself put the lie to that idea, but that hasn't stopped abortion "rights" advocates from making the same claim they have for decades. It's now known that small numbers of women died from abortion complications in the years immediately prior to Roe due to the secretive nature of the then illegal procedure. Most were done quietly in doctor's offices. The more dangerous procedures of the day, the real "back alley" abortions were performed by doctors like Gosnell, Carman, and the Jane Collective;

---

[53] David Jennings, the *Houston Chronicle*, "Will Houston's version of Kermit Gosnell be investigated and charged?", May 15, 2013.

in other words, pro-abortion activists more interested in keeping alive their romance with Margaret Sanger-style political activism than the patient's safety. There have to be more of these types of abortionists now in the post Roe liberated world of low regulation and tolerance for sloppy clinic work than ever. After Roe, back alley abortions have gone mainstream. It's even possible that, due to absence of regulation, legal abortion today has become more dangerous to women than the coat-hangered "back alley" of 1972.

With this number of enablers, it is inconceivable that there aren't numbers of Gosnell type clinics scattered around the country, safe from the un-prying eyes of reporters, and exempt by Supreme Court order from the regulation given to hair salons. The Court has never ruled that hair-dos are a fundamental constitutional right. If they had, hair styling would be in the same unregulated back alley as abortion.

Abortion activists don't really care if abortion is safe or rare. They just want it to be legal and *cheap*; or better yet, free. "Free" means paid for by taxpayers. Like the abortion clinics that complained that being regulated into cleaning up their clinics was just an anti-choice ruse to force them out of business, NARAL et al seem to think that abortion is a "fate" caused by pregnancy. For them, the absence of legal abortion services (regardless of quality) will exchange one million abortions a year, for one million maternal deaths from abortion a year. Women will be "forced" not to apply their contraceptive regimens with greater care, but into the arms of a million Kermit Gosnells. Every person who thinks like this is an "enabler" to Kermit Gosnell and every "doctor" like him.

Generations of Imbeciles
The Court

"Three generations of imbeciles is enough."
Supreme Court Justice Oliver Wendell Holmes

When in January of 1973, Roe v. Wade took the issue of abortion out of the hands of the voters and placed it irrevocably in the hands of a tiny number of unelected officials, few really understood the truly radical nature of the decision. It was, if anything, more radical than the similar Dred Scott decision of 116 years earlier. Scott had sued under existing law to gain his freedom from slavery. The 1857 court ruled that blacks had no rights that the rest of the human race was obligated to respect, but it set no new precedent, it didn't create slavery or a new class of "sub-citizens". These existed already. It took a bloody war to eliminate them entirely.

The 1973 Court on the other hand, did create an entirely new class of human non-persons, and did not authorize their mere enslavement, but authorized their killing. Even this understates the nature of the political power grab that the Court undertook.

Many people have gotten into the habit of speaking of 1973 "when Roe v. Wade was passed". Technically Roe wasn't "passed" it was decided. Should it be undone, it won't be "repealed" it will be overturned. Only laws are passed and repealed. Supreme Court decisions aren't. But as often happens, the ordinary citizen has understood the nature of this beast better than political theoreticians.

To all practical purposes, the Court *did* "pass" Roe; it engaged in the process of legislation that from a constitutional point should have been left to Congress. It was perhaps the most extraordinary extension of judicial power in the history of the country. There have been 55 million human beings killed in

American abortion mills since. That they were human beings is no longer under serious debate; abortion advocates like to claim that while they may have been human they weren't "persons". Thus by Court ordered fiat we now have a permanent underclass of human beings who may be killed on the basis of whim and convenience.

The level of ignorance about this is still astonishing. Many people who claim they support the Roe v. Wade decision have never heard of a case known as Doe v. Bolton. For all legal intents and purposes the two are the same case. They were decided simultaneously, and were intended to be read as a single decision.

Many people think that the Court permitted abortion only in the first trimester or when the mother's heath is in danger, and if you only read the Roe decision *alone* that's what Roe says. While Roe overturned a Texas law, Doe v. Bolton overturned a similar Georgia statute.

It was the simultaneous Doe decision that broadened the ruling to include the entire pregnancy, and to define a woman's health so broadly as to permit abortion on demand at any time. "Health" became anything "relevant to the well-being of the patient". This combination of decisions overturned every abortion law in the country.[54] Justice Byron White, one of only two dissenting Justices (the other was William Rehnquist) wrote in his dissent,

> *"The Court simply fashions and announces a new constitutional right for pregnant women and, with scarcely any reason or authority for its action, invests that right with sufficient substance to override most existing state abortion statutes. The upshot is that the people and the legislatures of the 50 States are constitutionally disentitled to weigh the relative importance of the continued existence and*

---

[54] Clarke D. Forsythe, *Abuse of Discretion*, (New York, NY: Encounter Books, 2013), p. 10.

development of the fetus, on the one hand, against a spectrum of possible impacts on the woman, on the other hand. As an exercise of raw judicial power, the Court ...judgment is an improvident and extravagant exercise of the power of judicial review that the Constitution extends to this Court.[55]

"Raw judicial power" isn't the way one might normally want a decision of this magnitude rendered, but that was the destined outcome, and the court took a few years to lay the judicial groundwork, so they could hear the case.

In 1971 Younger v. Harris, which had nothing to do with abortion, decided questions of Federal court jurisdiction, which the Court felt had to come before deciding on Roe/Doe.[56] Having given themselves latitude as to which cases they could hear, they then proceeded to U.S. v. Vuitch, a case that did pertain directly to abortion, and contained the elements of their later decision. In fact, the Court agreed to hear Roe the day after they decided Vuitch. Milan Vuitch was a Washington D.C. abortionist who was being prosecuted under the District's anti-abortion statute. The statute prohibited abortions unless they were deemed necessary to protect the life and health of the mother. Vuitch sued claiming the law was unconstitutionally vague with respect to its definition of health.[57]

The Court ruled that the concept of heath was not vague and upheld the statute. The concept of health that the law contained was exceptionally general and included the concepts of both physical and psychological health (including emotional well being). One can see why Dr. Vuitch thought the definition was vague. In fact Judge Gerhard Gesell of the Federal District Court thought so too and ruled

---

[55] Justice Byron V. White, "Dissent in the Cases of Roe v. Wade and Doe v. Bolton" January 22, 1973.
[56] Forsythe, p. 19.
[57] Mary Meehan, "Justice Blackmun and the Little People" *Human Life Review*, (Summer 2004).

in his favor, for the first time striking down an anti-abortion law. This was the decision that the Supreme Court over-turned, reinstating the law and the conviction.[58]

Dr. Vuitch was astute enough to consider this decision a victory, since the Court in the process of validating his prosecution had called abortion a medical procedure. Medical procedures are generally left to the discretion of the attending physician.

Vuitch himself noted "This is a big step forward. Now the government lawyer will be in the position of challenging my medical decision. What are the jury members going to decide when a lawyer tries to tell them that the doctor is wrong about a medical matter?" Thus the Supreme Court upheld the law while making it harder to enforce.

The Court needed to uphold one anti-abortion statute in order to strike down all of them two years later. It was the vague notion of "health" so vague that it could mean anything, that the Court needed to rule in Doe. This notion of "health" enabled the Justices to hold in Doe, that the health exception cited in Roe should be expanded to encompass the entire pregnancy. It's no wonder they agreed to hear Roe the day after they decided Vuitch.

For his part, Dr. Vuitch's celebration was premature. He was forced out of business by a malpractice suit in 1981.[59] After Roe made it impossible to prosecute him and all other abortionists for the practice of abortion, he fell afoul of the law in other ways. Since illegal businesses are by definition unregulated, his abortion clinic turned out to be the source of medical malpractice, and he was the subject of numerous suits to that effect. That's what happens when your formerly illegal practice suddenly becomes legal. No more operating without a license, not more surgery without anesthetic, no

---

[58] United States v. Vuitch, 402 U.S. 62 April 21, 1973.
[59] Forsythe, p. 213.

more lacerated uteruses; it's time to clean up the act; and the clinic. Old habits die hard. One woman was pronounced pregnant by Vuitch's clinic and offered an abortion. It turned out she was a reporter doing a sting and the urine sample she provided them to test for pregnancy was a man's. The report won a Peabody award,[60] but that didn't stop the New York *Times* from describing Vuitch as a "fighter for abortion rights".[61] The *Times* didn't mention the two women who died from Vuitch's abortions *after* Roe was decided.[62]

It turned out that the Supreme Court liked the definition of health it upheld in Vuitch and used it in Doe to expand the limited ruling of the Roe case to cover all abortions in all cases. It didn't mind enabling the prosecution of one abortionist to eventually make all abortions immune to prosecution. This is a useful legal process; putting language into a ruling to be exhumed for later use.

A well known example is the decision written by Justice Brennan in Eisenstadt v. Baird, a 1972 Massachusetts contraception case. Griswold v. Connecticut had already ruled that the privacy of the marital bedchamber could not be constitutionally intruded upon, and Baird extended the protection to unmarried persons as well.[63] Until this point contraception cases were not generally regarded as implying a freedom to abort. Couples, married or otherwise, might conceive a child in the bedroom, but never aborted one there. However, Brennan inserted a passage that altered the legal map entirely.

"If the right to privacy means anything, it is the right of the individual, married or single, to be free from unwarranted

---

[60] WDVM-TV, Washington, D.C., Mark Feldstein, Investigation of Dr. Milan Vuitch, 1984.
[61] New York *Times*, April 11, 1993, byline, Linda Greenhouse.
[62] Wilma Harris, 17 and Georgianna English, 32.
[63] Eisenstadt v. Baird, 405 U.S. 438 (1972) 405 U.S. 438, March 22, 1972.

governmental intrusion into matters so fundamentally affecting a person as the decision to bear or beget a child."[64]

Suddenly, privacy was no longer just about the privacy of the sexual act, but also a matter of choosing to have children, or not have them. Moreover, Baird wasn't intended to be about privacy at all. It was a case involving equal protection of married and single persons. That was the "buried bone".[65] The "bear or beget" phrase was inserted here by Brennan precisely because he knew that the Court was even then considering the Roe case.[66] It turned out to be a very useful phrase.

Brennan knew exactly what he was doing and forwarded his thoughts on using his Eisenstadt "Easter egg" in the context of Roe, which in March of 1973, was already being prepared. Brennan said as much in a memo to Justice William O. Douglas advising Douglas of the utility of his insertion for the coming abortion decision which appeared the following January.[67] All of this was done while the Court was short handed due to the near simultaneous retirements of Justices Harlan and Black. It was this rump Court of just seven Justices that decided Eisenstadt and that heard the first round of arguments in Roe and Doe.[68] Both were eventually (with much internal recrimination) reargued before the full Court.[69]

Vuitch, Baird, and Younger weren't the only cases that foreshadowed Roe v. Wade and Doe v. Bolton. Since much of the Court's logic turned on the concept of privacy, this required a

---

[64] Ibid., Brennan, 1972.

[65] Forsythe, p. 33.

[66] Edward Lazarus, *Closed Chambers: The Rise, Fall, and Future of the Modern Supreme Court,* (New York, NY: Penguin Books, 1999), p. 364-365.

[67] Clarke D. Forsythe, et al, "Constitutional Law and Abortion Primer", Advocates for Life, p. 7.

[68] Forsythe, *Abuse of Discretion,* p. 34.

[69] *Ibid.,* pp. 46-47.

reference to the 1965 Griswold v. Connecticut decision that struck down Connecticut's law against contraception; that law, the Court said violated a fundamental right to "marital privacy". In writing the majority Griswold decision, Justice William O. Douglas conceded that a straightforward right to privacy was nowhere mentioned in the Constitution. However, he wrote, it was to be found in the Constitution's "penumbras" and "emanations".[70] This sent some legal scholars scrambling to discover the meaning of the heretofore unknown legal term "penumbra".

Excepting the rare use by Justice Holmes, Judge Learned Hand and a few others, penumbra wasn't primarily a term from the law but from astronomy. During an eclipse of the Moon, the Earth's shadow has two distinct parts, the central umbra, within which the Moon is considered to be in total eclipse, and the penumbra, the lighter outer shadow which is often invisible in the light of the partially eclipsed Moon. It doesn't really have any clear legal meaning except to obliquely refer to a vague notion of indistinct association.

It did however neatly assert an opportunity for all manner of legalized obscurity whenever any court wants to describe the Constitution as "living".[71] Once privacy was established as a constitutional right, and the practice of ignoring the actual wording in the Constitution was established as a legitimate form of legal interpretation, the way was clear to declare abortion a constitutional right.

Although the Court was one that approved of wide latitude in the interpretation of "living" law, the decision in Roe was deliberately written to allow as little wiggle room for interpretation

---

[70] Griswold v. Connecticut, 381 U.S. 479 June 7, 1965.
[71] NOTE: Don't try describing the tax law as a "living document" to escape your taxes. This ruse is only available to judges who want to fudge the law. All others pay cash.

as possible. This is rare in court decisions; most courts like to decide issues on as narrow a basis as possible, so as to forestall setting wide precedents for sweeping change. Not in this case.

The Court struck down, not just the relevant Texas and Georgia Statues, but also every anti-abortion law in the country. Contrast this with the District of Columbia v. Heller case[72], which made a limited pronouncement on the individual's right to "keep and bear arms". Here, the Court did not strike down the entirety of the Firearms Control Regulation Act of 1975, much less every firearms control act in the nation. The decision was limited to aspects of the Act that required guns to be kept locked, unloaded and useless for self-defense, as well as restrictions prohibiting D.C. residents from owning handguns. Moreover, it applied *only* in federal enclaves like Washington, D.C.

The Court ruled that the right to keep and bear arms included handguns and was an individual right based on the Second Amendment as well as the ancient natural right to self-defense. It forthwith ordered the District to issue Mr. Heller a fire arms permit.

The District of Columbia promptly passed new regulations that denied Heller a permit. When he sued for summary judgment he was denied. It's unclear if Mr. Heller even today had ever been allowed to register his handgun in D.C. In any event, the District's already restrictive gun laws have been strengthened, not weakened despite a Supreme Court directive to the contrary. This is for a right that is actually *mentioned* in the Constitution. The words "the right of the people to keep and bear Arms, shall not be infringed" appear word for word in the Second Amendment. It's true that there's a preface which some find confusing "A well regulated Militia, being necessary to the security of a free State", but the Supreme Court did

---

[72] District Of Columbia et al. v. Heller, No. 07–290, June 26, 2008.

make it clear that the Amendment did not preclude but *required* a right to keep and bear arms *as an individual*.

There is no similar wording "A well regulated medical profession being necessary to good health care, the right of the people to abortion services, shall not be infringed". If you want to find the right to abortion in the Constitution you need to look at the "penumbras and emanations" rather than the actual wording of the law.

Somehow the Supreme Court found a right to kill a child, if it hadn't been born yet, in the penumbras, and decided that the right was so crucial to the Constitution that the Court needed to invalidate every anti-abortion law in the country and subsequent courts repeatedly struck down virtually all attempts to limit abortions.

But it's as hard as ever to get a gun for self-defense in the nation's capital. The Heller decision was supposed to be applied to the District of Columbia and all similar federal enclaves. Even in that limited form, it has not been enforced against the District.

Even so, it's true that the ruling was never intended to apply to the states. Court's like *limited* rulings remember? So, with that in mind, we turn to another limited ruling that of McDonald v. Chicago.[73]

Chicago's gun restrictions, while different in style, were as draconian as Washington D.C.'s. All guns had to be registered before purchase, but handguns could not be registered at all. The Court ruled in favor of McDonald's petition to be allowed to register and use a handgun for home defense. In doing so, it took Heller and applied it to all the states using the Fourteenth Amendment. One may wonder why they didn't just do that with Heller (after all the Fourteenth Amendment's been there since 1868) but the Court's

---

[73] McDonald v. Chicago, 561 U.S. 3025, August 20, 2010.

desire to be limited in its decisions is so firm that they ruled that Heller would only apply to federal enclaves and waited for someone like McDonald to come and broaden their constitutional interpretation to the rest of the country. More recently Illinois has passed legislation to permit individuals to own and carry guns.

No such restraint is visible in Roe/Doe. Not only did the Court make sure they had two relevant cases ready to decide simultaneously, but they also had all their precedent ducks lined up neatly ready to go. Getting them to rule 7-2 for an abortion right required none of the usual teeth-pulling that courts generally require. One may wonder why. After all, no ruling in any Second Amendment case could possibly have caused as much death and destruction as this one. Flood the market with Saturday night specials and you wouldn't kill a million people a year. Roe/Doe does exactly that.

And the right to keep and bear arms is actually in the text of the Constitution itself, not hidden invisibly away in the penumbras where only sympathetic judges can find it.

One reason the power grab by the 1973 Court was so raw was the insubstantial logic that Justice Blackmun brought to bear on the subject. It amounted to little more than lip service to the concept of legal justification. This was the result of the Court deciding to hear the "...two cases without any factual record" regarding the innumerable questions involving abortion that the law must face.[74]

Moreover, according to Fordham's Robert Byrn, the fundamental error in Roe was to bypass a decision as to whether a fetus should be considered a person and then, therefore, entitled to Fourteenth Amendment protection. Texas had urged that *"life begins at conception and is present throughout pregnancy, and that,*

---

[74] Forsythe, *Abuse of Discretion*, p. 21.

therefore, the State has a compelling interest in protecting that life from and after conception."[75]

In reply, the Court had this:

"...the word 'person,' as used in the Fourteenth Amendment, does not include the un- born; ... We need not resolve the difficult question of when life begins."[76]

The idea that human life begins at conception isn't difficult at all; Texas had no problem with it, and neither did the founders. The statement that the Fourteenth Amendment doesn't protect fetuses as persons is exceptionally dismissive, not least because it precedes the Court's notion that they don't need to decide when life begins.

As Robert Byrn notes, the Court had this exactly backwards. The Court presumed without argument that unborn children were not constitutional persons.[77] The original and fundamental error of the Court was to fail to address the humanity and personhood of the fetus. It should have first decided to examine whether or not a fetus was a human being, whether as such it was a person within the meaning of the Fourteenth Amendment, and if so, whether the state could justify any compelling reason to deny Fourteenth Amendment protection to the life of the fetus from the time of conception.[78]

It should have done so, by its own reasoning in the ruling itself.

"The appellee and certain amici argue that the fetus is a "person" within the language and meaning of the Fourteenth

[75] Roe v. Wade, *IX B.*
[76] Roe v. Wade, *IX A.*
[77] Robert Byrn, "An American Tragedy", *Fordham Law Review* (May 1973), 813.
[78] Byrn, p. 813.

Amendment. In support of this, they outline at length and in detail the well-known facts of fetal development.

If this suggestion of personhood is established, the appellant's case, of course, collapses, [410 U.S. 113, 157] for the fetus' right to life would then be guaranteed specifically by the Amendment."[79]

The Court should, therefore, have decided this fundamental question first; is the fetus a legal Fourteenth Amendment person? This, the Court failed to do. In fact, it began with a presumption that abortion was covered by the *woman's* privacy, and thereby ruled (in fact, assumed without argument) that the fetus is a non-person and, like Dred Scott, has no rights that anyone else is bound to respect.

Were the Court deciding the fate of any individual fetus (or any other child) the usual procedure would have been to appoint a court guardian to ensure that the presumptive right to life was not summarily over ruled. However, when considering the fate of all fetuses, the Court chose to ignore the problem, and simply assumed the result they intended to get.

The Court's reasoning, however flawed, was carefully crafted to avoid what it didn't want to discuss, and to presume what it did, and do so in such an order that it became in Byrn's words "irrebuttable". [80]

The Court's errors in logic were compounded by serious errors of history, largely because they relied almost exclusively and uncritically on one flawed source, historian Cyril Means.[81] Means

---

[79] Roe v. Wade, IX, A. at 728.
[80] Byrn, p. 813.
[81] Means, "The Phoenix of Abortional Freedom," 17 N.Y.L.F. 335 (1971) Means, "The Law of New York Concerning Abortion and the Status of the Foetus", 1664-1968, 14 N.Y.L.F. 411 (1968).

was a lawyer the National Association for the Repeal of Abortion Laws (NARAL) at the time, and was never an impartial source.

Blackmun claimed to think that restrictions on abortion were a recent thing and that it was doubtful that Common Law had ever restricted abortion. It's not the case that women have been immune from prosecution for the crime of abortion, and neither have doctors. Indictments for abortion go back to the Middle Ages. Abortion was a crime from the early days of the American Republic.

Nevertheless, Blackmun wrote in the decision:

"It is undisputed that at the common law, abortion performed before "quickening"-the first recognizable movement of the fetus in utero, appearing usually from the 16th to the 18th week of pregnancy—was not an indictable offense. . . . [I]t now appear[s] doubtful that abortion was ever firmly established as a common law crime even with respect to the destruction of a quick fetus."[82]

The idea that this was "undisputed" is nonsense. There was some question among early American courts over whether abortion before "quickening" could be a *prosecutable* crime. Quickening is the time of pregnancy when a woman begins to feel the baby moving about in the womb. Once quickening has begun, there can be no doubt that the woman is pregnant. Modern pregnancy testing makes this antique concept obsolete, but in the 19th century and before, proving the crime of abortion meant proving that the woman charged was in fact pregnant. Before quickening, there was no scientific way to make such a determination. This meant proving the charge was difficult or impossible; that doesn't imply an approval of early stage abortion in 18th or 19th century America. It just means that

---

[82] Roe v. Wade, *VI 3.*

prosecutors' options were limited by the science of the day. Abortion was never regarded as a "liberty" much less a right. [83]

However, the Court's wording allowed it to present what was a radical departure from constitutional jurisprudence as merely *restoration* of a right to women that they, more or less, had all along.

The Court put it like this:

> "*It is thus apparent that at common law, at the time of the adoption of our Constitution, and throughout the major portion of the 19th century, abortion was viewed with less disfavor than under most American statutes currently in effect. Phrasing it another way, a woman enjoyed a substantially broader right to terminate a pregnancy than she does in most States today . . .*"[84]

The Court also claimed that the abortion laws that (it says) began to appear only after the Civil War were primarily designed to protect women from a dangerous medical procedure rather that for any concern about the well being of the unborn child. The fact remains that laws as far back as the 11th century, both civil and ecclesiastical punished abortion as a crime. By the 13th century abortion of a formed and moving fetus was condemned.

Henry de Bracton, the earliest compiler of common law, wrote around 1250:

> ""*Should anyone strike a woman quick with child or give her a potion which produces an abortion, if the fetus is already formed or animated, especially if it is animated, he commits homicide.*"[85]

---

[83] Byrn, P. 815.
[84] Roe v. Wade, *VI 5*.
[85] Henri de Bracton, *The Laws and Customs of England*, III, ii, 4.

The difficulties of prosecution in cases of abortion continued for centuries thereafter, but none of this translates into a "right to terminate". Byrn notes that the English Common Law was finally made statute by Parliament in 1803. Pregnancy and fetal development were only vaguely understood at the time and English and American law reflects that. This all changed in 1827 with the discovery of the ovum, and with it a new understanding of conception. Within a decade English law began to be rewritten to include the new understandings of science. Since at least the 13th century of Bracton, common law extended its protections to the fetus from the moment it was scientifically practical to establish its existence.[86]

The Roe Court, nevertheless, proceeded to claim that with respect to American laws beginning in the nineteenth century, most anti-abortion statutes were enacted to protect women from unsafe medical practices and did not reflect a concern for the well being of the fetus. Absent this insistence, it would have been more difficult for the Court to rule so brazenly that the fetus was never considered a person by the framers of the Constitution.

"The few state courts called upon to interpret their laws in the late 19th and early 20th centuries did focus on the State's interest in protecting the woman's health rather than in preserving the embryo and fetus."[87]

Instead of relying on Means, the Court might have looked at the language of any number of relevant case laws.

"...to protect the life of the child also, and inflict the same punishment, in case of its death, as if the mother should die."
New Jersey 1881

---

[86] Byrn, p. 826.
[87] Roe v. Wade, *VII.*

The statute was *"intended specially to protect the mother and her unborn child from operations calculated and directed to the destruction of the* one *and the inevitable injury of the other."*

Colorado, 1872

"Does not the new being, from the first day of its uterine life, acquire a legal and moral status that entitles it to the same protection as that guaranteed to human beings in extrauterine life?"

Alabama, 1916

"[T]he abortion statute is not designed for the protection of the woman . . . only of the unborn child and through it society . . . ;"

Idaho, 1934

"We hold that the anti-abortion statutes in Oklahoma were enacted and designed for the protection of the unborn child and through it society; "

Oklahoma, 1936

"...to protect the health and lives of pregnant women and their unborn children from those who intentionally and not in good faith would thwart nature by performing or causing abortion and miscarriage.

Virginia, 1950

"...designed to protect the life of the mother as well as that of her child."

Washington (State), 1936 [88]

---

[88] All quoted in Byrn, pp. 828, 829.

When the Fourteenth Amendment was passed in 1868, in the aftermath of the Civil War at least twenty-eight of the thirty-seven states criminalized abortion. Seven or eight more followed suit in the years immediately following adoption of the Amendment. While the "great evil" being remedied at the heart of the Amendment was slavery, it was also intended that *no one else* should be so degraded. The framers of the Amendment fully intended that no human being should be arbitrarily designated a non-person.[89]

In another little known corner of the 1973 ruling the Court made this astonishing assertion:

> *"The privacy right involved, therefore, cannot be said to be absolute. In fact, it is not clear to us that the claim asserted by some amici that one has an unlimited right to do with one's body as one pleases bears a close relationship to the right of privacy previously articulated in the Court's decisions. The Court has refused to recognize an unlimited right of this kind in the past. Jacobson v. Massachusetts, 197 U.S. 11 (1905) (vaccination); Buck v. Bell, 274 U.S. 200 (1927) (sterilization)."*[90]

In 1927 Justice Oliver Wendell Holmes affirmed a state's right to forcibly sterilize a woman named Carrie Buck on the pseudo-scientific grounds that she was "feebleminded". She wasn't. Justice Holmes wrote infamously in his majority opinion that

> *"It is better for all the world, if instead of waiting to execute degenerate offspring for crime, or to let them starve for their imbecility, society can prevent those who are manifestly unfit from continuing their kind. The principle that sustains compulsory vaccination* [Jacobson v. Massachusetts] *is broad*

---

[89] Byrn, p. 837.
[90] Roe v. Wade, supra, at *154.*

enough to cover cutting the Fallopian tubes. Three generations of imbeciles are enough."[91]

In 1973 in its Roe v. Wade decision the Supreme Court re-affirmed both Buck v. Bell and the forcible vaccination case of Jacobson v. Massachusetts that was the precedent for Buck. The implication in Row is that while the Court was declaring an unlimited right to choose abortion, it was simultaneously denying a universal right for women to choose to carry a child to term. Thus the Court has affirmed a right of the state to force abortion on an unwilling woman in the same way that it affirmed a similar right to forcibly sterilize Carrie Buck. Should the state find that a pregnancy might produce an infant it judges to be mentally defective in utero, it can, by this ruling, order an abortion whether the woman wants it or not. So at the same time as it marked out an entirely new "constitutional" right to obtain an abortion, the Court also appropriated to itself and other agencies of the state the right to take over entirely a woman's reproductive system by forcing her to abort the child she carries. "Keep your laws off my body" indeed.

The odor of state mandated medical procedures swirls around the Roe decision, and can only be intensified when the state takes over (as by law it will) medical care completely. This has resurrected the specter of eugenics that many had thought long gone with the defeat of the Third Reich. Forced abortions aren't common in the United States yet, but they are in China to the tune of 400 million since the 1970's, about the same time Roe was decided. There is nothing to be done constitutionally in a post Roe world should the government decide to exercise its right to abort or, inevitably, euthanize any one it chooses.

Something else to consider was the nature of the individual plaintiffs who brought the cases. Roe v. Wade and Doe v. Bolton

---

[91] *Buck v. Bell*, 274 U.S. 200 (1927).

were both argued by lawyers, of course, but lawyers need clients, other than themselves, or they have a fool for an attorney. Being a fool is not a career disqualification for any form of employment within Washington D.C. city limits, but here, at least, the legal teams came up with one individual each to represent. The names "Jane Roe" and "Mary Doe" were pseudonyms. We know them today as Norma McCorvey and Sandra Cano respectively.

McCorvey was a teenager at the time on her third pregnancy when she sought an abortion in Texas. She had initially claimed that the pregnancy was the result of rape, in the hope that this would make it easier to get the abortion she wanted. Her lawyer, Sarah Weddington wanted to establish a more general right to abortion and so ignored the rape story. What they really needed was a client who would not flee Texas and get a legal abortion in another state.

McCorvey later recanted the rape story. Over the course of many years, where she had at first been a staunch supporter of abortion rights, she began a long conversion process, first becoming a devout baptized Christian, then Roman Catholic and eventually actively opposed to abortion.

Sandra Cano's story is even more convoluted.[92] Whereas McCorvey had at least originally wanted and tried to get an abortion, Cano (originally Sandra Race Bensing) has many times testified that she never wanted, intended to get, or tried to get an abortion. She had gone to a legal-aid office to begin divorce proceedings and signed a number of papers she assumed were all related to the divorce. In fact one was an affidavit, which read in part:

"On March 25, 1970, she applied to the Abortion Committee of Grady Memorial Hospital, Atlanta, for a therapeutic abortion under 26-1202. Her application was denied 16 days later, on

---

[92] Forsythe, *Abuse of Discretion*, p.94.

April 10, when she was eight weeks pregnant, on the ground that her situation was not one described in 26-1202 (a)." [93]

Cano has testified repeatedly that nothing in the affidavit was true, that indeed she made no such application to Grady Hospital. Extensive searches since have produced no evidence that any such application ever existed.

The next section of the affidavit reads:

"Because her application was denied, she was forced either to relinquish 'her right to decide when and how many children she will bear' or to seek an abortion that was illegal under the Georgia statutes." [94]

Recall the decision of the Court that privacy in pregnancy is not an absolute right, and can be over ridden for reasons of vaccination, forcible sterilization *or forced abortion*. They weren't kidding about that. Cano's attorney in collusion with Cano's mother set up an appointment (again without Cano's knowledge) for an abortion that Sandra didn't want, had never sought and assuming she would be given a choice in the matter was never about to agree to. When Cano found out what her mother and attorney had done, she fled the state.[95]

In any event, it's clear enough that the attorneys and the Court didn't get the contents of the Doe v. Bolton case from Mary Doe, Sandra Cano, or anyone else who might be described as a plaintiff. Cano subsequently filed suit in Georgia[96] to get the courts to review and hopefully overturn both Roe and Doe, but was denied at all levels. Nowhere in the legal system did the courts show much

---

[93] Doe v. Bolton, 410 U.S. 179 (1973) II, (2).
[94] Ibid. section (3).
[95] Senate Committee on the Judiciary, Testimony of Sandra Cano (The former Doe of Doe v. Bolton), June 23, 2005.
[96] Cano v. Baker, 435 F.3d 1337 (2006).

interest in the actual plaintiffs allegedly behind either case, and in the case of Mary Doe cared not at all save for a brief inquiry as to whether such a person actually existed. The best and truest answer to that question would have been "No".[97]

What's astonishing is that neither plaintiff in the most notorious decision of the twentieth century ever had an abortion, legal or illegal. Both now are actively opposing the results of that Court decision. Indeed, one of them had nothing to do with the court proceedings at all, and both have renounced the whole business. Cano, for her part, is and *has always been* pro-life.[98]

They have more in common than might be at first apparent. Both were grindingly poor, both dropped out of school, both became pregnant as teenagers, both were victims of family abuse, both were used by ambitious attorneys to seek a backdoor around the Constitution. Both came, after serious soul searching, to see the decision as a prelude to an American holocaust. In many ways either could be seen as a sister to Carrie Buck. Dred Scott, Buck v Bell, and Roe v Wade are *"Three generations of error ..."* [99]

"We let the feminist word warriors hide the fetal Holocaust that surrounds us every day just as effectively as the Nazis hid their extermination of the Jews." [100]

---

[97] Forsythe, *Abuse of Discretion*, p. 95.
[98] Cano, p. 378n19.
[99] Byrn, p. 862.
[100] Michael Bauman, "Beware of Feminist Euphemisms" *Life Advocate*, May/June, 1999 Volume XIII Number 6.

Fudging it
Myths of Abortion History

"if it doesn't work out, fudge it..."[101]
David Tundermann

MYTH: "Back Alley" Abortions killed thousands.

This is a myth that has been repeated endlessly and was once given sanction by Columnist Ellen Goodman.[102] Goodman herself has since recognized that the figures were inflated, largely by abortion proponents, taking many estimates from the 1930's (before the widespread use of antibiotics). Dr. Bernard Nathanson of the National Association for the Repeal of Abortion Laws (NARAL) eventually confessed that the figures were widely used and widely known to be a fiction. [103]

The actual CDC figure for illegal abortion related deaths in 1972, one year before Roe, was 39. Since abortion was already legal in some states, there is a figure for legal abortion related deaths as well, which was an additional 49.[104]

For the most part, abortion proponents knew as well as Nathanson did that abortion in the decades immediately prior to Roe was not particularly dangerous. As we've seen, Planned Parenthood

---

[101] Tundermann was a Yale Law student working for the pro-abortion Waddington team at the time of Roe.
[102] Ellen Goodman, "Not just a march on Washington," Boston *Globe* (April 25, 2004).
[103] Nathanson, *Aborting America,* p. 193.
[104] "Morbidity and Mortality Weekly Report", Centers for Disease Control Surveillance Summaries, 9/4/92, p. 33.

Medical Director Mary Calderone noted in the 1950's how safe (then illegal) abortion really was. [105]

She attributed this partly to antibiotics and also to the fact that 90% of illegal abortions were being done by physicians, who "must do a pretty good job if the death rate is as low as it is."[106] Therapeutic (to save the mother's life, and therefore legal in all 50 states) abortions were generally done in hospitals.

All this was widely known to the Planned Parenthood Conference on 1955 where abortion deaths were discussed. None of this deterred pro-abortion advocates from claiming figures of tens of thousands of deaths taken from the 1930's. The figure is still quoted in some advocacy circles. Therapeutic abortions by the time Calderone wrote were a vanishing rarity; she noted even then that abortion to save a mother's life was "hardly ever necessary."[107]

Alan Guttmacher, later President of Planned Parenthood wrote in 1954 that abortions which were "absolutely essential to preserve a woman's life are relatively few."[108] Later as Director of New York's Mt. Sinai Hospital Obstetrics Department he approved many abortions as "therapeutic" in order to make them legal under New York State's pre-Roe laws forbidding abortions for any other reason. In effect, he had anticipated the Doe concept of unlimited flexibility in the concept of "health" 20 years before the Supreme Court made the concept constitutional doctrine. Eventually doctors

---

[105] Mary Steichen Calderone. M.D., "Illegal Abortion as a Public Health Problem" *American Journal of Public Health*, (VOL. 50. NO. 7, 1960), p. 949.

[106] Ibid.

[107] Ibid. pp. 948, 949.

[108] Alan Guttmacher, "The Shrinking Non-Psychiatric Indications for Therapeutic Abortions" Harold Rosen, *Abortion in America: Medical, Psychiatric, Legal, Anthropological, and Religious Considerations*, (Boston, MA: Beacon Press, 1967).

like Guttmacher and Warren Hern have been willing to certify that "any pregnancy" is a threat to a woman's life and health.[109]

If abortions were generally done by physicians prior to Roe, consider the current practice where the overwhelming number of abortions are performed in clinics with minimal assistance from the doctor; the prepping is generally done by clinic staff. Where complications set in, a clinic should generally refer the patient to a local emergency room. There are several hundred clinics in the country which specialize in only one procedure: abortion. This specialization requires that they do a rapid high volume business with time for only minimal consultation or reflection. Current law has made this industry difficult to regulate. Attempts to do so are often met with court injunctions.

In part this is because the Roe Court chose to interpret its own authority with a certain liberality. The Court was not shy about making medical judgments, particularly that viability occurs only at the second or third trimester. Trimesters and viability are medical concepts that the Court appropriated arbitrarily for the purpose of creating an absolute right to abortion. Viability, the ability of the child to survive outside the womb, should be properly understood as a statement about current medical technology, rather than as the Court assumed, a statement about the nature of the fetus. Viability has been pushed back significantly since 1973, and will no doubt be pushed back further as medicine makes continued progress. Moreover, viability construed as survival *without medical support* can't even be applied to infants after birth. Viability with medical support, which includes intensive care units, incubators, and on occasion surgery in the womb to improve the infant's chances is an

---

[109] *"I will certify that any pregnancy is a threat to a woman's life and could cause 'grievous injury' to her 'physical health."* -Warren Hern, Frank J. Murray, "Daschle bill may not ban anything; Abortionists could use own judgment," *Washington Times*, May 15, 1997.

exceedingly fluid concept. Nevertheless, the Court insisted on using it to declare when a state may have the authority to regulate a certain medical procedure. No other medical procedure has ever been similarly singled out, with the result that regulation of abortions nearly impossible to regulate. Generally hair stylists are more tightly regulated than abortion clinics. By declaring a constitutional right, the Court gave abortion a protection from state intrusion that no other medical procedure has.[110]

Subsequent decisions have confirmed this. In 1986 the Court again took up the abortion issue in Thornburgh v. American College of Obstetricians & Gynecologists.[111] Here a Pennsylvania law had required the women contemplating abortion be presented with state sponsored literature that describe the development of the fetus on a two week basis. It also gave a list of public and private agencies willing to help women who decide to carry their child to term, providing assistance whether she decided to keep the child or put it up for adoption. In other words, it provided her with alternatives as part of an attempt to guarantee informed consent (something required for every other medical procedure). Justice Blackmun, still on the Court, wrote that any such materials can "serve only to confuse and punish her and to heighten her anxiety..." Blackmun failed to describe how literature could be considered punishment except to call it "inflammatory". Justice Sandra Day O'Connor wrote in concurrence that "any regulation touching on abortion must be invalidated if it poses an unacceptable danger of deterring the exercise of that right."[112] Deterrence in this context means that some women might change their minds about abortion once they find out what it does.

---

[110] See Daniel J. Castellano, M.A., "Legal Issues of Roe v. Wade," (2006, rev. 2011) Repository of Arcane Knowledge, (arcaneknowledge.org).
[111] Thornburgh v. American College of Obstetricians & Gynecologists 476 U.S. 747 (1986) p. 795.
[112] *Ibid.* p. 829.

Chief Justice Burger had supported the original Roe decision. Here he begins to withdraw his support, recognizing for the first time the implications of the original ruling. He displays remarkable cluelessness writing, "Can it possibly be that the Court is saying that the Constitution forbids the communication of such critical information to a woman…" because it "might have the effect of 'discouraging abortion' as though abortion is something to be advocated…"

Had he communicated better with Justice White in *his* dissent from the Roe decision Burger would have been better informed. Justice White knew perfectly well in 1973 that

> *"The common claim before us is that for any one of such reasons or for no reason at all, and without asserting or claiming any threat to life or health, any woman is entitled to an abortion at her request…"* [According to this] *"…the Constitution of the United States values the convenience, whim, or caprice of the putative mother more than the life or potential life of the fetus…the people and the legislatures of the 50 States are constitutionally dissentitled to weigh the relative importance of the continued existence and development of the fetus, on the one hand, against a spectrum of possible impacts on the mother, on the other hand."*[113]

It took until 1986 for Chief Justice Burger to realize what Justice White knew in 1973; that this indeed, was what Roe had wrought. The implication was exactly that the people and the legislatures of the 50 States were not entitled to even provide information necessary for informed consent lest it discourage even one abortion.

---

[113] Roe v. Wade ante p. 113.

MYTH: The fetus is a type of "potential life".

"It must be remembered that Roe v. Wade speaks with clarity in establishing not only the woman's liberty but also the State's 'important and legitimate interest in potential life'".[114]

The phrase "potential life" refers to the actual fetus, which is in no sense potential. The life of the fetus is real; the child from the moment of conception as a zygote, then an embryo, then a fetus is indubitably alive. Justice Stevens one of the more radical pro-abortion Justices on the Court liked to insist that to claim otherwise is to illegitimately impose a theological judgment in violation of the establishment clause of the First Amendment. The idea that conception begins life is neither a theological nor religious assertion. It is a scientific fact established by centuries of research into the process of human reproduction. It is a fact found in the introductions of innumerable embryology textbooks. It may or may not agree with the policies of various religious denominations; today the later is probably more likely among liberal Protestant churches. The United Church of Christ for example is officially pro-choice.

Eventually in 1992, with Casey v. Planned Parenthood, another Pennsylvania case, the Court managed to permit information being given to an abortion patient, although it upheld virtually all of Roe otherwise. This turned out to be a close run thing. Four Justices were finally ready to overturn Roe entirely. Only two were prepared to uphold it in its entirety and reject all Pennsylvania regulations. Thus the fundamentals of Roe were upheld by a five to four vote. However, the plurality agreeing to permit some regulation of abortion was only three Justices.

---

[114] Planned Parenthood Of Southeastern Pennsylvania v. Robert P. Casey, No. 91-744 505 U.S. 833 June 29, 1992.

The "swing" vote here as in so many other cases was Justice O'Connor. She had written compellingly in dissent for the Akron case (1983).

"The Court also recognized that the State has 'another important and legitimate interest in protecting the potentiality of human life.' ... I agree completely that the State has these interests, but, in my view, the point at which these interests become compelling does not depend on the trimester of pregnancy. Rather, these interests are present throughout pregnancy."[115]

The State has a compelling interest in the life of the fetus *"throughout pregnancy"*. Here again she mistakenly refers to the fetus as potential, and not just potentially alive, but also potentially human. The fetus is demonstrably both human and alive, not "potentially" so. However, in claiming a legitimate state interest in the life of the human fetus, she comes perilously close to stating an outright opposition to Roe. Justice Powell certainly thought so.

In writing his majority opinion upholding Roe he noted

"Today, however, the dissenting [O'Connor] opinion rejects the basic premise of Roe and its progeny. The dissent stops short of arguing flatly that Roe should be overruled. Rather, it adopts reasoning that, for all practical purposes, would accomplish precisely that result."[116]

By the time of Casey (1992) O'Connor had evolved. This is what "swing votes" do. They swing back and forth. It's an extraordinarily powerful position to be in, a sort of constitutional "kingmaker" where a single vote one way or the other can decide

---

[115] Akron v. Akron Center for Reproductive Health, Inc. (No. 81-746) 462 U.S. 41.
[116] Ibid.

policy for nations, and millions of citizens. In the Akron decision O'Connor was one of a three-vote minority with no opportunity to be the swing vote. In a two to three to four situation, as with Casey, the potential is far greater for one woman to make her mark.

O'Connor wrote the deciding plurality decision that upheld Roe in the Casey decision substantially downgrading her estimate of State interest in the life of the fetus. Whereas in Akron she had expressly denied the validity of the viability criterion, by the time she got to Casey she had mellowed. In Akron she had written defending the State's interest in the life of the fetus throughout pregnancy.

> *"The choice of viability as the point at which the state interest in potential life becomes compelling is no less arbitrary than choosing any point before viability or any point afterward."*[117]

In Casey, however, expressing the will of the plurality she wrote,

> *"We have seen how time has overtaken some of Roe's factual assumptions: advances in maternal health care allow for abortions safe to the mother later in pregnancy than was true in 1973, and advances in neonatal care have advanced viability to a point somewhat earlier. But these facts ... have no bearing on the validity of Roe's central holding, that viability marks the earliest point at which the State's interest in fetal life is constitutionally adequate to justify a legislative ban on non-therapeutic abortions... Whenever it may occur, the attainment of viability may continue to serve as the critical fact, just as it has done since Roe was decided; which is to say that no change in Roe's factual underpinning has*

---

[117] Ibid.

left its central holding obsolete, and none supports an argument for overruling it."[118]

The inestimable Justice Antonin Scalia dissented as follows:

"*But 'reasoned judgment' does not begin by begging the question, as Roe and subsequent cases unquestionably did by assuming that what the State is protecting is the mere 'potentiality of human life.' The whole argument of abortion opponents is that what the Court calls the fetus and what others call the unborn child is a human life.*"[119]

Indeed it is a human life. This has long been an established scientific fact. By assuming without evidence or justification that a fetus is only "potential" (as if it didn't really exist yet) the Court preserved a necessary rationale for a decision that it very much wanted to make. Nevertheless, the so-called potentiality of the zygote/embryo/fetus is a myth created *ex-nihilo* by the 1973 Court. Without it the house of cards legal edifice of Roe would collapse, as the Roe Court expressly recognized.[120]

While the Casey Court seems to abandon the strict scrutiny standard, it replaces it with a vague standard of "undue burden". In other words, Pennsylvania can regulate abortion unless it places an undue burden on the woman seeking one. The word "undue" is never explained. How they reconcile this with the Roe decision's declaration that abortion is a fundamental right (just as if it were mentioned in the First Amendment) is also never explained.

---

[118] Planned Parenthood v. Casey No. 91-744.

[119] Planned Parenthood v. Casey No. 91-744, Justice Scalia et al dissenting.

[120] "The appellee and certain amici argue that the fetus is a 'person' within the language and meaning of the Fourteenth Amendment....If this suggestion of personhood is established, the appellant's case, of course, collapses."

Casey legitimizes a 24-hour waiting period, informed consent, and parental consent requirements holding that they did not constitute an "undue" burden. In Akron, O'Connor thought such a waiting period would be a good idea.[121] If abortion really were a fundamental right on a par, say with the First Amendment, however, a 24 hour waiting period would be considered undue indeed.

> *"The appropriate analogy, therefore, is that of a state law requiring purchasers of religious books to endure a 24-hour waiting period, or to pay a nominal additional tax. The joint opinion cannot possibly be correct in suggesting that we would uphold such legislation on the ground that it does not impose a "substantial obstacle" to the exercise of First Amendment rights. The "undue burden" standard is not at all the generally applicable principle the joint opinion pretends it to be; rather, it is a unique concept created specially for this case, to preserve some judicial foothold in this ill gotten territory."[122]*

So, the Casey Court, after considerable gymnastics decided to let sleeping dogs lie.

> *"We do not need to say whether each of us, had we been Members of the Court when the valuation of the State interest came before it as an original matter, would have concluded, as the Roe Court did...we are satisfied that the immediate question is not the soundness of Roe's resolution of the issue, but the precedential force that must be accorded to its*

---

[121] Akron, p. 474. "No other medical procedure involves the purposeful termination of potential life. The waiting period is surely a small cost to impose..."
[122] Casey, Scalia dissent.

holding. And we have concluded that the essential holding of Roe should be reaffirmed."[123]

So near and yet so far.

MYTH: Abortion was a "Common Law" liberty before the 19th century.

While the number of abortion deaths that Goodman originally quoted can reasonably be called an urban legend, this myth is simply a deliberate distortion. It derives from a paper by Cyril Means, a lawyer for NARAL at the time of the Roe decision. It became the source for Justice Blackmun's "analysis" of abortion history, but Means primarily relied on only two early cases and misconstrued them both. Perhaps "disconstrued" would be a better word, since "misconstrued" has overtones of accidental misunderstanding. There is a distinction to be made between misinformation and disinformation, the latter being a knowing and deliberate act. The Means articles, prepared for NARAL to be submitted to the Court during the Roe arguments, is largely an example of legal disinformation.

The Means analysis has since entered the realm of legend. It is still referred to almost casually by legalists trying to defend abortion rights as if there hadn't been extensive research performed since that debunked it. For that matter, there was plenty of evidence at the time to show that Means analysis was flawed. These references have found their way into amicus briefs filed with the

---

[123] Casey, p. 2808.

Court in cases since Roe. These include Webster v. Reproductive Health Services and Planned Parenthood v. Casey.[124]

The fact remains that, as most of the Roe team must have known, early common law regarded abortion not as a liberty, but as a crime. The early statutes in American law were intended not as a repeal of common law, but a reinforcement of it. Law against abortion was made statutory as early as 1821 in the United States and 1803 in Britain. These did not invent new law, but codified accepted English Common Law as it had developed since the middle ages. Common law prosecutions of abortion cases in the Colonies was primarily limited by evidentiary concerns (then as now, prosecutors had to prove their case) rather than any principle in favor of the alleged liberty of abortion. Abortion laws in the Colonies were enforced as vigorously as medical knowledge at the time permitted.

MYTH: Laws against abortion were only to protect the mother not the fetus.

This is another one of Means' "fudge it as necessary" items.

Early cases concerning abortion make it clear that protecting the fetus was the universal intent of laws against abortion. Some went so far as to call it the murder of the fetus. It's hard to see how that could be construed as protecting the mother from dangerous medical procedures. The Roe Court went out of its way to overlook a plethora of decisions from a variety of jurisdictions all affirming that the law's design was to protect the unborn human child. The courts in Maine, Vermont, Iowa, Colorado, New Jersey, Oregon, New Mexico, Maryland, Alabama, Utah, Idaho, Oklahoma, Georgia,

---

[124] Ramesh Ponnuru, *The Party of Death: The Democrats, the Media, the Courts, and the Disregard for Human Life*, New York, NY: Regnery Publishing, 2006, p. 105.

Virginia all mentioned protecting the child or fetus as the intent of anti-abortion law.[125]

The 1917 Oregon Court went so far as to say that,

"From the moment of conception a new life has begun, and is protected by the enactment. The product of conception during its entire course is imbued with life, and is capable of being destroyed as contemplated by the law. By such destruction the death of a child is produced."[126]

Copious court rulings were echoed by the Supreme Court of Idaho when in 1934 it ruled that the statutes had been enacted "not for the protection of the woman, but to discourage abortions because thereby the life of a human being, the unborn child, is taken."[127]

The Supreme Court's 1973 Roe assertion that the *"... few state courts called upon to interpret their laws in the late 19th and early 20th centuries did focus on the State's interest in protecting the woman's health, rather than in preserving the embryo and fetus..."*[128] is so off the mark that Justice Blackmun and his colleagues had to know it was false.

The "few state courts" were in fact "...at least sixty-four decisions from forty States."[129]

---

[125] Paul Benjamin Linton, "Planned Parenthood V. Casey: The Flight From Reason In The Supreme Court," *Saint Louis University Public Law Review* [Vol. 13:1] 1993, pp. 109-110.

[126] State v. Ausplund, 167 P. 1019, 1022-23 (Or. 1917).

[127] Nash v. Meyer, 31 P.2d 273, 280 (Idaho 1934).

[128] Roe v. Wade, *VII*, p. 148.

[129] *Linton*, p. 115. [Interestingly on January 11, 2013 the Alabama State Supreme Court issued a ruling that included the following: "The decision of this Court today is in keeping with the widespread legal recognition that unborn children are persons with rights that should be protected by law."]

MYTH: Abortion was widely and safely practiced in early times.

Finding accurate figures for illegal abortion at any time is a difficult business, since most criminals know that keeping accurate records of their crimes is a good way to get caught. How often abortion occurred in the ancient world is a subject for guesswork only. However, it was mentioned enough in ancient texts to conclude that it was a well-known procedure, and its appearance in repeated records of criminal trials throughout the medieval period testifies to the fact that it must have been at least somewhat common. Of course, the alternative of infanticide, especially among the ancient Greeks and Romans who freely accepted the practice means that abortion had at least one form of competition, and one that was generally safer for the mother. The ancients rightly saw little difference between abortion and infanticide.

Plato in his *Republic* required abortion for middle-aged women to limit population. His republic was an ideal state, a theoretical construct, not an actual political entity where abortions were carried out. Roman law gave the husband, and only the husband, the right to order an abortion, which Rodney Stark speculates is the reason most women might have undergone such a dangerous procedure. Husbands were instructed "not to order their wives to abort without good reason, but there were no penalties specified".[130]

Prior to the modern understanding of cleanliness very little medical practice could be considered safe, including both abortion and childbirth. Puerperal fever (pyaemia), or childbed fever was known at least as far back as the ancient Greeks. It wasn't until the

---

[130] Rodney Stark, *The Triumph of Christianity*, (New York, NY: Harper Collins, 2011), p. 132.

75

nineteenth century that its nature as an infection, caused often by the doctors and midwives themselves, became clearly understood. It occurred most frequently in childbirth, miscarriage and abortion.

Joseph Dellapenna noted that famed midwife Martha Ballard's first death of a patient happened when she was dealing with a scarlet fever epidemic.[131] Lack of knowledge of how disease was transmitted led to many deaths, not just in childbirth or abortion.

Ignaz Semmelweis discovered the infectious cause of the disease in 1848, and once antiseptic procedures were introduced into his Vienna hospital the death rate declined from around 25% to less than one percent. Eventually, Pasteur and Lister would bring vindication to Semmelweis. His recommendations for hand washing had no scientific explanation at the time. Physicians ignored Semmelweis' recommendations and went on ignorantly killing their patients for more than another twenty years. It took Joseph Lister's publications in *The Lancet* and *The British Medical Journal* in 1867 to expound the work (although Lister himself was unaware of Semmelweis)[132] and Pasteur to apply it to antisepsis in medicine.

Semmelweis eventually went mad, perhaps in part because of the refusal of the medical community to adopt simple hand washing procedures that he had already proven would save thousands of lives. Part of the problem was also Semmelweis himself.[133] His own dogmatic attitude and long time refusal to publish[134] led to equally

---

[131] Joseph W. Dellapenna, *Dispelling the Myths of Abortion History*, (Durham, NC: Carolina Academic Press, 2006), p. 5.
[132] Sherwin B. Nuland, *The Doctors' Plague: Germs, Childbed Fever, and the Strange Story of Ignac Semmelweis*, (New York, NY: W. W. Norton & Company 2004), p. 178.
[133] Irvine Loudon, *The Tragedy of Childbed Fever*, (Oxford, UK: Oxford University Press, 2000), p. 100.
[134] He did eventually in 1861 publish *The Aetiology, the Concept, and the Prophylaxis of Childbed Fever*.

dogmatic reactions to his ideas. Ignored and increasingly alone, his family had him committed involuntarily to a mental institution. There he was beaten savagely by the guards and left with untreated festering wounds in a cell where he died two weeks later.

Two thousand years earlier, ancient procedures involved hooked probes and knives inserted into the cervix to kill and dismember the fetus. Then the abortionist would insert his (unwashed) hand into the cavity and extract the parts. The absence of cleanliness alone must have caused many deaths.

Ancient physician Aulas Cornelius Celsus wrote in his *De Medicina*, that removing a dead fetus (caused either by abortion or miscarriage) required surgery "which may be counted among the most difficult; for it requires both extreme caution and neatness, and entails very great risk."[135] Celsus describes how to insert the physician's greased hand (and sometimes both hands) into the cervix all without thought of cleanliness or anesthesia. This requires a patient's vigorous "strength of mind".

Then there are the pessaries and potions that were used to kill the fetus which were as likely to kill the mother as well. Pennyroyal is mentioned in Aristophanes and appears to have been on the list of approved ancient drugs. The dried leaves were used in cooking but the oil of the plant is highly toxic to humans even in small quantities. Non-surgical methods of abortion generally involved poisons administered either orally or by insertion into the cervix. Either method could be fatal to mother, child or both.

In addition to fatal complications, sterility was a frequent result, which often made a young woman incapable of further contribution to the population. Roman girls were often married and pregnant by age twelve. Widespread sterility and fatal abortion was

---

[135] Aulas Cornelius Celsus, *De Medicina*, Book VII. 28.

complicated by a preference for sons which led many a paterfamilias to order the death by exposure of a girl child. Stark estimates the gender ratio of the Roman Empire at large at about 140 males to 100 females.[136] This translates in modern parlance to 714 females per 1000 males, an exceedingly low ratio; lower than 20th century India or China. It makes for fertility rates far below replacement level. This is a recipe for population and societal collapse. Rarely did a Roman family raise more than one daughter to adulthood, perhaps only one percent.[137]

The effectiveness of many ancient remedies is also open to question, especially ones like amulets worn on the ankle.[138] Soranus and Hippocrates recommended vigorous jumping and frequent baths. Galen recommended bloodletting and various sorts of vigorous exercise including weight lifting, carriage rides over rocky roads, and being shaken by strong men.

George Devereux[139] lists an astonishingly long list of methods adopted in primitive societies. Generally they seem to favor those that might cause trauma to the fetus, and would be reflected by the causes of spontaneous miscarriage. Exercise, climbing, falling, lifting, carrying heavy loads, being punched in the belly, all seem to recall the ancient methodology. Devereux proposes his list uncritically, even when listing supernatural remedies, so it's unclear

---

[136] Stark, *The Triumph of Christianity*, p. 130. (referencing Josiah Cox Russell, *Late Ancient and Medieval Population Control*, (Philadelphia PA: American Philosophical Society,1958).

[137] Jack Lindsay, *The Ancient World: Manners and Morals,* Putnam's Sons, 1968 (Referenced by Stark, *The Rise of Christianity,* (New York, NY: Harper Collins, 1997), p. 97.

[138] Stark, *The Rise of Christianity*, p. 125. (The amulets were apparently thought to be more contraceptive than abortifacient in nature.)

[139] George Deveruex, *A Study of Abortion in Primitive Societies*, (New York, NY: Julian Press, 1955).

how seriously he meant to take some of this,[140] but the echo from ancient times is unmistakable.

On the other hand the effectiveness of what Malinowski[141] called "mechanical" abortion is considerably more reliable. However, the trick here (as with abortifacients, drugs, pessaries and the lot) is to kill the fetus without undue damage to the mother. Devereux describes an instance of a painful dangerous abortion performed only to demonstrate the technique, wherein a pregnant woman was beaten severely on the abdomen by a pair of older women until she bled. "She aborted a few hours later."[142] The abortion was effective enough, but the patient could well have died or suffered permanent injury.

This sort of thing can also be inadvertent, of course; men have been known to beat their pregnant girlfriends senseless resulting in miscarriage. (Exodus 21:22-25 seems to have been written for this.[143]) Anyone who picks up on how injury to a pregnant woman can cause injury or death to her baby would be able to infer a possible form of induced abortion. It should be needless to say that the more effective the method, the more dangerous to the mother. Devereux goes so far as to suggest that suicidal tendencies

---

[140] Devereux, pp. 27-35.

[141] Bronislaw Malinowski, *The Sexual Life of Savages in North-Western Melanesia*, (New York, NY: Eugenics Publishing, 1929, 168-169.

[142] Devereux, p. 20.

[143] *"If men fight and hurt a pregnant woman so that she gives birth prematurely, and yet no harm follows, he shall be surely fined as much as the woman's husband demands and the judges allow. But if any harm follows, then you must take life for life, eye for eye, tooth for tooth, hand for hand, foot for foot, burning for burning, wound for wound, and bruise for bruise."* (WEB)

are a "powerful motive force behind the invention of abortifacient techniques."[144]

It's certainly known everywhere that killing the mother will almost certainly kill the child. Dellapena states flatly that insertions, battery and serious injury, as well as other traditional techniques were neither safe nor effective.[145]

Early writers also noted the dangers of abortion. St. Basil, of Caesarea wrote in 374,

> *"The woman who purposely destroys her unborn child is guilty of murder. With us there is no nice enquiry as to its being formed or unformed. In this case it is not only the being about to be born who is vindicated, but the woman in her attack upon herself; because in most cases women who make such attempts die."*[146]

Any form of poisonous ingestion whether orally or as a vaginal suppository (a pessary) could be hazardous. If the drug was given in small enough quantity, it might be safe, but was less likely to be effective. The greater the dose, the more likely that it would have the desired effect of killing the fetus, but also more likely to have the undesired effect of killing the mother. One pessary of apparent Japanese provenance was even reported to have used mercury, dangerous in just about any dose or manner of ingestion.[147]

---

[144] Devereux, p. 28.
[145] Dellapena, p. 31.
[146] St. Basil the Great, Letter to Amphilochius, Bishop of Iconium (Letter #188) *First Canonical Epistle.*
[147] Dellapena, p. 51.

It was pessaries that the original form of the Hippocratic Oath warned physicians against.[148]

Among certain African tribes and much of Melanesia, abortion is widely regarded as equivalent to suicide.[149] Devereux notes that such a suicide may be an expression of a desire to die to escape the pregnant woman's predicament, but if death is the only way out, how safe can these abortions be?

Given the vast number of cultures that have existed (civilized and pre-civilized), from ancient times to modern, it's impossible to prove that there never was there an instance of someone devising a safe effective home abortion remedy.

Even so, the best advice to give anyone contemplating a technique they got from an anthropology text is "Don't try this at home."

---

[148] *"I will not give a lethal drug to anyone if I am asked, nor will I advise such a plan; and similarly I will not give a woman a pessary to cause an abortion."*
[149] Devereux, p. 149.

Removing the Misery of the World
Fourth Trimester Abortion

"Thousands of ethicists and bioethicists, as they are called, professionally guide the unthinkable on its passage through the debatable on its way to becoming the justifiable until it is finally established as the unexceptional."[150]

Father Richard John Neuhaus

Jim Holt, writing in 2005 for the *New York Times* notes that "This year ... a new chapter may have begun in the history of infanticide."[151] He was referring to the "Groningen Protocol" named for the city in the Netherlands where the authors of the protocol work. The Groningen Protocol is a set of rules carefully set out which define when a physician may euthanize an infant. A number of informal and unwritten "rules" had been in place in the Netherlands, and it was rare for a doctor to be prosecuted for euthanasia even before it was legal.

A committee of the University Medical Center in Groningen in consultation with the Groningen prosecutor's office devised the guidelines to provide health care givers a set of rules to guide their thinking in the most difficult cases of infant deformity and suffering. Normally, euthanasia, which has been legal in the Netherlands for a number of years, is a process that could only be initiated by a patient who wished to die. This is impossible in the case of infants. The guidelines state categorically that the process in the case of babies must be, and can only be, started by the parents of the infant.[152]

---

[150] Richard John Neuhaus, "The Return of Eugenics," *Commentary*, (April, 1988).

[151] Jim Holt, "Euthanasia for Babies?" New York *Times*, (July 10, 2005).

[152] Dutch Law actually makes voluntary euthanasia legal for anyone over the age of 16.

In addition to the consent of the parents, the case must be one of "the presence of hopeless suffering, with no means of alleviating the suffering" for the child, and must take place with extensive medical consultation and the death must be "carefully executed".[153]

Authors of the Protocol expect around 600 cases a year in the Netherlands where euthanasia of an infant will be at least considered. Presumed candidates for euthanasia are infants with no chance of survival, those for who the prognosis is very poor, and are treatable only with intensive care, including those with extensive brain damage, organ failure, or blood oxygen deficiency (hypoxemia) and those with unbearable suffering with no hope of relief.[154]

Holt's *Times* article uses as its first example babies born with partial brains a condition known as anencephaly. It would be hard to imagine a more tragic or extreme example. Anencephalic infants often die within moments after birth, although some do live longer. One lived for two and a half years with the aid of a ventilator. Others can live from a few months to a year without extraordinary medical care.

However, anencephaly is an irreversible condition with a poor prognosis, and it is widely accepted that such babies should be given palliative care only and allowed to die. Many do die as soon as care is withdrawn. A baby with anencephaly is also a clear candidate

---

[153] Verhagen, E., Sol JJ, Brouwer OF, Sauer PJ., "Deliberate termination of life in newborns in The Netherlands; review of all 22 reported cases between 1997 and 2004," Academisch Ziekenhuis, Beatrix Kinderkliniek, (Postbus 30.001, 9700 RB Groningen). e.verhagen@bkk.azg.nl.

[154] Eduard Verhagen, M.D., J.D., and Pieter J.J. Sauer, M.D., Ph.D "The Groningen Protocol — Euthanasia in Severely Ill Newborns," The *New England Journal of Medicine*, (March 10, 2005, N Engl J Med 2005; 352:959-962).

for euthanasia under the Groningen Protocol, as well as those with extreme hydrocephalus (fluid in the brain often causing swelling of the head) and some types of spina bifida and Down syndrome.

Children with milder forms of spina bifida can live reasonably full, if disabled, lives. Many grow to be productive successful adults. John Mellencamp and Hank Williams are examples. Some are confined to wheelchairs, and a few have become well known athletes at the Paralympic level.

Down syndrome children often also live full joyful lives. Some have even enjoyed successful acting careers. Down is a chromosomal condition also known as trisomy 21 associated usually with mild to moderate intellectual disability. At one time Down infants were not expected to live more than a few years, but in recent years life expectancy has risen dramatically. Dale Evans Rogers wrote a well-known biography of her Down child, Robin, who died from complications of the syndrome when she about two years old. The book, *Angel Unaware*,[155] became a best seller.

One would think that neither John Mellencamp nor Hank Williams would have been good candidates for the Groningen Protocol, and while the Rogers' were advised to institutionalize their daughter they found that they were able to care for her throughout her short life. The Protocol is primarily, claims to be, exclusively concerned with the most extreme cases.

If euthanasia were really to be left to only the most extreme cases, few would have any problem with it. It doesn't work that way. The moment one set of standards becomes acceptable the automatic

---

[155] Dale Evans Rogers, *Angel Unaware*, (Grand Rapids, MI: Fleming H. Revell Company, 1953). ("Be not forgetful to entertain strangers: for thereby some have entertained angels unawares." *Hebrews* 13:2)

workings of society begin to explore ways to expand the practices to suit new, larger classes of problems. It is not coincidental that the Groningen Protocol was conceived in the Netherlands, the first country to permit euthanasia and assisted suicide. The Protocol itself was developed as an expansion of already accepted euthanasia practices, and applied them to a new class of individuals. Voluntary euthanasia, once accepted, becomes a stepping-stone for involuntary euthanasia, and what better class of individuals than babies who are in terrible suffering? Who could oppose alleviating the suffering of newborn infants?

The original euthanasia law was written to be very strict. Only those in unbearable physical pain, with no hope of improvement may request euthanasia. No mention is made of non-terminal illness. Nevertheless, some psychiatry patients have requested euthanasia or physician-assisted suicide (PAS) where no underlying physical disease is present. While many euthanasia requests come from cancer patients, a 2005 study noted that about half of the cancer euthanasia deaths also involved symptoms of clinical depression.[156] It's not surprising that someone suffering from intractable pain due to cancer would also be experiencing symptoms of depression. However, since the addition of depression to the other symptoms of cancer substantially increases the likelihood that a patient will request assisted suicide, some have suggested that the depression be treated first before a request for euthanasia or assisted suicide be considered.

In any case, because Dutch law is so specific about the requirement that there be constant extreme pain before a request can be considered, the stereotype of the euthanasia subject as a terminal

---

[156] Marije L. van der Lee, Johanna G. van der Bom, Nikkie B. Swarte, A. Peter M. Heintz, Alexander de Graeff and Jan van den Bout, "Euthanasia and Depression: A Prospective Cohort Study Among Terminally Ill Cancer Patients," *Journal of Clinical Oncology*, (September 20, 2005).

cancer patient in excruciating pain persists as almost *the* definition of what euthanasia is all about. Even so, uncontrollable extreme pain is a rarity in today's medical environment. Advances in pain relief and management mean that almost no one needs to suffer the effects of long-term pain. Those who do are almost always victims of their doctor's ignorance of the latest in pain management and palliative care. Very few doctors are experts or specialists in pain therapy.

Writing in the same journal as the above study, Ezekiel Emanuel has noted that many of the stereotypical assumptions about euthanasia and assisted suicide, even those encoded into Dutch Law, need to be re-examined. The traditional image of the dying patient in excruciating agony begging to die is a prevalent one, but despite this *"...there is woefully little evidence supporting this image."* Pain is generally *"not a key factor motivating terminally ill patients' interest in euthanasia or PAS..."* Far more frequently it is psychological factors, not intractable pain that motivate a request to die. [157]

Others have suggested that the main reason most people either request or politically support the idea of euthanasia and assisted suicide is that they fear the loss of independence that extended hospital stays conjure up. They don't want to be tied to a wheelchair, or hooked up to tubes, catheters, and waste bags. A fear of a loss of dignity and a desire for control over one's person and life are likely far more potent motivators in the patient's mind than uncontrollable pain.

The idea of unbearable suffering (other than physical pain) is a loose concept, subject to multiple definitions, malleable, even fluid standards, and the shifting winds of public opinion. It includes the

---

[157] Ezekiel J. Emanuel, M.D., PhD., "Depression, Euthanasia, and Improving End-of-Life Care," *Journal of Clinical Oncology*, (2005).

idea of loss of dignity, a concept that defies quantification; *how much* dignity does one have to loose? Being unable to reach the bathroom in time would surely cause a loss of dignity. One such instance, however upsetting, shouldn't be grounds to request euthanasia. General incontinence certainly means a loss of dignity, although surely not *all* dignity. Moreover, some people bear the ravages of age with greater dignity, greater stoicism than others. Much depends on the individual's determination to live life well despite its hardships, despite the body's gradual decay and increasing decrepitude. Many who at one time might have thought life would be unbearable confined to a wheelchair, bed, respirator find ways of maintaining a sense of dignity and humanity despite the tubes, monitors and ventilators. Much more depends on the individual's faith, resilience, determination, and sense of the worthiness of living life for its own sake.

The Project to Educate Physicians on End-of-life Care at the Institute for Ethics at the American Medical Association has developed a handbook for doctors regarding end-of-life issues including physician assisted suicide. It notes that with greater palliative care and pain management for all patients much suffering could be reduced *"reduced sufficiently to eliminate their desire for hastened death."*[158]

And these are just the beginning of complexities for adults who are sentient, and able to rationally consider their rights and options. Already Netherlands doctors have approved the euthanasia of a woman in the severe stages of dementia who could no longer recall her original reasons for contemplating a voluntary death. That she was unhappy was obvious. Beyond that, her ability to rationally

---

[158] Emanuel LL, von Gunten CF, Ferris FD., "Physician-Assisted Suicide," The Project to Educate Physicians on End-of-life Care The Robert Wood Johnson Foundation, (Powerpoint presentation, 1999).

reconsider her original request (made well beforehand when she was clear headed) was seriously limited.[159] This is a very long way from a do-not-resuscitate order, or the original euthanasia concept of the dying patient writhing in pain.

When it comes to discussing new-born infants, where a feared loss of dignity and independence are not factors, and where pain is usually controllable to a high degree, advocates like to pretend that they aren't charting new territory. Every new step is merely a small expansion on an earlier victory. New territory *is* being charted, but in such small steps as to seem innocuous and not noticed. That's how slippery slopes work. However, when the first supposedly easy, obvious example turns out not to exist, somebody has some explaining to do. Some accounting should be proffered before we move on with the next seemingly innocuous step.

Abortion has been called the Swiss Army Knife of ethics; once you have it, you can open anything.[160] Euthanasia of infants, did not spring from nothing. We begin with euthanasia of adults who can give their consent and proceed to those who cannot give their consent. We proceed from abortion to infanticide by a similar path. Dehydrating and starving a patient to death was unthinkable 20 years ago. Now it is legal in all 50 states.[161] At one time, no one would have imagined that food and water might be classified as medical treatments. Now, it's routine. A mere reclassification allows us to withhold "medical treatment" (notice that we're no longer talking about heroic or extraordinary procedures, much less a respirator) and thereby "allow to die" anyone whose life we think *ought not to be*

---

[159] *ProLiving - a Disability perspective on euthanasia and physician-assisted suicide*, November 8, 2011, http://proliving.blogspot.com/
[160] Editorial on the30th anniversary of Roe v. Wade and Doe v. Bolton By Dave Andrusko, http://www.nrlc.org/archive/news/2003/NRL01/editb.html
[161] Wesley J. Smith, *The Culture of Death: The Assault on Medical Ethics in America*, (New York, NY: Encounter Books, 2000).

worth living. "I wouldn't want to live like that" becomes life unworthy of life (in German: "lebensunwertes Leben").

Whether infanticide comes via a loose definition of abortion or a loose definition of euthanasia doesn't make a great deal of difference. Both approaches are simultaneously possible. The culture of death can advance along several roads at once. Since potential suffering can be diagnosed before birth there need be little difference on aborting a fetus that appears to have Down syndrome and "euthanizing" it afterwards.

It's true that "problems" like Down syndrome can be eliminated with a judicious use of abortion and euthanasia. The only thing standing in the way of eradicating Down syndrome is the decision of some mothers to carry their Down babies to term. Women who make such a choice can be subjected to extraordinary pressure to abort and suffer social ostracism afterwards if they fail to make the "correct" choice. Melinda Tankard Reist's book *Defiant Birth*[162] profiles a number of women who have decided to have their babies over the objections, often strong objections, of doctors, nurses, even friends and family members. The subtitle *Women who Resist Medical Eugenics* refers to the eugenic desire of many to have a society without "defective" people, a desire now deeply imbedded in the medical community and academic elites. The pressure follows pre-natal testing, which may be merely inconclusive or just hint at a possibility of a problem.

Often women who choose to proceed to term discover that the warnings were for nothing and their babies are born perfectly normal and healthy. The other mothers, who had babies when the warnings were accurate, even include those who had anencephalic

---

[162] Melinda Tankard Reist *Defiant Birth: Women who Resist Medical Eugenics,* (N. Melbourne, Vic. Australia: Spinifex Press, 2006).

babies. Such children rarely live more than a few hours or days. The pressure is always to discard anything less that perfect while it's still a fetus and legal to do so. It shouldn't be surprising that such an unthinking mentality leads to a casual attitude towards fetuses and babies in general, the very thing on display at the Gosnell clinic in Philadelphia, and which lead to the casual snuffing out of life on hundreds of occasions. This was a world that was "a perverse universe unto itself, where death had become as common as breathing, and the dead a collective pile of dust."[163]

This is also about the eugenic search for the "good birth" that accompanies the euthanasia desire for the good death. Both words come from the Greek "eu" for "good". Parallel words like eudaimonia and eupraxophy do as well. That eugenics should be having a modern renaissance is disturbing to many who thought that they'd seen the last of it in 1945. We're reminded and warned that on the contrary, this generation of mothers chronicled by Reist may be the last to have children without the approved imprimatur stamp of governmental and societal approval.

Once "fourth trimester abortion"[164] is no longer seen as a contradiction on terms, the pressure on these parents will continue indefinitely after their child is born. That's the idea.

"Misery can only be removed from the world by the painless extermination of the miserable."
	Nazi Physicist Gerhardt Hoffman writing as Ernst Mann, 1922.[165]

---

[163] Robert H. Abzug, *Inside the Vicious Heart*, Oxford University Press, New York, NY: 1985, p. 44.
[164] Mark Steyn coined the phrase "fourth trimester abortion". It was the title he used for an article in *National Review Online* in September 2011.
[165] Quoted in Lifton, R. J. *The Nazi doctors: Medical Killing and the Psychology of Genocide*, New York, NY: Basic Books, 1986.

Nothing to Do With a Healthy Baby
After-Birth Abortion

"...are human embryos human beings?
Indeed they are, and contemporary human embryology and developmental biology leave no significant room for doubt about it."[166]

Robert P. George, and Patrick Lee

A pair of Italian bio-ethicists created quite a stir in early 2012 with a paper in a philosophical journal on the subject of infanticide. Publications in academic journals, not least those of the philosophy profession, generally don't attract public attention. The writings are dry, aimed at a technical elite, and filled with abstract terminology not easily understood by the general public. The assumed audience for these publications is generally quite small.

They also operate on a set of assumptions that may or may not be understood by the general populace. In the fall of 2011, scientists at CERN in Switzerland claimed to have measured neutrinos traveling (ever so slightly) faster than light. As any Star Trek fan knows this won't become possible until the 22^d century, and is utterly beyond our current understanding of physics.

Nevertheless, the scientists involved claimed that while they were as reluctant as the next fellow to dump all of modern physics into the dustbin, they couldn't find any fault in their measurements. This is the physicist's version of a cry for help. The folks at CERN really, really wanted some assistance from their colleagues to explain what the heck was going on. Since faster than light travel would, in the words of one physicist enable you to "be your own grandmother" a fate everyone wants to avoid, the stakes couldn't be

---

[166] Robert P. George, Patrick Lee, "Acorns and Embryos", *The New Atlantis*, (Number 35, Spring 2012).

higher. Thankfully, the kind folks at CERN have saved the world from becoming it's own grandmother (grandfather's apparently weren't on the worry list for now). They've since decided that their timer was off and that there was nothing wrong with their neutrinos in the first place. What a relief.

While many people know that you're not supposed to go faster than light, the minivan in the garage is in no danger of being arrested by the galactic police for speeding. Your minivan maxes out at around 120 just like everybody else. There probably isn't one person in a hundred that can explain what the speed of light is (about 300,000 Km/second) or why you're not supposed to be able to go faster than it. Presumably the grandmother story was just an allegory designed to explain to us ordinary folks something that was over our heads. There's a lot of that in physics.

After the story broke on Giubilini 's and Minerva's article called "After-birth abortion: why should the baby live?"[167] the authors and their publisher, like the scientists at CERN, were quick to point out that the opinions expressed in the paper were not intended for distribution to the public at large and that these sorts of things should be left to the professionals who were academically better equipped to understand the nuances of the theory. Not everyone took comfort in these reassurances. In short (and in laymen's terms) the argument put forth was simple. Since we've long ago accepted as obvious that a woman has the right to kill her offspring while it is still in the womb, why not afterwards? Academic journal or no, this turns out to be a lot easier to understand than physics.

---

[167] Alberto Giubilini and Francesca Minerva: "After-Birth Abortion" Journal of Medical Ethics 23 February 2012. (*J Med Ethics* doi:10.1136/medethics-2011-10041.

"We can terminate for serious foetal abnormality up to term but cannot kill a newborn. What do people think has happened in the passage down the birth canal to make it okay to kill the foetus at one end of the birth canal but not at the other?"[168]

We can terminate for a lot more reasons than fetal abnormality. The point is valid, and it was probably first raised by someone opposed to abortion. The argument says "Abortion is just like baby-killing". Giubilini 's and Minerva's paper says "Why yes it is, and why aren't we proceeding with a lot more baby-killings, now that abortion's been declared OK?" This turns the original *"reductio ad absurdum"* point on its head.

Reductio ad absurdum, if you don't recognize it, is Latin for reduction to absurdity. The idea is to show that an idea or theory implies something ridiculous or obviously false. It's a well established fact of logic that if premises lead to a false conclusion, then the premises themselves must be false as well. The problem is that grade inflation limits the range of what most people regard to be obviously false.

The abstract for Giubilini's and Minerva's paper explains everything:

Premise 1: Abortion is widely accepted for essentially any reason. Premise 2: Late term fetuses and newborns are essentially the same kind of thing. Conclusion: If we can kill fetuses we should be allowed to kill babies *"in all the cases where abortion is* [allowed], *including cases where the newborn is not disabled."*[169]

---

[168] John Harris, interview with *The Sunday Times*, Harris is a member of the U.K. Human Genetics Commission and a professor of bioethics at Manchester University.
[169] Giubilini and Minerva.

"Cases where the newborn is not disabled" means "where the baby is perfectly healthy". It's certainly the case that abortion is widely permitted where the fetus is perfectly healthy, and also when the mother is perfectly healthy as well. The mother's life need not be in danger and with the possible exception of partial birth abortions in the U.S. abortion in almost all circumstances is legal and culturally accepted. Canada has no anti-abortion laws whatsoever. Giubilini and Minerva seem to be recommending infanticide at the mother's whim. (As with abortion, fathers will have no say.)

Giubilini and Minerva say explicitly that they have no idea how long this permission to kill after birth should last, so they refuse to *"suggest any threshold..."*[170]

Just as the Supreme Court claimed *"...we need not resolve the difficult question of when life begins."*[171], so, the question "How old is too old to kill a child" is bypassed. In other words having decided when it's OK to kill a kid, they don't want to talk about when it's not. Typical philosophers: leaving us hanging at the end. Having solved the really tough philosophical question, the details can presumably be left to amateurs. In any case newborns would be better off if birth defects were the only justification for infanticide. As it is here, if the mother really wanted a boy, Giubilini and Minerva it's open season.[172] More children are aborted and killed worldwide for reasons of sex selection than any other.

The authors do seem to refer the rationale of undetected birth defect as a reason to post-birth abort however. They spend most of

---

[170] Ibid.

[171] Roe v. Wade, *IX A.*

[172] "The House on Thursday rejected a measure that sought to impose fines and prison terms on doctors who perform ... sex-selective abortion."
Jennifer Steinhauer "House Rejects Bill to Ban Sex-Selective Abortions" *The New York Times*, (May 31, 2012).

their introduction to that subject. Of course, birth defects are often detectable before birth when legal abortion is available, but they point out that prenatal testing isn't always infallible, and in some cases isn't done at all. Treacher-Collins syndrome (facial deformity accompanied by physical difficulties life respiratory problems) can be a tough one to catch.[173] So can Down syndrome.[174]

Trisomy 21, (also known as Down syndrome) is a genetic disorder named after the physician who discovered it in 1866, Dr. John Langdon Down. It is one of the most popular reasons for abortion among parents concerned about birth defects. Although most individuals with Down syndrome live happy, loving lives, and live significantly longer than they did even a few decades ago, an estimated 92% of pregnancies diagnosed for Down syndrome are aborted.[175] This has resulted in a sharp drop in the number of people with the syndrome and it's led some to imagine that we could soon see the elimination of this kind of birth defect. We could "cure" cancer in the same way.

The societal pressure on a parent who is considering carrying a baby to term when there is a possibility of Down syndrome can be intense. It may continue with even greater intensity after the child is born. Physicians will often try and coerce mothers into an abortion they would prefer not to have, sometimes even lies and insults are not off the table.[176]

The widespread use of pre-natal testing is creating a very large number of such parents. Whether via amniocentesis or ultrasound pre-natal tests are never guaranteed to be accurate. Like

---

[173] Giubilini and Minerva.

[174] Ibid.

[175] Susan Donaldson James, "Down Syndrome Births Are Down in U.S." ABC News November 2, 2009.

[176] Jane Lebak *Carrying to Term Pages*, "Dealing With The Clueless". http://www.janelebak.com/ctt/tips-clueless.html

all medical tests they have their false positives and false negatives. The latter have, since Roe v. Wade, created a whole new class of lawsuit known as "wrongful birth" lawsuits. This has the effect of pressuring doctors to pressure patients always in the direction of abortion as the preferred "treatment", even for tests that are clearly inconclusive. How could it be otherwise? The odium of eugenics invariably wanders into these discussions. *"How perfect must a person be to deserve health insurance, a job, a parent's love, or life itself?"*[177] One wonders.

The fact remains that most abortions have nothing to do with preventing birth defects. Pro-abortion advocates still insist that women want, need and have a right to have a free choice about terminating the life of their fetus at any stage of pregnancy. The operative phrase for abortion is what it's always been; it should be available "early as possible and as late as necessary".

Giubilini and Minerva's idea would rid us of a whole series of complications by simply removing the prohibition of "aborting" a child after its been born. In the process they've confirmed the assertions of anti-abortion activists who've been claiming for years that there was no difference between abortion and infanticide. The term "as late as necessary" has here been extended indefinitely. They propose no date and no time from to decide when an after birth abortion should not be permitted. They conclude that a fetus is a human being, just as a newborn is, but neither is a person with a right to life.[178]

The late philosopher Mary Anne Warren had a list of criteria that she used in this context to determine if an individual could be considered not just a human being, but also a person. She claimed

---

[177] Natalie Angier, "Ultrasound and Fury: One Mother's Ordeal," *The New York Times*, (November 26, 1996).
[178] Giubilini and Minerva.

that there are six criteria for determining if an individual is a person or not.

Sentience
Ability to feel emotion
Ability to reason
Ability to communicate
Self-awareness
Moral agency or awareness

While one might be a person of one were lacking one or several of these, someone lacking all six could not be considered a "person".[179] Different philosophers inevitably come up with differing lists of "properties" that an individual must possess in order to qualify for personhood. This lends an air of arbitrariness to the theory. The various lists may have much in common, but they are always the product of differing intellects, and reflect therefore the personal choices and preferences of the writer making them up.

All this is made necessary by the fact that embryology has finalized the question of when human life begins. This is as settled as science gets. A fertilized egg *is a human being* and remains so until its death. The argument that a human being doesn't come into existence (or even that we don't know when it comes into existence) is no longer available. If one is to promote abortion in the face of settled science, one has no choice but to divide the human race into two separate and profoundly unequal populations; those who can be killed and those who can't.

The inevitability of infanticide is demonstrated by the growing list of pro-abortion activists who have given up trying to

---

[179] Mary Anne Warren, "On the Moral and Legal Status of Abortion," from *Biomedical Ethics*. 4th ed. T.A. Mappes and D. DeGrazia, eds. (New York, NY: McGraw-Hill, Inc. 1996), pp. 434-440.

exclude children from the list of killable humans. Their logic is inexorable. One can choose to grant all humans the right to life, or grant it to only some. What's no longer a convenient option is to assume that birth is some kind of bright line dividing humans from tissue in the womb, from a precious child to a disposable parasite. The boundary line will inevitably slip, has already slipped, and will continue to slip further and further into the human family.

Resistance is futile.

Paid for by the Crown
Canadian Law

"A female person commits infanticide when by a willful act or omission, she causes the death of her newly born child, if at the time of the act or omission she has not fully recovered from the effects of giving birth to the child and by reason thereof or of the effect of lactation consequent on the birth of the child her mind is then disturbed."

Canadian Criminal Code, Part VIII, section 233

"Every one who causes the death, in the act of birth, of any child that has not become a human being, in such a manner that, if the child were a human being, he would be guilty of murder, is guilty of an indictable offence and liable to imprisonment for life."

Canadian Criminal Code, Part VIII, section 238

"223. (1) A child becomes a human being within the meaning of this Act when it has completely proceeded, in a living state, from the body of its mother, whether or not (a) it has breathed;
(b) it has an independent circulation; or (c) the navel string is severed."

Canadian Criminal Code (R.S.C., 1985)

There was a time when in both British and Canadian law a mother who killed her newborn infant could be tried and convicted of murder. While ancient pagan societies like Greece and Rome routinely practiced infanticide, by the time the Judeo-Christian ethic took over western society, the killing of a baby was considered to be murder of the worst sort.

Prior to the 19th century women in the dock for killing their own children would be subject to the death penalty by hanging. By the Victorian era a new public sympathy began to emerge for these women, especially if (as they usually were) unmarried. Increasingly juries began to see unwed mothers as needing sympathy as much as censure, and when a mandatory death sentence would accompany a conviction, many juries simply refused to convict, even in the face of overwhelming evidence. This form of jury nullification eventually became so widespread in Great Britain that Parliament was forced, beginning in 1922, to introduce a lesser charge, in effect a new crime, of infanticide, with a 5 year maximum sentence. While the U.S. has no separate infanticide law, Canada, New Zealand, Australia and the U.K. have all adopted a separate type of homicide for mothers killing their own newborns. Medical research seemed to provide a scientific basis for regarding women, especially in the time following childbirth as a biologically distinct set of offenders apart from men. Some have loosely termed this the "raging hormones theory"[180] and with the advent of modern feminism it has become controversial.

Nevertheless, the seemingly scientific reference to "the effect of lactation consequent on the birth of the child" remains in the language of the Canadian infanticide statute. The actual scientific basis of the effect of lactation as a mitigating factor in crime is still rather unclear.

Canadian law provides three types of homicide; murder, manslaughter, and infanticide. American law only provides for the first two.[181] In Britain, but not in Canada, in addition to being a lesser charge for prosecutors to use against a defendant, infanticide is considered a form of defense argument analogous to "mental defect" available to the defense.

---

[180] Bernadette McSherry, "The Return of the Raging Hormones Theory: Premenstrual Syndrome, Postpartum Disorders and Criminal Responsibility," *Sydney Law Review* (15 Sydney L. Rev. 1993).

[181] Terms like "third and fourth degree murder" are mostly obsolete having been replaced by degrees of manslaughter, although some jurisdictions may still use them.

In times past, the primary mitigating factor considered for unmarried women who had killed their own children was the widespread stigma attached to unwed motherhood. Women would be sent into seclusion for the term of their pregnancies and often the child would then be offered up for adoption. A woman abandoned by the man who had fathered the child could be subject to extreme societal pressure. If the father were known, of course, he could also be subject to considerable pressure to "do the honorable thing" by marrying the mother of his child. Many stable families were created in this way.

However, from time to time, a women might panic at the birth of a child without a father and kill the child. The Victorian sympathy for these women found expression in many ways. They created homes for unwed mothers, giving them a place to stay during the pregnancy, away from wagging tongues and prying eyes (that is, away from society's stigma) and homes for foundlings (abandoned children). It is not commonly remembered how renowned the Victorian era was for it's numerous works of charity, and for it's charitable institutions. It's more often remembered as a time of patriarchy, which it was, but the stigma of unwed motherhood, as painful as it may have been, also certainly had the effect of reducing the prevalence of illegitimate children. In the process it also reduced the likelihood of child murder by the mother.

Still, systems of social ostracism generally don't eradicate the behavior they seek to stigmatize; they only reduce it. Removal of the stigma results in an increase in the behavior that was once disproved of. Today, the removal of the stigma of unwed motherhood (we now call them "single moms") is complete. If anything, single motherhood is now seen as a badge of honor rather than a sign of personal weakness.

However, the notion of the suffering single women with children is a useful idea; too useful to do without, so decades after it ceased to be relevant it is still claimed that unmarried pregnant women are more to pitied than censured even when they commit homicide. The device of claiming victim class status is the central political tool of identity politics, and it is ever-present in criminal court cases.

We can illustrate this with a variety of examples. We need not limit ourselves to Canadian law, but as Canada is a more liberal venue even than the United States, which is reflected in its legal system, it's as good a place as any to start.

In 2005, Katrina Effert, then 19, gave birth to a son in her parent's basement, which she proceeded to kill and discard by throwing the body over the neighbor's fence. She then lied to the police claiming initially that she had not even been pregnant, and then blamed her boyfriend for the crime. Eventually the police sorted out her lies and she was tried and convicted of second-degree murder in the death of her son, whose name was Rodney, and sentenced to life in prison with the possibility of parole after 10 years. On various technicalities the verdict was overturned and she was retried and again convicted and sentenced, but the "compassionate" Canadian legal system still wasn't satisfied with its own workings and the conviction was again overturned. The Court of Appeals set aside the second-degree murder conviction and replaced it with a conviction on the lesser charge of infanticide. They then returned the case to the lower Court for sentencing. The prosecution asked for a four-year prison term, although the maximum sentence is five years.

Instead Judge Joanne Veit of the Alberta Court of Queen's Bench gave the defendant a suspended 3 year sentence and 100 hours of community service. Canada has no anti-abortion statutes at all, and the Crown pays for all abortions, so abortion is completely legal and free. Referring almost entirely to the legal practice of abortion (i.e., not infanticide, the crime the defendant was actually convicted of) Judge Veit ruled that *"while many Canadians undoubtedly view abortion as a less than ideal solution to unprotected sex and unwanted pregnancy, they generally understand, accept and sympathize with the onerous demands pregnancy and childbirth exact from mothers, especially mothers without support... Naturally, Canadians are grieved by an infant's death, especially at the hands of the infant's mother, but Canadians also grieve for the mother."[182]*

The defendant was living with her parents at the time, who apparently have stood by their daughter throughout the trials, her father calling one of the convicting juries "heartless bastards". Katrina doesn't seem to have been *all that* "without support".

So, because Canadian society allegedly had no problem with abortion, someone convicted of infanticide should also be allowed to go free. In fairness, the Judge did also note that there were no aggravating factors to the "crime". No aggravating factors with the possible exceptions of the extreme youth and vulnerability of the victim, lying to the police about having sex, blaming her boyfriend for the killing, and disposing of the baby's body in a careless, callous (and illegal) way; no aggravating factors at all.

This elaborates the "logic of abortion" to apply to a new group of individuals not officially mentioned in the abortion law, children; *" -- that's to say, someone who has managed to make it to the post-fetus stage."[183]* This is not the last time we will encounter

---

[182] Judgment on the case of Her Majesty the Queen v Katrina Ann Effert, The Honourable Madam Justice J.B. Veit, Dated the 20th day of June, 2009, (Docket: 050485499Q1)

[183] Mark Steyn, "Fourth-Trimester Abortion," *National Review Online*, September 13, 2011 http://www.nationalreview.com/corner/277027/fourth-trimester-abortion-mark-steyn.

the merger of the concepts of fetus and child. The ancient Greeks and Romans understood that there was no distinction to be made between abortion and infanticide; so do most anti-abortion pro-life advocates. Now abortion supporters are joining the bandwagon albeit for their own purposes.

Abortion is usually defined as the termination of a pregnancy. In this case the defendant wasn't pregnant when she killed her son, Rodney. It was no longer a matter of doing what she pleased with her own body. She chose to carry her pregnancy to full term and gave birth to a healthy baby boy, a "citizen" of Canada, if we may speculate; all this despite the fact that abortion in Canada is both legal and paid for by the Crown.

The judge apparently dissatisfied with trying a case of infanticide (downgraded from the original two murder convictions) decided to rule on another case entirely; a case not before her court, an "offense" with which the defendant had not been charged, for which no evidence had been presented, by either prosecution or defense, (which would have been quite a trick, since in Canada the "offense" of abortion *doesn't exist*). The case before Judge Veit involved the crime of infanticide, not the *non-crime* of abortion. Infanticide is in most other "civilized" countries indistinguishable from murder. Under Canadian Law (which also apparently allows a judge to rule on any case she pleases, rather than the one before her court) this is considered hairsplitting. If you don't want to convict the defendant of the crime she's been charged with, pretend she's been "charged" with something that's perfectly legal and rule on that.

If Canada had something like the safe haven laws found in the U.S. the legal travesty that Judge Veit's Court found itself in might have been avoided. Safe haven laws are designed to give parents, especially mothers, a legally safe way to discard their infant without killing it. This allows one parent, usually without the consent of the other, to drop off an infant at a hospital, police or fire

104

station within a period after the child's birth. They're generally allowed to do so anonymously under the assumption that abandoning a living child is preferable to killing it. This has the side effect of giving the state's imprimatur of approval to child abandonment, not something that most states *should* want to do. It is hoped that providing a consequence free way out will save at least the lives of some children. All 50 American states and Puerto Rico (beginning with Texas in 1999) have adopted (if that's the word) some form of infant safe haven law; in Europe these are also called "baby Moses" laws or "hatchery" laws. Some babies are indeed surrendered under such statutes, while others continue to be illegally abandoned, a significant portion of which die as a result.

The age at which a child may be surrendered, which parent may do so, and degrees of anonymity and freedom from legal liability vary from state to state. Some states provide for a surrendering parent to change her mind, and some also provide for the non-surrendering parent to challenge for custody.

As of 2008 only Nebraska had no age limit on abandoned children, apparently leading to a boom in abandoned teenagers in that state, with parents crossing state lines to take advantage of Nebraska's liberalism. Since then the Nebraska Legislature has set the age limit at 30 days.[184]

Canada has no similar safe haven statute. On occasion, when seeking information about an abandoned child, Canadian prosecutors have made public their intention to not prosecute an individual case. At the same time, some Canadian prosecutors have tried to charge mothers with criminal acts against their unborn children, if, for example she is addicted to drugs that will harm the child. Courts in Canada have routinely thrown these cases out, as Canadian Law

---

[184] "Nebraska lawmakers vote to limit safe-haven law," CNN, November 22, 2008.

simply does not recognize that any human being exists prior to birth. According to Canadian Law there is no one there to protect, and prosecutors are routinely forbidden by the courts to seek legal remedy against mothers who by lifestyle or deliberate act harm their babies before birth.

Canada is a signatory to the international treaty embodied in the United Nations Convention on the Rights of the Child, which makes some obscure mention of the rights of unborn children. It is exceedingly vague, making only reference to pre-natal care. Only the United States has not ratified the treaty.

The Geneva Declaration of the Rights of the Child in 1924, as well as the U.N.'s reaffirmation of it in 1959 were more strongly worded stating that

> *"the child, by reason of his physical and mental immaturity, needs special safeguards and care, including appropriate legal protection, before as well as after birth"*.[185]

By 1989 the U.N. Convention was more mindful of abortion "rights" terminology, so while it mentioned a "right to life" it set no age at which that right might begin. While the Convention requires children be provided rest, leisure, recreation and play, the words "born or unborn" are absent from the treaty. The treaty does contain nearly 30 pages of "reservations" and counter objections to elements of the text.

> *"The Syrian Arab Republic has reservations on the Convention's provisions which are not in conformity with the Syrian Arab legislations and with the Islamic Shariah's principles, in particular the content of article 14 related to*

---

[185] Adopted by UN General Assembly Resolution 1386 (XIV) of 10 December 1959.

the Right of the Child to the freedom of religion..."[186]

"The Government of the Republic of Tunisia considers that article 7 of the Convention cannot be interpreted as prohibiting implementation of the provisions of national legislation relating to nationality and, in particular, to cases in which it is forfeited."[187]

Etcetera, etcetera, etcetera.

Like the U.N., Canada wants nothing to do with the abortion controversy, however much that controversy may seek her out. As long as judges continue to invoke the issue of abortion as justification for leniency in murder and infanticide cases they'll just have to live with it. Meanwhile, one outlet that might have been used by Katrina Effert and those like her (a safe haven law) is not available in her country. If Judge Veit were genuinely concerned for the level of support that the Katrina Efferts of Canada get, she might have mentioned this. On the other hand, since in Judge Veit's court, penalties for the Katrina Efferts of Canada are minimal, why bother?

All of this must be quite a setback for Canadian pro-life advocates. For years they've argued that human life begins at conception. In Canada, it doesn't even begin at birth.

Or maybe Canadians are ahead of the ethical curve. Having legalized abortion, they want to make child murder safe, legal and rare.

---

[186] CHAPTER IV HUMAN RIGHTS, Convention on the Rights of the Child, 1989.
[187] Note 53, Chapter IV.11, Multilateral Treaties Deposited with the Secretary-General.

Moral Schizophrenia
The Peterson Case

"What so false as truth is,
False to thee?
Where the serpent's tooth is
Shun the tree--- "

Robert Browning[188]

In 2005 Scott Peterson was convicted in Redwood City, California of murder and sentenced to death. The murder victims in this case were Peterson's wife Laci, and their son Connor. Laci and Connor had gone missing in December of 2002 and it was not until the following April that the body of Connor was found washed up on a California beach. The following day the badly mauled body of Connor's mother was discovered and both were identified by DNA testing. As they had been in the water of San Francisco Bay for about 4 months, the poor condition of the bodies prevented any definitive cause of death being determined.

While not initially considering Scott a suspect in the case, Police became more suspicious over time as news of Scott's extramarital affairs became evident. He had mentioned that Christmas 2002 would be his first without Laci, some weeks before her disappearance and death, which prosecutors took as evidence of intent to commit murder. They charged Scott Peterson with two counts of murder, one in the first degree for Laci, and one in the second degree for Connor.

What made this case national news, apart from its sensationalist aspects was the fact that Connor Peterson died before he was born. Laci was carrying him at the time of her death, and thus

---

[188] "A Woman's Last Word", Robert Browning, published in *Men and Women*, 1855.

108

by some legal counts he was a fetus, not a baby, and according to some theories, at least, not a person at all. However, California had a fetal death statute allowing prosecutors to treat Connor's death as murder. Thus the killing of a pregnant woman counts as two murders, whether or not the killer knew she was pregnant. At the same time, of course, California law exempts the killing of a fetus *during an abortion.*

Thus, in effect, it's murder if the mother wants the child, and abortion if she doesn't. The law is giving the mother exclusive right to decide if her baby will be considered a human being or not. The statutes dodge the exact nature of the individual being killed.

About two dozen states have statutes that allow prosecution of anyone who harms an unborn child in a crime (something other than actual abortion). This means that included in the choice of reproductive freedom a woman can choose whether or not the unborn child can be considered a human person (entitled to protection under the law as the Connor was) or is merely a clump of blood and tissue. If the baby is wanted, it's a person, if not it's tissue. This is part of the confusing set of implications that follow from the current state of abortion law.

Meanwhile the New Jersey Supreme Court issued an abortion related ruling in 2006 in the case of Acuna v. Turkish. Sheldon Turkish was Rose Acuna's obstetrician-gynecologist. When her pregnancy was six to eight weeks along she went to Dr. Turkish to ask about an abortion. She wanted to know, she said, if the fetus was a baby. He reportedly replied something along the lines of "Don't be stupid. It's only blood...[or tissue]".[189] She proceeded with the abortion three days later. After complications developed from what was called an "incomplete abortion". The nurse apparently told Acuna that "the doctor had left parts of the baby inside of you."

---

[189] Supreme Court of New Jersey, Acuna v. Turkish, September 12, 2007.

Since this seemed to conflict with what the doctor had told her, she investigated on her own and decided that the doctor had misinformed her and proceeded with a malpractice lawsuit. She argued that the doctor should have informed her that she was carrying a human being.

Although doctors are required to make sure that patients give informed consent to any procedure including abortion, the Court ruled against her complaint, reasoning that "Despite defendant's 'don't-be-stupid-it's only blood' remark in describing the developmental stage of her embryo, [Acuna] understood that without [an abortion or] miscarriage, she would give birth to a child in seven more months."[190]

Well, sometimes she gets to say it's a human being, sometimes not. Sometimes the doctor says it's just blood and tissue, or just a clump of cells. In reality, there is no point in the life of an embryo/fetus when it can be characterized as just a clump. An embryo is an organized system developing according to its own internal rules along a definable path, which ends only in death. It is a living human organism from the moment it comes into existence. It is no more a clump of cells than a baby, a toddler or an old man.

Fetal homicide laws however necessary they may be tend to muddy the waters. Susan Estrich told her USA Today readers "The Peterson case, as with many in the past, has nothing to do with abortion."[191] It may be true that the case was about many other things, but the fetal homicide law under which Connor Peterson's father was charged with his murder is one example of an increasing level of schizophrenia underlying public attitudes on abortion. The inability of the legal system to decide what characteristic the fetus

---

[190] Ibid.
[191] Susan Estrich, "Laci Peterson's unborn child becomes pawn in abortion debate", *USA Today*, (April 29, 2003).

has (or lacks) that gives it (or deprives it) of a right to life is a reflection of society's own ambivalence. The default position should have been on the side of life. If a fetus is the kind of thing that can be a murder victim then it has a right not to be aborted.

This is lost on Estrich as she concludes her column with the following astonishing comment. "Conner Peterson didn't live long enough to be born, but he had a right to live...".[192]

Really? He had a *right to live*?

Isn't that *exactly* what the abortion debate is all about...the right to life of an unborn child? *Any* unborn child?

Apparently not, since the law only grants the right to life in certain special cases. If the mother of the child wants her baby and intends to let it live, and if she is murdered then the dead child is retroactively granted the right to live after he's dead. If the mother should by some miracle escape her killer, and the next day decide she no longer wants her baby, she may kill him. Moreover, if a man stabs a pregnant woman and kills the child but the woman survives, he might be convicted of murder, depending on the state. Yet that same woman would have had the right to kill the same child at the same stage of development in an abortion clinic.

What clearly has escaped Estrich is that if Connor Peterson had a right to live, then Laci Peterson had *no right* to an abortion. To be sure, it took the murder of both to reveal society's uncertainties. Abortion proponents need all the confusion they can muster to continue to promote abortion rights. Otherwise it would be crystal clear to anyone that the moment society concludes that Connor Peterson had a right to live, the abortion debate *would be over*.

---

[192] Ibid.

Unfortunately for the rest of us, it gets more confusing. Consider young Sarah Marie Switzer who was operated on in the womb for spina bifida. Life magazine published a photo of her surgeon's finger cradling her hand during the surgery. She was born (again; for good) two months later. Her doctor often performs surgery on similar patients and says he often talks to them to reassure them. He also performs abortions on fetuses with spina bifida. He says it's "an increasingly difficult position to be in".[193]

Like Samuel Armas, also operated on for spina bifida, Sarah didn't "reach out" for her doctor's hand. During this kind of surgery babies, like their mothers, are anesthetized. Both children were at about the same stage of development as those killed in the Kermit Gosnell clinic in Philadelphia - without the anesthetic. Moreover, the babies aborted by the same doctor who performed Sarah's surgery are not given the same anesthetic for what must be equally painful "surgery". Babies are anesthetized; fetuses are not, even if they may both be at the same stage of development.

No wonder doctors are finding this "an increasingly difficult position to be in".

Still it's not an *unusual* position to be in. It's not uncommon, in hospitals with maternity wards that also perform abortions, for one to go from one operating theater where doctors are frantically trying the save the life of a premature baby, to another just down the hall where other colleagues are performing abortions on fetuses at exactly the same stage of development (with perhaps the same condition, spina bifida, motivating each team). In one ward it's "Baby with spina bifida: kill it." In the other it's "Baby with spina bifida: perform extraordinarily expensive and heroic surgery to save

---

[193] "Baby Samuel and Mother Doing Well after Fetal Surgery," *WorldNet Daily*, 16 February, 2000. Quoted in Randy Alcorn, *Pro-life Answers to Pro-Choice Arguments* (Colorado Springs, CO: Multnomah Publishers, 2000), p. 94.

it." Who can blame the rest of us for being confused, especially with the same doctor doing *both* procedures? Perhaps we should at least be a little grateful if the doctor displays some of the same confusion.

Sarah Marie Switzer and Samuel Armas are now both healthy teenagers.

The fetal homicide law under which Scott Peterson was convicted dates from a 1969 attack on a pregnant woman named Teresa Keeler that did not result in her death but did kill her unborn baby girl. California prosecutors tried to charge the attacker, Teresa's former husband Robert Keeler, with murder. The California Supreme Court threw out the charges on the grounds that a fetus is not a human being. A fetus is a human being by every meaning of the word. Here, as elsewhere, courts take to themselves the power to decide if a human being is a human being *for the purposes of law*, whether or not it agrees with the "natural order"[194]. They do not believe that the right to life is "unalienable" but is rather conferred on human beings by the court, as the court pleases. This prompted the California legislature to pass a law stating otherwise. More than half the states have passed such laws since 1969. Note that 1969 is before the 1973 decision on Row v. Wade. The U.S. Congress has now passed a federal version, The "Unborn Victims of Violence Act" of 2004.

It's not implausible for pro-abortion types to imagine that such laws are meant to chip away at Roe v. Wade, despite the pre-Roe provenance of the original law. After all, that says nothing about the motivations of those who have sponsored similar laws since 1973. Despite the fact that Roe-style escape clauses are factored into every such law, and these specifically exempt abortions (no law would survive court scrutiny without one) complaints persist that

---

[194] See Kass v. Kass, New York State Court of Appeals, 1998.

fetal homicide laws are trying to sneak around a woman's "right" to abortion.

The suspicion seems natural enough, and much opposition to fetal homicide laws arises from a concern that women's reproductive rights not be limited however indirectly or symbolically. Some anti-abortion activists may well be using public outrage over certain exceptionally heinous crimes to advance a pro-life agenda. The real need for fetal homicide laws derives from court reluctance to define fetal personhood in the absence of a statute passed by the legislature. Add to this the reality of some highly publicized cases (like the Peterson case) that mobilize public anger and which compel lawmakers to do "something". What must be realized is that the moral confusion at the center of the controversy is deliberate. Without it we might cure our moral schizophrenia, and our spiritual discontent as well. Moreover, the confusion is a direct result of the wording of the Roe decision itself.

> "… *unborn children have been recognized as acquiring rights or interests by way of inheritance or other devolution of property, and have been represented by guardians ad litem. Perfection of the interests involved, again, has generally been contingent upon live birth. In short, the unborn have never been recognized in the law as persons in the whole sense.*"[195]

A fetus can be a person, in that he can inherit. It can be a person in that he can be a murder victim. A fetus is a person when it he treated as a patient, in fetal surgery, being given anesthetic for pain. He can also be a person who has a court appointed guardian in a court proceeding, something the Roe Court refused to do. That would have declared the fetus as a person at the opening bell. On the other hand,

---

[195] Roe v. Wade 410 U.S. 113, 1973.

without such an appointed counsel, the interests of fetuses could not be fairly represented, also deciding the issue before arguments were heard. Since the most relevant party was not represented in Court in 1973, it would be interesting to see what might have happened otherwise. Such objectivity among the justices was not available.

Indeed it seems that in law, a fetus is a person under every, and any, circumstances *except* abortion, and that, only because of the way the Court ruled in Roe. Fetal protection statutes are always carefully written to provide one, and *only* one exception; abortion, and that, only because Harry Blackmun said so in 1973.

It's historically questionable to state that "the unborn have never been recognized in the law as persons in the whole sense", and since Roe, abortion is the only sense in which the unborn *cannot* by law be regarded as persons for the purposes of the right to life.

Meanwhile the state of Oregon has a mandatory add campaign to remind people that "Pregnancy and alcohol don't mix", not that they want to force *their* morality on everyone else.

Is this a great country or what?

The Moral Circle
More Schizophrenia

"And well may the children weep before you;
They are weary ere they run;
They have never seen the sunshine, nor the glory
Which is brighter than the sun:"
Elizabeth Barrett Browning[196]

The confusion of our moral sensibilities is the inevitable result of our inability to confront the central fact of abortion. It deliberately kills a young human being. This fact, however poorly understood in its moral implications, is no longer a subject of debate. It has now become a matter of settled textbook science. Even so, it is an openly agreed on fact that legal jurisprudence has consistently refused to acknowledge. Lawyers, judges, courts and legislatures habitually dance around this universally known fact like medieval scholastics. As a result, doctors, nurses, parents and teachers are required by law to engage in the same malignant dance.

Historically, we can trace the origin back to the Roe and Doe decisions themselves. The Court deliberately failed to make clear the nature of the being whose killing they were authorizing. By claiming ignorance of a fact that the Court was not in ignorance of, they ruled out of order any subsequent argumentation in favor of the right of an unborn child to live. The Court expressly gave permission to destroy life that they deemed unworthy of life. It did so at the urging of a small number of lawyers, all on one side of the case: Sarah Weddington, and Linda Coffee for Roe, Margie Pitts Hames, for Doe and Cyril Means, author of a propagandized report on the history of abortion and lawyer for NARAL at the time of the decision. Weddington, Coffee and Hames argued formally before the

---

[196] "The Cry of the Children" Elizabeth Barrett Browning, published in *Blackwood's Edinburgh*, 1843.

Court, but it was the Means flawed history article that the Court adopted as authentic without further historical inquiry. It was as if the Court had deliberately set out to rule as it did from the beginning.

Squaring this moral circle[197] has become a major industry since 1973. It has lead to confusion, and the organization of death on an industrial scale; 55 million human dead in the U.S. alone, 400 million in China more than the dead from all the wars and socialist tyrannies of the 20th century combined. Nothing the Third Reich or any Soviet committee of commissars could have imagined comes close. If, as estimated there are around 43 million abortions worldwide each year[198], then the total number of aborted children since 1973 would be in the neighborhood of 1.8 billion.

Still, we can take heart that there are still individuals, even including some prosecutors and politicians who are trying to poke holes through the chinks in the Supreme Courts legal armor despite being repeatedly assured that "resistance is futile".

The result is a series of legal chimeras like "Laci and Connor's Law" (also known as the "Unborn Victims of Violence Act"), which gives the protection of law to some unborn children that the Roe Court sought deliberately to deny. The technical legal term is "child in utero" which the law defines as a "victim", but only if injured or killed in a narrowly constructed list of Federal crimes of violence.

---

[197] "Squaring the circle" is philosophy speak for an impossible task; you can't make a circle a square and vice versa.

[198] "Facts on Induced Abortion Worldwide," (November 2105) Alan Guttmacher Institute report (the Guttmacher Institute is the research arm of Planned Parenthood). The report lists 45.6 in 1995, 41.6 in 2003 and 43.8 in 2008.

The child is a fetus or clump of cells if the sensitivities of the mother and her aborting doctor need soothing, but is a human being if she intends to *not abort* the child. This includes but is not limited to the case of a pregnant wife being murdered by her philandering husband when the fetus/child dies as well. It includes the death of said fetus/child when a pregnant woman is caught between two quarreling men, is struck by one or both and the resulting injury causes the death of the fetus/child. (See *Exodus* 21 for further information.[199])

The Unborn Victims of Violence Act is part of the ancient legal traditions of Moses and Hammurabi, but it cannot square the circle. It leaves unanswered the specific nature of the being that is injured; it *must* do so by fiat from the Supreme Court of the land. No statute that does not bow before the 1973 legal travesty of Roe will survive court scrutiny, and this is because the Court refused to settle the central question of the humanity of the child.

The Court stated with absolute clarity its muddling of the situation.

> *"We need not resolve the difficult question of when life begins. When those trained in the respective disciplines of medicine, philosophy, and theology are unable to arrive at any consensus, the judiciary, at this point in the development of man's knowledge, is not in a position to speculate as to the answer..."*[200]

This creates a number of difficulties. First, the idea that resolving the question of when life begins is "difficult" is plainly

---

[199] *Exodus* 21:22-25 reads in relevant part *"If men strive, and hurt a woman with child, so that her fruit* [unborn child] *depart from her* [die], *... then thou shalt give life for life, Eye for eye, tooth for tooth, hand for hand, foot for foot, Burning for burning, wound for wound, stripe for stripe."*
[200] Roe v. Wade, 410 U. S. 160.

false. A consensus from any or all of the fields mentioned is not difficult. It is common knowledge that life begins when it is conceived, neither before nor after. It would be no speculation at all for the "judiciary" to decide that what everybody else knows. Moreover, the reference to "this point in the development of man's knowledge" is troubling. The term "this point" refers to human knowledge in January of 1973. The judiciary might have begun its "speculations" the following month or year and have been confident that additional knowledge would be available. More importantly, the state of human knowledge in 1973 was nowhere near as blinkered as the Court would have all subsequent generations believe.

Three years prior to the Roe decision, the journal *California Medicine* had written about the

> *"... curious avoidance of the scientific fact, which everyone really knows, that human life begins at conception and is continuous whether intra- or extra-uterine until death."*[201]

The journal makes no reference to medical, philosophical or theological difficulties deciding the starting point of human life. It commences when it is conceived and this is a well-known *"scientific fact"*.

The Court knew what it was doing of course. It was kicking up dust for the purpose of claiming poor vision. In doing so, it ruled out any argument in favor of fetal humanity without discussion or argument. The Court simply ruled arbitrarily and capriciously that an unborn child was not a human being at any stage prior to birth, in direct contravention of what everyone knew to be true. It's only justification for this ruling was to apply the label of "speculation" to widely known scientific fact. There can be little doubt that the Court

---

[201] "A New Ethic for Medicine and Society," *California Medicine: The Western Journal of Medicine*, (113, no. 3, 1970), pp. 67-68.

knew full well the fraudulent nature of its statement and went ahead with it anyway.

It's no wonder that we experience a sense of confused schizophrenia when we try to sort out the legalities from the ethics. You can kill a child when he's within the womb but not without; someone else can't kill him if he's an intentional pregnancy and you want him, but he's no different from a hamburger that you shouldn't have eaten and want to regurgitate, if you decide you don't want him. It can go either way. (This also all applies if it's a "her".)

Dr. George Flesh explained in an article for the September 1999 L.A. *Times* why he had given up doing abortions. He had postponed an abortion for a week due to complications with the mother's cervix. Within that week the couple changed their minds and Dr. Flesh delivered a healthy little boy seven months later. He kept in touch with the couple and their son that they named Jeffrey. He played with the boy by the pool at their tennis club.

> *"The connection between the six-week-old human embryo and a laughing child stopped being an abstraction for me. While hugging my sons each morning, I started to think of the vacuum aspirator that I would use two hours later."*[202]

Little Jeffrey is now a healthy child. Sarah Marie Switzer and Samuel Armas are now both healthy children. Ana Rosa Rodriguez is now a healthy child, although missing her right arm from a botched abortion.

> *"Today we find obstetricians referring to a conceptus as a 'baby' when the mother wants the child and as "a product of conception" when the mother does not."*[203]

---

[202] Dr. George Flesh "Why I No Longer Do Abortions" (LA *Times* Sept. 12, 1991).
[203] *Dellapenna* p. 926

A doctor who saves a baby in utero from a life of spina bifida by pre-natal surgery in the morning can go down the hall in the afternoon and abort a baby at the same stage of development for no reason more compelling than a changed mind; the same kind of changed mind that saved little Jeffrey, but in the other direction.

> *"Abortion attempts to make conception a reversible fact; it happened only if you want it to happen."*[204]

The idea that abortion is just like contraception is no less a fiction when a court certifies it as a "right". Some things are impossible no matter how badly you want them. The court can make up any number of fantasies it likes; it can't change the biological facts of human nature. It can't change the biological fact that an embryo and then a fetus is a human being. It can't change the moral fact that a human being is a person. It can't change the biological/moral fact that killing a human embryo/fetus is killing an innocent human person. What it *has* done is declare that *for the purposes of the law*, the killing of innocent human persons is not always illegal, nor does it require much in the way of justification. Neither has it clarified a sensible criterion that distinguishes between human persons who have a right to life and those who don't.

It is irrational to suppose that a child is killable inside but not outside the womb, that a child is a murder victim if the mother wants it, but mere product of conception (POC) if not, that the mother or society or a court confers humanity or personhood on a child by arbitrary choice. This is a throwback to the way the ancient Roman paterfamilias would welcome or discard his progeny in the first nine days of a new child's life. These are not examples of progress.

---

[204] Sidney Callahan "The First Stage of Life is Life" (LA *Times* June 19, 1991), p. B7.

"A woman who is pregnant against her wish lives at war with her body. The fetus is a foreign body…"[205]

A fetus is indeed foreign; it is an entirely different person from the mother. Why is she only at war if she doesn't want to be pregnant, and why is she at war with *her* body, if the fetus is the foreigner? If she is at war with *her* body, why strike out at that *other* person's body who is not at war with her. Why not commit her act of war against the one she's (allegedly) at war with and leave the baby out of it?

This may be *moral* schizophrenia but it's also a spiritual disorder. The confusion begins with the ideology that motivated the Roe/Doe cases in the first place. *"We need not resolve the difficult question of when life begins,"* said the Blackmun Court, so they just made something up. Resolving the question of human life, however difficult, was precisely the Court's first duty. Failure to resolve that question should have obligated them to rule in favor of life. Instead they gave a blank check to everyone to abort as many babies as they wanted for any reason.

Any shooter on the range knows that if you can't resolve the question of who or what might be down range, the one thing you *don't* do is to open fire. Every presupposition must be made in favor of preserving and protecting life. That's why you look both ways before you cross the street. That's why hunters make sure of their target (and what's behind it) before they pull the trigger. That's why you watch your kids in the pool. That's why you may drive them to school and pick them up at the end of they day. That's why you tell them never to talk to strangers. When in doubt, *be careful*:

---

[205] Marielouise Janssen-Jurreit, *Sexism-The Male Monopoly of History and Thought,* (New York, NY: Farrar, Strauss and Giroux, 1976).

"therefore choose life, that both thou and thy [children] *may live."*
206

The Supreme Court might have figured that simple rule of jurisprudence out if they hadn't been in so eager to give a victory to their ideological allies. They thought they'd settled the issue. They did the opposite. Once their example of slovenly reasoning was set into the legal record, the consequences began to flow, pushed hard by the pump of liberalism/progressivism. Contradictions (as with "square" circles) are not the kind of things that can be resolved, no matter how vigorous the court defense. Set out to "settle" a question by contradicting the known facts of embryology, biology, previous law, and basic morality, and all the dancing legal gymnastics in the world can't prevent chaos.

Abraham Lincoln, in arguing a court case of his own once asked a jury "How many legs does a dog have if you call the tail a leg?" Lest the jurors be inclined to give the "obvious" answer of five, Lincoln reminded them of what they already knew that "Calling a tail a leg doesn't make it a leg." Legal positivists like to imagine that the law is whatever a court says it is. Courts like to rule that "It is not true, however, that the legal order necessarily corresponds to the natural order."[207] A human being, as a natural entity can be declared a non-human or non-person, if the court wants to do so. Presumably, they can declare a dog's tail a leg for purposes of deciding legally that a dog has five legs.

Fortunately, we have Judge Burke's eloquent dissent in the Burn v. N.Y. Hospitals case.

"This argument was not only made by Nazi lawyers and Judges at Nuremberg, but also is advanced today by the

---

[206] *Deuteronomy* 30:19.
[207] Robert M. Byrn, v. New York City Health & Hospitals, Court of Appeals of New York, 1972, Judge Brietel writing for the majority.

Soviets in Eastern Europe... To equate the judicial deference ... in a local zoning case with the case of the destruction of a child in embryo which is conceded to be "human" and "is unquestionably alive" is an acceptance of the thesis that the "State is supreme", and that "live human beings" have no inalienable rights in this country. The most basic of these rights is the right to live, especially in the case of the "unwanted" who are defenseless... Human beings are not merely creatures of the State, and by reason of that fact, our laws should protect the unborn from those who would take his life...

We began our legal life as a Nation and a State with the guarantee that these were inalienable rights that come not from the State but from an external source of authority superior to the State which authority regulated our inalienable liberties and with which our laws and Constitutions must now conform. That authority alone ... also tests the Constitutions and the United Nations Convention against genocide which forbids any Nation or State to classify any group of living human beings as fit subjects for annihilation... It is the inalienable right to life in the nature of the child embryo who is "a human" and is "a living being"... The Appellate Division and the majority agree that the "state", as in Nazi Germany, could decide what human beings are persons or nonpersons".[208]

No court can make a dog with five legs, a man a slave (Dred Scott notwithstanding), nor can it fashion an "imbecile" out of a normal woman, (Buck v. Bell notwithstanding) nor create a "right" to kill, no matter how many spectral penumbras are consulted. The Court would have had better luck (and made better law) with a Ouija board.

---

[208] Ibid., Judge Burke dissenting.

Doubtful Dogma
Eugenics and Bioethics

"One of the most remarkable features in our domesticated races is that we see in them adaptation, not indeed to the animal's or plant's own good, but to man's use or fancy."
Charles Darwin[209]

"We must breed a race of thoroughbreds."
Margaret Sanger[210]

When Darwin first proposed his theory of evolution he reasoned that humans had been breeding livestock, domestic animals and pets for several thousand years. Those who own dogs and cats are the beneficiaries of this practice. Dogs have been around humans for about 10,000 years and their owners have deliberately bred them for a variety of traits. Some dogs are excellent hunting companions, others specialize at sheep herding, and many of the ones you know are mongrelized crossbreeds that may have no specialty at all, except playing with your kids. Many mutts are especially hearty and healthy due to the absence of inbreeding, that otherwise might lead to congenital defects of the heart, hip or temperament. The story is the same with cats, except that cats have been around humans for only about 5,000 years with the result that they retain more of their original wildness, as any cat owner can tell you.

Humans have known about this for a long time. You just mate any two of the same species, both with the trait you want them to pass on, and you'll have a whole litter of hunting dogs, mouse catching cats, or race horses.

---

[209] Darwin, *On the Origin of Species,* John Murray publishers, London, 1859, Chapter 1.
[210] Margaret Sanger, *The Pivot of Civilization*, (New York, NY: Brentanos, 1922).

Darwin wondered if, since this kind of artificial selection for traits worked so well, nature might also select for certain traits, and over time, breed all the variants of species that we know today. Thus he reasoned from a well-known process of artificial selection to a revolutionary concept of evolution by *natural* selection.

It took him a while to figure out a mechanism in nature that would make natural selection work. It's all well and good to say that it all works by "natural processes", but without further explanation that's one step removed from blaming it all on God. Scientists go to the most extraordinary effort to avoid this. Then, by simple happenstance Darwin found himself reading Thomas Malthus' *Essay on Population.*[211] Malthus was convinced that population inevitably increased until it exceeded the available food supply, whereupon the "surplus population" died off. That this is untrue for human populations escaped Malthus' notice, but Darwin adapted it for his theory on natural selection. Oddly enough, Darwin's competitor evolution-wise was Alfred Russell Wallace who had independently read the same passages from Malthus and come to the same conclusion. Darwin figured that Russell was getting ready to publish and ended his own dithering thus beating Russell to the punch. It is for this reason alone that we speak of "Darwinism" rather than "Wallace-ism". He who publishes first gets the credit.

Contrary to what many people believe, Darwin was not immediately scourged and driven from polite (or religious) society. Indeed, many religious people had no trouble whatever accepting his new theory. Darwin himself was conventionally religious, although in later years his faith became more "agnostic". This was not due to his scientific ideas but to the death of his favorite child, Annie who died at the age of 10 of scarlet fever. Darwin himself is buried in that most august of religious venues, Westminster Abbey.

---

[211] Thomas Robert Malthus, "An Essay on the Principle of Population," (London, UK: Joseph Johnson Publisher, 1798).

However, it wasn't long before followers of Darwin's theory (and late in life Darwin himself) began to take the original reasoning from artificial to natural selection, and reverse it once again, applying it to human beings. If evolution produced the "survival of the fittest" (not Darwin's favorite phrase but popularized by Herbert Spencer) why shouldn't the human species produce the "best" in itself by artificial means. From this idea has been deduced much mischief. What became known as "Social Darwinism" produced an ideology of the strong dominating the weak in human affairs that came to be used by socialist regimes, from National Socialism in Germany to Bolshevist socialism in the Soviet Union.

Social Darwinism, however, had its origins in democratic societies with the writings of organizers like Margaret Sanger (founder of Planned Parenthood), Alfred Kinsey, Clarence Gamble, and Francis Galton, cousin of Charles Darwin. Darwin himself in his late work, *The Decent of Man*[212], published 12 years after *Origin of Species*, speculated that humans should themselves take over the planning of their own evolution.

Social Darwinism (by this time better known as "eugenics") claimed that those at the top of the social food chain must have gotten there on their own merits and breeding; in other words by virtue of the doctrine of the "survival of the fittest", those at the top of the social register must be the fittest. It was up to them to ensure their own breeding (by making lots of babies. It was also up to them, as leaders of society, to make sure that the lower classes had fewer children, through education about birth control if possible, forced sterilization if necessary. In the famous case of Carrie Buck taken all the way to the Supreme Court, Supreme Court Justice Oliver Wendell Holmes commented that "Three generations of imbeciles are enough"[213] and decided that Carrie Buck was "feeble minded"

---

[212] John Murray publishers, London,1871.
[213] Buck v. Bell, 274 U.S. 200 (1927).

and should be sterilized against her will. There was never any real evidence that Carrie was anything but perfectly normal, and before her sterilization had a normal daughter who made it to the honor roll in school. This daughter, Vivian Buck, was the supposed third generation of imbeciles, diagnosed at the ripe old age of six months.[214]

It's easy to forget today, but Eugenics was, as recently as the mid 20th century, a popular movement in the United States and Europe. In the 1930's it formed the basis of articles written by respected physicians arguing for forced sterilization, "euthanasia" and infanticide. Among the most well known was a book published in 1920 by Karl Binding and Alfred Hoche called "The Permission to Destroy Life Unworthy of Life". They described the taking of "unworthy" life (including the terminally ill, the mentally ill, and the deformed; anyone who might be severely disabled) as a "healing" procedure. This work became one of the central theses used to justify extermination of whole populations of Europeans in the 1930's and 1940's.

It is uncomfortable to realize, but eugenics type procedures are still recommended to "improve the species". Former US Surgeon General Joycelyn Elders once noted that "abortion has reduced the number of children afflicted with severe defects. The number of Down syndrome infants in Washington State in 1976 was 64 percent lower than it would have been without legal abortion."[215]

This is eugenics without the name.

Down syndrome appears to be declining because many Down babies are being aborted. This is so much the case that couples who know in advance that a child will be born with Down are strongly

---

[214] Stephen Jay Gould, "Carrie Buck's Daughter," *Natural History* magazine, (July 1984).
[215] Joycelyn Elders testifying before the U.S. Congress, 1990.

pressured to abort, and are often looked down on afterwards if they choose not to do so.[216] The current emphasis is on Down syndrome because it's easy to detect by pre-natal testing. More conditions and syndromes will follow as our science gets better. One writer calls this "medical cleansing". That's not a new kind of detergent; it's akin to *ethnic cleansing* which is a fancy name for genocide.

It's not just among our cultural "elites" that we find this naïve eugenics mentality. Ordinary people ask why we allow handicapped children to continue to live. ("Imagine being deaf and blind; what kind of life is that?") We may call it "naïve" because not everyone is prepared to imagine just where this kind of thinking leads. One has to wonder if it's possible that so many people have never heard of Helen Keller.

It's true that animals don't let the runt of the litter survive. It's not true that this is an example for humans to emulate. We all know people who have cats (just to pick one example) and when a litter is born, sometimes there's a "runt"; one that's smaller than the others. In the wild such a kitten would be neglected to death. In most (human) families it's singled out for special protection. A veterinarian who was once given a kitten with three legs assuming that he would find a home for it. He decided he liked the little one so much he kept it. The kitten quickly learned to do everything the other cats did, including climb over everything everywhere. We behave differently from cats (both with respect to our pet cats *and* with respect to our children) because we're not cats. If we want to continue to be distinguished from the beasts we will have behave differently from dogs, cats and cattle.

Eugenics and the concept of feeblemindedness are based on pseudoscience with no basis in fact. Carrie was committed to a mental institution by her foster parents after being raped and

---

[216] Reist, *Defiant Birth*, 2006.

impregnated by a cousin. It's been suggested that family embarrassment may have been the real reason for the commitment. It may also be that being pregnant she was assumed to be promiscuous. Also, since her mother was thought to be feebleminded, it was assumed that all *her* offspring would also be feebleminded, including Carrie and all her children.

This junk science was very fashionable stuff once. Unfortunately judges, even Supreme Court Justices aren't experts in anything but the law, and when they decide to venture outside of it, they have to rely on the testimony of trusted "experts". Sadly many experts are also enamored of fashionable nonsense, which is assumed to be "scientific" but isn't.

We're no more immune to junk-science now than they were in Carrie's day. As for the socialist tyrannies of the 20th century, it's been estimated that these governments have killed something like 100 million people, at least as many as were killed in the wars of the same century, started by the same governments. There are so many dead that the number can't be reliably estimated even to the nearest million.

We could eliminate any disease if all we cared about was not having to look at it. Cancer would disappear if we used all our screening tests to kill everyone who showed signs of malignancy. Malaria would vanish if we exterminated everyone who came down with it. (We could also eliminate malaria by re-introducing the vigorous use of DDT, but that would be environmentally incorrect.)

If we could find a pre-natal test that would predict everyone who would develop cancer or malaria or muscular dystrophy, we could do away with telethons. There is no disease that couldn't be eliminated by this form of early detection. This is how eugenicists "improve" the species, by getting rid of everyone who isn't perfect. It's no less eugenics if it's done before birth.

The term "eugenics" was coined by Darwin's cousin Francis Galton. Galton can reasonably be said to have invented the field. It was Galton's reading of *The Origin of Species* that inspired him to devote the rest of his life to the study of manipulating human heredity and reproduction.

Much of early eugenics, which quickly became popular in the U.S., emphasized sterilization (including forced sterilization) but there was also a "euthanasia" component that tended to stay in the background. Official numbers of those sterilized in the U.S. are around 60,000. Buck v. Bell has never been overturned. In fact, it was *reaffirmed* in Roe v. Wade. Most state sterilization laws have been abandoned by general consent.

One early and telling case (by no means the only one) was the 1915 death of baby Bollinger. The Bollinger baby, born with a number of birth defects was allowed to die over a period of five days with the permission of his parents by the family physician Dr. Harry Haiselden. While surgery was available to fix at least some of the child's infirmities, Dr. Haiselden strongly recommended that the parents, Anna and Allen Bollinger, withhold their consent for these procedures on the grounds that if the child survived, it would suffer a life of pain and deprivation.[217]

This sort of thing may once have been a fairly common agreement between doctors and parents of deformed newborns. The difference here is that Dr. Haiselden wrote to the local Chicago newspaper, publicizing and defending his actions. His series of articles was noticed by the New York *Times*, and the Washington *Post*, gaining considerable notoriety. Thus began a highly publicized campaign to promote his ideas on infant euthanasia. He bragged

---

[217] Martin S. Pernick, *The Black Stork: Eugenics and the Death of "Defective" Babies in American Medicine and Motion Pictures since 1915*, (London, UK: Oxford University Press, 1999), p. 4.

about his decision arguing not only that "it is our duty to defend ourselves and the future generations against the mentally defective"[218], but also that such individuals are objects of pity and should be spared a life of pain. He claimed to have been in the active practice of allowing similar babies to die in his practice for the previous 10 years, and went on to participate in five more known cases.

He became involved in, directly or indirectly, in a number of subsequent cases of parents asking for the death of their own afflicted babies. After two years he revealed that he had moved from "passive" euthanasia to using a narcotic to ease and accelerate the process. Parents cited Haiselden as a precedent to their own doctors and on occasion even asked Haiselden to consult or intervene on their behalf.

Haiselden's Kevorkian-like desire for publicity went to far as to appear in a filmed fictionalizing of the Bollinger case, where he played a character based on himself. The silent film, known as "The Black Stork" was shown regionally throughout the U.S. possibly as recently as 1942.[219]

While the subject of considerable condemnation he also garnered support from sources as widely different as Clarence Darrow, and of all people, Helen Keller. Keller, born blind and deaf, was a well-known advocate for the disabled, particularly for the visually and hearing impaired. She was also at the time an activist member of the Socialist Party and the Industrial Workers of the World, and her support for the disabled did not extend to *all* forms of disability. She wrote a letter recommending jury-like panels of doctors to decide on which babies should be put to death. The panel

---

[218] Natalie Oveyssi "The Short Life and Eugenic Death of Baby John Bollinger" *Psychology Today*, Oct. 12, 2015.
[219] Pernick, p. 6.

would act "only in cases of true idiocy, where there could be no hope of mental development." She concluded that "we must decide between a fine humanity like Dr. Haiselden's and a cowardly sentimentalism."[220]

Haiselden briefly became a progressive cause-célèbre gathering support not just from Darrow and Keller, but also from historian Charles Beard, Federal Food and Drug founder Harvey Wiley and Baltimore's Catholic James Cardinal Gibbons. Others criticized Haiselden's actions and publicity seeking, including Jane Addams, Julia Lathrop and Massachusetts General Hospital's Urology Department founder Hugh Cabot.[221]

A string of newspaper editorial endorsements for both sides of the controversy followed. There were numerous investigations as well with state attorneys unable to reach sufficient agreement to make prosecution possible. These continued with each of Haiselden's subsequent infant cases, but the only action was from the Chicago Medical Society which expelled him for being a publicity hound.[222]

After about two years of headlines the issue lost it's appeal to the press and disappeared from view. Haiselden moved to Cuba where he died in 1919, but his brief time in the media floodlights got him hailed as a eugenics pioneer. However briefly, the eugenics debate moved beyond the emphasis on birth prevention; it displayed the additional possibility of the passive or active killing of "defectives" who might range from mild birth defects to birth "monsters".

---

[220] Helen Keller to *The New Republic*, Dec. 18, 1915 "Physicians' juries for defective babies".
[221] *Pernick*, p. 6.
[222] Ibid, pp 9-10.

Few remember Helen Keller as a socialist supporter of the Soviet Union or a eugenicist, so the best-known American eugenicist was probably Margaret Sanger, founder of Planned Parenthood. Sanger's nominal interest was promotion of birth control, but her eugenic motivations are now widely accepted. She was convinced that many minority populations, constituted a set of inferiors that could be limited by reducing their ability to breed. Persuading them to adopt population control measures was high on her agenda.

In a 1932 article for her own publication, *Birth Control Review*, called "A Plan for Peace" she outlined a series of points for the country, which included recommendations for "sterilization and segregation" of "tainted" populations, to protect the country from the "burden" of overpopulation by the "feebleminded" and *"to give certain dysgenic groups in our population the choice of segregation or sterilization."*[223]

Sanger called for "corralling" the entire population of undesirables segregated and supervised (she estimated about 5 million mental and moral degenerates) on "farm lands" purchased to contain them for "their entire lives".[224] She didn't specifically define the phrase "dysgenic groups". "Dysgenic" means the opposite of "eugenic". The word implies that which ever group turns out to be *dysgenic* has something wrong with its genes. As usual, the eugenicist enforces the rules with a firm "choice" between voluntary and forced sterilization.

Sanger's 1921 book *The Pivot of Civilization* cited three social systems as capable, to varying degrees, of dealing with society's ills; philanthropy and charity (at best merely ameliorative

[223] *Birth Control Review*, (Vol. XVI No. 4, April 1932), pp. 107-108.
[224] Margaret Sanger, "A Plan for Peace", *Birth Control Review* April 1932, pp. 107-108.

at worst paternalistic) Marxism (too limited and superficial) and eugenics, far and away for her the most promising.

> *"The Eugenist points out that heredity is the great determining factor in the lives of men and women. Eugenics is the attempt to solve the problem from the biological and evolutionary point of view… Eugenics thus aims to seek out the root of our trouble, to study humanity as a kinetic, dynamic, evolutionary organism, shifting and changing with the successive generations, rising and falling, cleansing itself of inherent defects, or under adverse and dysgenic influences, sinking into degeneration and deterioration."*[225]

The April 1933 issue of *Birth Control Review* (its sterilization issue) featured on its cover a map of the U.S. showing which states had enacted sterilization laws and which had not. The issue began with an excerpt from Justice Holmes' decision in Buck v. Bell. "The principle that sustains compulsory vaccination is broad enough to cover cutting the Fallopian tubes. Three generations of imbeciles are enough."[226] The issue went on with articles on "Eugenic Sterilization" by Paul Popenoe, "Selective Sterilization" by E. A. Whitney, M. D., "Birth Control and Sterilization" by Havelock Ellis, "Eugenical Aspects of Legal Sterilization" by Harry H. Laughlin, "Defective Families" by C. 0. McCormick, M. D. and "Towards Race Betterment" by Theodore Russell Robie, M. D.

The same issue also published an article by Dr. Ernst Rüdin titled "Eugenic Sterilization: An Urgent Need". While focusing in the essay with voluntary sterilization Rüdin noted the need for "systematic and careful propaganda...where sterilization is advisable", beginning with the directors of medical facilities and schools, individual medical practitioners and finally with individual

---

[225] Sanger, *The Pivot of Civilization*, 1921.
[226] Buck v. Bell, 274 U.S. 200 (1927).

patients. Rüdin claimed here to see no need for compulsory sterilization although "Whether in the far future something of the sort might be required cannot be predicted now I do not foresee any such necessity..."[227] He considers the sterilization of individuals whether mentally ill or just "subnormal", but quickly moves on to those who are not abnormal at all, but may be "carriers" of disease while not being sufferers themselves; and to their families. All should be vigorously persuaded to have themselves sterilized. At the same time the exceptional, the talented, the elite should be encouraged to reproduce at an accelerated rate. He notes in passing that "The oft-encountered objection that genius or talent is frequently associated with insanity has no solid foundation." (He might have noticed that genius often fails to reproduce at all, J.S. Bach being the notable exception. The list of great geniuses from Beethoven to Newton who produced few or no children has been commented on by David Stove.[228])

Rüdin was at the time of his April 1933 article for Sanger the director of the Kaiser Wilhelm Institute for Genealogy in Munich. He quickly shed whatever reluctance he had to forced sterilization, and was one of the forces behind the Law for the Prevention of Hereditarily Diseased Offspring enacted in the Third Reich in July of 1933. In 1934 (not the "far future" he claimed) he remarked to the German Society for Racial Hygiene that...

---

[227] Ernst Rüdin, "Eugenic Sterilization: An Urgent Need" *Birth Control Review*, (Vol. XVII No. 4, April 1933), p. 103.

[228] *"Men of the highest genius who were childless include Newton, Faraday, and Mendel; Vivaldi, Handel and Beethoven; Gibbon Macaulay and Carlyle, Plato Aquinas, Bacon, Locke, Leibnitz, Hume, Kant and Mill...Copernicus, Swift, Adam Smith, Samuel Johnson, Haydn, Dalton, Francis Galton himself..."*

David Stove *Darwinian Fairytales*, (New York NY: Encounter Books, 1995), p. 44.

"Not until the political activity of Adolph Hitler, and only through his work has a thirty-year long dream of translating racial hygiene into action finally become a reality... We can hardly express our efforts more plainly or appropriately than in the words of the Fuehrer: 'Whoever is not physically or mentally fit must not pass on his defects to his children. The state must take care that only the fit produce children.'"[229]

The sad fact is that National Socialism didn't exclusively invent the racial ideology of the Third Reich. For that, they looked, at least in part, to the United States. In *Mein Kampf*, published in 1924, Hitler noted his interest in legislation in American states such as Virginia and California for their eugenic programs.[230] Both the Carnegie Institute and the Rockefeller Foundation helped fund the American eugenics project. In 1912 the Carnegie Institute funded a report by the American Breeders Association regarding ways to eugenically improve the human species. As usual with American proponents the emphasis was on birth control and sterilization, but the committee also considered "euthanasia" as a potential, if partial solution to be considered.[231]

We've encountered Paul Popenoe earlier. His text, *Applied Eugenics*, published in 1918 with Roswell Hill Johnson, mentions

---

[229] Ernst. Rüdin, "Aufgaben and Ziele der Deutschen Gesellschaft fur Rassenhygiene," (Archiv Fur Rassen- und Gesellschafts- biologie 28 1934), pp. 228-29.

[230] *"There is today one state in which at least a weak beginning toward a better conception is noticeable. Of course, it is not our model German Republic, but the American Union..."*
Mein Kampf Volume Two, Chapter 3.

[231] Bleeker Van Wagenen, "Preliminary Report of the Committee of the Eugenic Section of the American Breeder's Association to Study and to Report on the Best Practical Means for Cutting Off the Defective Germ-Plasm in the Human Population" (Eugenics Education Society, London, 1912). College of Law Faculty Publications, Georgia State University Archive, Paper 74.

"execution" as a possible method of control. They stop short of recommending it, in part because it violated the "spirit of the times", and "is not considered seriously by the eugenics movement". He does not shy away from coercive methods, however, which he says he intends to interpret "very broadly".[232]

"Execution" as such remained on the back burner in the United States, but the fact remains that American eugenicists were convinced that they needed to limit the gene pool of large groups of peoples considered defective. In another age this has been called "ethnic cleansing", but ethnic groups weren't the only targets of eugenicists. Anyone who might be determined to be "feeble-minded", suffering from intellectual impairment, Down syndrome (then known as "Mongoloidism" - individuals were known as "Mongoloid idiots"). Many alleged "idiots" were suffering from nothing more than extreme poverty, but Popenoe and Johnson lump them all together as "tribes" of various sorts of "Jukes, Nams, Kallikaks, Zeroes, Dacks, Ishmaels, Sixties, Hickories, Hill Folk, Piney Folk and the rest, with which the readers of the literature of restrictive eugenics are familiar."[233] That heredity should be considered responsible for their problems was more article of faith than science. While the mentally ill *might* from time to time harbor a few geniuses, the feeble minded had nothing whatever to offer society, and this pseudo-scientific classification amounts to an obsession among American Eugenicists like Popenoe and Sanger.

At the same time, it would be a mistake to ignore the racial element to eugenics. Madison Grant's *The Passing of The Great Race; or The Racial Basis of European History*[234], published in 1916 put forth a racial hygienist ideology of the racial superiority of the

---

[232] Paul Popenoe & Roswell Hill Johnson, *Applied Eugenics,* (New York, NY: Macmillan, 1918 p. 192.
[233] Ibid., p. 176.
[234] Madison Grant, *The Passing of The Great Race,* (New York, NY: Charles Scribner's Sons, 1916).

"Nordic" peoples, which was popular for a time among American eugenicists, but which fell out of favor before World War II. It was, however, taken up by German eugenicists who took the term "Nordic" and changed it to "Aryan". Nazi ideologist, Alfred Rosenberg himself preferred "Aryo-Nordic", but the difference was semantic.

Grant's fear was that Nordic protestants were being out-bred by immigrants from non-European stock as well as what he called "Negroids" and "Mongoloids". He claimed that Nordic people were committing "race suicide" through intermarriage and that the solution was sterilization, quarantine, segregation, and ghettoization of undesirable individuals and races.

Much of this theory fell out of favor, in part because of the "Germanic" implications of "Nordic" theory. Sympathy for all things German was at low ebb during and after World War I. Nevertheless, sometime between the world wars dedicated American eugenicists looked again to Europe for leadership, in particular to Germany.

Grant's *The Passing of the Great Race,* greatly admired by Hitler, recommended stronger medicine than occasional sterilization as a eugenic methodology. It also went beyond the category of infants to "an ever widening circle of social discards". Grant wanted a national system of "rigid selection" that would feed and nourish "social failures" but would also make sure that they were never allowed to reproduce;

> "...*beginning always with the criminal, the diseased, and the insane, and extending gradually to types which may be called weaklings rather than defectives, and perhaps ultimately to worthless race types.*"[235]

---

[235] *Ibid*, p. 28.

After World War II when the Holocaust became widely known, and gave eugenics a very public black eye, it went underground, busily renaming organizations, re-tooling the message for a new audience, and scrubbing the public relations image. It never disappeared. The name "eugenics" itself isn't much mentioned any more, and many people have never heard the word. But eugenics as a concept never disappeared and is creeping back into public consciousness via progressive ideology.

The spirit of eugenics means the exact opposite of what the Declaration of Independence calls the equality of all men, "endowed by their Creator with certain unalienable rights". Progressivism recognizes no concept of inherent natural rights at all, but adopts the legal positivist notion that all rights come from the state and its laws as interpreted by the courts. Progressivism does not recognize that "all men are created equal", and, significantly, neither does eugenics. Some men, for the purposes of progressive eugenics are always "more equal" than others, and so some human beings may be declared by court order to be non-persons for the purposes of law. Such non-persons may be enslaved (Dred Scott v. Sandford) or sterilized (Buck v. Bell) or aborted (Roe v. Wade).

This provides so much fertile ground for so much mischief.

The World of Slippery Slopes
"The Most Influential Philosopher Alive"

"So, let's start again, without the preconceptions imposed on us by millennia of religious teachings, and ask: what makes it wrong to kill any being?"[236]

Peter Singer

Peter Singer is a bio-ethicist philosopher at Princeton once called the most influential philosopher alive. He's been interviewed many times, and appeared throughout the world as a speaker. In Germany and Austria where his views have reminded many of the Nazi pasts of both countries, he often has run into serious opposition. He argues in favor of routine infanticide.

In 2005 Marvin Olasky interviewed Singer for a *Townhall* article as follows:

> *"If the 21st century becomes a Singer century, we will also see legal infanticide of born children who are ill or who have ill older siblings in need of their body parts..."*[237]

Olasky asked Professor Singer what he thought of parents breeding children specifically to use the child's body parts in other children. Singer replied that it might be *"difficult to warm to parents"* like that but it wouldn't be *"really wrong in itself"*, nor *would there be anything wrong with a society where such parts farming of children were routine.*[238] Difficult to warm to indeed, but Singer is right about one thing. Such a society is essentially inevitable once traditional moral restraints (what he calls "preconceptions") are removed.

---

[236] Peter Singer, "Making Our Own Competency Should Be Paramount Decisions about Death", *Free Inquiry*, (August/September 2005).
[237] Marvin Olasky, Townhall.com December 2, 2004, "The Most Influential Philosopher Alive".
[238] Olasky.

Of course, not all bio-ethicist are as extreme as Singer; on the other hand not all are as moderate. John Harris has this comment on euthanasia of newborns as an extension of abortion.

> *"We can terminate for serious foetal abnormality up to term but cannot kill a newborn. What do people think has happened in the passage down the birth canal to make it okay to kill the foetus at one end of the birth canal but not at the other?"*[239]

If we continue the logic of his argument (and we must) we have to ask what has happened to a 1 week newborn and a 2 week newborn, or a 2 month or....

This is the difficulty that Singer and others have found themselves in. If we decide that just being human isn't enough, and we formulate criteria to distinguish between mere humans and persons, we find that our rules may apply to animals (making them persons, à la Singer[240]) or may *not apply* to a host of human beings who by our new criteria don't count as persons any more. It's hard as the dickens to keep from killing whole categories of humans to whom we *might* ordinarily want to give the right to life; otherwise we ourselves might become "difficult to warm to". We move from embryos to infants to the disabled, from abortion to euthanasia to whatever, in a series of tiny steps. The only solutions are to either stop killing embryos, or to let our "killable" category expand. The choice we make here is a test of character.

---

[239] John Harris Interview with *The* [London] *Sunday Times*. In fairness to Harris he has said that he does not advocate infanticide as a "policy". "I have never advocated or defended infanticide as a policy proposal. I would not and do not advocate the legalization of infanticide on the basis of any alleged ethical parity of infanticide with abortion." (*Practical Ethics*, University of Oxford, Feb. 29, 2012).

[240] Singer is a famous advocate of animal rights.

As Singer indicated, also expanding are our ideas about what we can do with the after-remains of the now deceased product of conception. Later term abortions particularly, will leave behind a number of body parts, which may be useful to other children (those we want to keep) or as subjects of research. Embryonic stem cells are no longer the only embryonic or fetal parts that are subjects of medical research. Recent videos of abortion providers negotiating the price of livers, hearts, legs, muscles and other partial remains of the babies they kill in utero have caused a sensation on the Internet. Once we step onto the slippery portion of the slope there's no way to stop, slow down, to even guess where our new ethical trajectory will take us. Will we go from killing fetuses to killing children, or go to breeding children for their organs? Yes.

Ever see a couple of kids who had to share a room? They try to demarcate who has which side of the room with a line; "You stay on your side, I'll stay on mine." It's only a matter of time before one of them ends up deciding that his side of the room includes the line itself; then he's standing just a wee bit over the line, then a little more, etcetera, etcetera, etcetera.

Someone once said, "The world is full of slippery slopes".

Yes it is.

Singer takes a lot of heat for his ideas (at least those ideas that get publicized outside of academia) but that's because he's well known, not because his ideas are more radical than others. They've become pretty "main stream" in bio-ethics departments in universities.

He resents the comparisons that many make to early eugenicists and the Nazis. He's said by those who have met him exceptionally mild mannered. More importantly, he doesn't single out Jews, homosexuals, Gypsies and other minorities the way the

Nazis did. Singer is no Nazi and it's a serious *mistake* to think of him as one.

The German "euthanasia" or "*sterbehilfe*" program proposed in the 1920's and implemented in earnest in 1939 didn't single out minorities either. It was proclaimed to be a benefit, indeed, ironically, a benefit that Jews were considered unworthy to receive. It began with the "*gnadentod*" or mercy death of children, quickly spread to adults, first the terminally ill, then the mentally disabled, first by voluntary request and then by outside decision "on behalf of" those who were considered incompetent to make their own choice. It began with lethal injection and proceeded to gas by carbon monoxide. Soon fake showers were constructed for the administering of the gas to larger numbers of people, a system transplanted intact to the extermination camps. In the Hadamar hospital alone, 10,000 people were gassed in the first eight months of 1941.[241]

Binding and Hoche in their 1920 work insisted that guidelines should make every effort to ensure that all euthanasia be voluntary, ruling out involuntary "mercy killings" insisting that each "permitting of killing which requires violating the will to live of the actual or potential victim is ruled out" and there must be no "reason to doubt the sincerity of his consent."[242]

It all sounds very reasonable, but even so, Binding and Hoche were well outside the mainstream in the 1920s. When the Third Reich came to power in 1933, they found their champion. Even here, the beginnings were modest. Child euthanasia for only

---

[241] Cathleen A. Cleaver and Edward Grant, "Lessons From History's Most Calamitous Experience", *Assisted Suicide & Euthanasia, past & present*, by J.C. Willke, MD et al, (Cincinati, OH: Hayes Publishing Company, 1998).
[242] Alfred Hoche, Karl Binding, "The Permission to Destroy Life Unworthy of Life".

the most severe cases was the original program, but adult terminal patients were quickly added to the protocol, followed by the mentally ill. Everything was justified on the grounds of a healing compassion but one not too encumbered by an "exaggerated concern for humanity".[243] None of this was originally anti-Semitic, because as noted euthanasia was considered a compassionate act and, Jews were considered unworthy of compassion, even one without "exaggerated concern for humanity".[244]

Moreover, much of the theory that informed the practices of the Third Reich came originally from main line thinkers like Margaret Sanger (founder of Planned Parenthood), Alfred Kinsey founder of the still functioning Kinsey Institute, and Clarence Gamble (of Procter and Gamble).

Singer wrote in 2005,

"During the next 35 years, the traditional view of the sanctity of human life will collapse... only a rump of hardcore, know-nothing religious fundamentalists will defend the view that every human life, from conception to death, is sacrosanct."[245]

Hoche wasn't a Nazi, but his writings were among the founding documents of Nazi eugenics. In the 1920's he wrote that,

"...a new age will arrive --- operating with a higher morality and with great sacrifice --- which will give up the requirement of an exaggerated humanism and overvaluation of mere human existence."[246]

---

[243] Cleaver and Grant, 1998.
[244] Ibid.
[245] Peter Singer "The Sanctity of Life" *Foreign Policy*, (August 30, 2005). http://www.foreignpolicy.com/articles/2005/08/30/the_sanctity_of_life.
[246] Binding and Hoche, 1920.

In Singer's brief article for *Foreign Policy* in 2005 he claims that public clamor will make the "new ethic" inevitable by making opposition to it politically impossible. *"Terri Schiavo's... case produced a surge in the number of people declaring they did not wish to be kept alive in a situation such as Schiavo's."*[247] Here we see the common "I wouldn't want to live like that" so often voiced in public opinion polls. It doesn't follow that *Terri* didn't want to live like that.

Singer goes on to claim that eventually, *"we will respect the right of autonomous, competent people to choose when to live and when to die."*[248] It was just a few lines above that his best example was someone who was *not* "autonomous" nor was she able to make any choice on her own. Terry Schiavo's death wasn't voluntary, it was decided for her by others. She was starved to death *by court order*. Singer tries to explain it like this.

> *"...it is difficult to think of any morally relevant properties that separate human beings with severe brain damage or other major intellectual disabilities from nonhuman animals..."*[249]

As usual with pro-abortion/pro-euthanasia bioethicists Singer must use the definition of "personhood" as that of having "relevant properties". Each bioethicist has a proprietary list of such properties, stated or unstated. While the lists are similar they are still peculiar to each individual, and thus have a sense of the arbitrary about them. Singer thinks that by 2040 only *"know-nothing religious fundamentalists"* will imagine that every human life is sacrosanct. The suggestion is dripping with condescension, but it's not obvious

---

[247] Singer *Foreign Policy*, (2005).
[248] Ibid.
[249] Peter Singer "Making Our Own Competency Should Be Paramount Decisions about Death", *Free Inquiry*, (August/September 2005).

that the only alternative to his kind of utilitarianism is theology. Immanuel Kant (1724-1804) proposed a version of non-utilitarian morality based "on reason alone". Whatever else one thinks about Kant's categorical imperative,[250] it isn't in any obvious sense theological. Indeed, it's expressly designed to be not based on religious doctrines at all. There are arguments against Singer's new moral age of permissiveness that make no reference to the book of *Genesis* or God.

Singer deals with one such that he calls the "slippery slope". He cites "studies" in the Netherlands and Belgium that, he says, show no abuse of the current permissive laws allowing euthanasia. Other writers have had no trouble coming up with plenty of evidence of abuse, bioethicist Wesley Smith[251] is among the best. This leaves Singer open to the charge of cherry picking his "studies", but the more obvious slippery slope objection remains simply this. He's ignored the biggest slippery slope of them all, the Third Reich. He can't credibly claim that arguments like his (and Binding/Hoche, Margaret Sanger, Madison Grant etc.) can't lead to totalitarian extremes, because it has already happened. Perhaps he makes the lesser claim that the "new ethic" won't make the rest of us become *actual* Nazis.

Or perhaps not, but it's still incumbent on him, and others like him, to show the end to the slope of slipperiness. Until then, we're entitled to ask, "Where will all this end?" As long as bioethicists continue to use each small victory to expand the scope of permissible action there can be no assurance of any end in sight. In fact, nothing in any utilitarian list of properties that make up the definition of so-called "personhood" provides any assurance.

---

[250] The imperative states that in general we should treat human beings as "ends in themselves" never "as a means only".
[251] Wesley J. Smith, *The Culture of Death: The Assault on Medical Ethics in America*, New York, NY: Encounter Books, 2000.

Once again we must refer to Father Neuhaus.

"Thousands of ethicists and bioethicists, as they are called, professionally guide the unthinkable on its passage through the debatable on its way to becoming the justifiable until it is finally established as the unexceptional."[252]

Defining food and water as "medical treatment" thus allowing dehydration and starvation of patients as a means of "withdrawing treatment" would have horrified the world 20 years ago, (and not just because it violated our notion of man in God's image). Now, it's legal in all 50 states. And bioethicists like Singer continue to press for more "liberalization" of our laws and our morality. Pro-life advocates have always claimed that abortion would lead to infanticide.[253] Singer confirms that idea.

"One point on which I agree with opponents of abortion is that, from the point of view of ethics rather than the law, there is no sharp distinction between the foetus and the newborn baby."[254]

Singer has been advocating the legitimacy of infanticide for some time, and *not just* for disabled babies. His notion of a lack of distinction between the newborn and the fetus is indeed shared with abortion opponents, and this implies the permissibility of infanticide in *every* case where abortion is permitted.[255] Since Singer is comfortable with the fact of 55 million abortions (give or take a million) since Roe v. Wade, he's presumably comfortable with 55

---

[252] Richard John Neuhaus, "The Return of Eugenics", *Commentary* Magazine, (April 1988).
[253] See the John Harris, interview with *The Sunday Times* quoted above.
[254] Singer, interview with *The Independent*, (September 11, 2006).
[255] See Giubilini and Minerva, "After Birth Abortion; Why Should the Baby Live?" " (*J Med Ethics* doi:10.1136/medethics-2011-100411).

million infanticides. He's also advocating terminating the elderly, and various classes of the disabled. This requires him to be comfortable with yet another 55 million. Each. The simple logic of his position s inexorable.

Is that slippery slope enough? To be sure, it's not going to turn any of us into literal Nazis. The National Socialist Workers Party of Germany is defunct, and swastika arm bands have been out of style for a couple of decades. No bioethics department is going to bring them back. But if Singer's ethical system of rules and definitions doesn't cause us to consider what the previous paragraph describes as a "holocaust", then a better (not necessarily new) ethics *really is* needed.

If all that separates us from tens of millions of babies, elders, and disabled being "aborted" and euthanized is a belief in man as the image of God, then we all need to return to the faith of our fathers.

Embryos and Syllogisms
The Inevitability of Infanticide

"It remains true that, on my view, neither abortion nor the killing of newborns is obviously a form of murder."[256]
Mary Anne Warren

For many years, anti-abortion activists have suggested that approving of abortion would inevitably lead to infanticide. This is what philosophers technically refer to as a *"reductio ad absurdum"* argument. The phrase is Latin and it's not hard to translate, even by those who don't know Latin. It means, as you might imagine, "reduction to the absurd".

The idea is to take the logic of an argument to its fullest conclusion in hopes of showing that the end point is an absurdity. The purest form of the argument is to show that an idea implies a contradiction. A contradiction is the simplest and most obvious form of falsehood, but it's not the only kind of false statement. The point of *reductio ad absurdum* is to show that an idea implies something that is obviously false, something that any sane person would agree is false, and reject.

The logic behind it is simple and non-controversial. No true statement can imply a contradiction; indeed, no true statement can imply anything that is false. If the falsehood is sufficiently obvious, then everyone should be able agree to it. This is sometimes called self-annihilation, or indirect proof.

In our present context, the point is to show that arguments in favor of abortion lead us to justify, not only abortion but also infanticide. The hope is that any sane person would never condone

[256] Mary Anne Warren, "On the Moral and Legal Status of Abortion" from *Biomedical Ethics*. 4th ed. T.A. Mappes and D. DeGrazia, eds. (New York, NY: McGraw-Hill, Inc. 1996).

infanticide. Normally, the murder of a child is considered the most monstrous form of murder. Infanticide, the killing of children, is the "*absurdum*" portion of the argument.

Abortion proponents have been increasingly sensitive to this argument for a number of reasons. There is the scientific fact that we have learned an enormous amount about conception and the gestation of the human fetus. The television series by *National Geographic* called *Inside the Womb* is a visually stunning representation if this explosion of knowledge. The original program was so successful that *National Geographic* came out with a series of programs based on the original; these showed the womb view of the development of dogs, cats, elephants, human twins and multiple births.

The series was made possible by the development of sonograms that have recently become genuinely sophisticated; *National Geographic* relied on what are known as 3d and 4d sonograms. Three-dimensional images can be taken into a 4th dimension by the addition of viewing the developing baby in time.

This has been an aid, not only to the documentary maker, but also to obstetricians caring for their patients. It enables parents to see their babies before they are born, to scan for abnormalities and birth defects, and to determine before birth, the sex of the child. It is only in recent times that we haven't had to wait for the moment of birth to call out joyfully, "It's a girl" or "It's a boy!" Now we can know weeks ahead of time.

Sonograms are a double-edged sword. Mothers who see their babies in the womb are less likely to have an abortion. They see all too well that what's inside them is not a mere clump of cells, but looks and acts (from smiles to yawns) like a baby. What they see, *is* a baby. This is no doubt part of the motivation behind a number of state laws mandating the viewing of a sonogram before a woman makes the final decision to have an abortion. While it has its political purposes, it also provides an expectant mother with information that is vital to her ability to make an informed consent. In any other context, it wouldn't be controversial. The wide availability and popularity of sonograms is sometimes credited with the modest, but clearly measurable, decline in the number of abortions over the last decade or so.

However, sonograms can also scan for deformities, and can provide reasons to promote the abortion of Down syndrome babies and other forms of "defect". In Communist China and elsewhere, they are used extensively for sexually selective abortions to weed out girls and promote the birth of boys.

Much has been learned in recent research in the science of embryology. What embryology has to say about human origins in instructive, if only to provide us with a basis in fact to make informed moral judgments later. We need to take a moment to understand it.

All somatic cells (that is, cells other than sex cells, sperm in the male, eggs or ova in the female) have an identical genetic makeup however differentiated they might be in their function in the body. That differentiation into various types of cells, brain cells, muscle cells, skin cells and so forth begins at conception. All cells contain the same basic genetic information, but within each type, only part of that information is "active".[257]

Each somatic cell has 23 chromosomes each from the mother and father for a total of 46. As noted sex cells, sometimes called "gametes" are different from all the other cells of the body, in part because they each (either a sperm or an egg) contain only 23 chromosomes. Were this not the case they couldn't join with a

---

[257] Robert P. George and Christopher Tollefsen, *Embryo*, (New York, NY: Doubleday, 2008), p. 30.

152

gamete from the opposite sex to create a new organism with the requisite total of 46 chromosomes. Thus, neither form of gamete can be considered in any sense a human being. It is only when one of each participates in the process of fertilization does a new individual organism come into being.

While fertilization itself is a process, there is a moment in that process where the unique genetic form of the new human being, including its sex takes place. After a sperm has penetrated an egg, each individual gamete, with its 23 chromosomes begins to merge with the other. A male nucleus and female nucleus (23 chromosomes each) merge to form a new individual with the requisite 46 chromosomes. By this time the sperm and egg have each ceased to exist as separate entities, and we now have a new human individual. This organism is initially comprised of a single cell called a zygote.

The zygote contains within its own nature all the genetic material and instructions to create a fully formed human organism. It proceeds without any external direction to divide and differentiate itself into all the cells of the human body. Although it contains half its genetic material from the mother and half from the father, it is identical to neither. It is a completely genetically unique individual. All its growth and development is determined from within.

"It possesses the active capacity for self development toward maturity using the information it carries."[258] It only needs sustenance (food) and a congenial environment, which is usually, but these days not exclusively, a womb.

This means that the newly formed zygote is not part of another organism in the way that skin or muscle or brain cells or even sperm and egg cells are. It is a new and unique separate individual, which may or may not be living in a woman's womb. It

---

[258] Ibid, p. 41.

153

serves no role in the body of the parent in the way that brain or skin cells do.[259] While a sperm or an egg have life expectancies in the order of hours, a zygote has a life expectancy of seventy or eighty years.[260] By the eighth week, the zygote has developed into an embryo, which contains all the major organs, and has a distinctly human shape.

> *"A human embryo is not something different in kind from a human being, like a rock, or a potato, or a rhinoceros. A human embryo is a whole living member of the species Homo Sapiens in the earliest stage of ... natural development."*[261]

None of this, so far, is controversial. It is, in fact, settled science. It can be found in any good embryology textbook. These scientific facts, many of which have been discovered since the 1973 Roe v. Wade decision provide the proponents of abortion with a problem. It is simply no longer scientifically plausible to suggest that a zygote or embryo is not in fact a human being, but merely a "potential" human being. We know differently now.

If they wish to continue to defend the practice of abortion (and they do) they need to come up with something else. They have. This can be briefly described as something called "personhood theory". The idea is that although an embryo or fetus may indeed be a human being, it is not a "person"; that is it isn't the kind of thing to which we normally have moral obligations. Only when the individual becomes a person, do we begin to have obligations to it, for example, it becomes wrong to kill it, and one can be tried for murder if one violates the right to life of that person. Prior to that point, it's open season on non-persons.

---

259 Ibid, p. 40.
260 Ibid, p. 41-42.
261 Ibid, p. 50.

According to this theory, the human race must be divided into two profoundly unequal classes of human beings; persons and non-persons. Ideally, one might become a person at birth. This would at least avoid the *reductio* argument we discussed above. All and only non-persons may be aborted, and fortunately for us, since personhood begins at birth, we wouldn't be required to tolerate child murder to protect a woman's right to reproductive freedom.

There is a fly in this ointment. Philosopher John Harris has put the question as succinctly as possible. "What do people think has happened in the passage down the birth canal to make it OK to kill the foetus at one end of the birth canal but not at the other?"[262]

The question is rhetorical. Harris knows, everyone knows, that *nothing* has happened in that short journey. Whatever the fetus is at the inner end of the canal, it is the same thing as when it comes out the other, gets slapped by the doctor, who announces, "It's a boy!"

In other words, if it's a baby on the outside, that's what it is on the inside. If it's a fetus on the inside, that's what it is on the outside. If you can kill it on the inside, you can kill it on the outside, although some abortionists still prefer the legal fiction of the "partial birth" abortion. There, the baby remains with its head inside where the doctor rams a scissors through the base of the skull. If the kid goes a few more inches down the birth canal, the mother looses her right to reproductive freedom. Even post-birth "abortion" had to be the subject of legislation before abortionists could be compelled to quit doing it. Gosnell shows that even then, *they didn't stop.*

According to personhood theory a person must have certain properties, usually a list of things like sentience, self-awareness etc. If it isn't awake, or doesn't feel pain and has no awareness of death,

---

[262] Harris..

155

and so forth, then it's not a person and it should be OK to kill it. It really has no way of caring one way or the other. If it doesn't care, why should we?

Philosopher Mary Anne Warren, who passed away in 2010, had one of the best known and best argued versions of the theory. Her article, "On the Moral and Legal Status of Abortion", was originally published in the journal *Monist*.[263]

For Warren, a person generally has a number of defining characteristics.

These are:

Sentience
Ability to feel emotion
Ability to reason
Ability to communicate
Self-awareness
Moral agency or awareness

One might be a person if one lacked one or a few of these (as with a comatose patient) but not if one lacks all six. Since an unborn zygote/embryo/fetus has none of them, it cannot be considered a person; it is not the sort of thing which can be the object of moral obligations. It has no rights that an actual person has any obligation to respect.

This bears repeating. Fetuses are by this standard inferior beings, "so far inferior that they [have] no rights which [persons are] bound to respect."[264]

While not random, or even necessarily badly chosen, the list of characteristics is in one sense arbitrary; it varies of necessity, from

---

[263] *Monist* 57:1 : 43-61
[264] Roger Taney, Dred Scott v. Sandford, 1857.

one philosopher to another. There is another larger problem. While it is certainly true that no fetus has any of Warren's characteristics of personhood, neither does a newborn infant. In fact, a one year old or even an eighteen month old doesn't have all of them either. A child, by this analysis doesn't become a person until *well after birth.*

There are a variety of reasons for this. Human beings have substantially larger brains than other mammals. This means humans have a significantly larger skull relative to body size than, say kittens or puppies. A cat, which can live to be over twenty years old, becomes an essentially mature adult at about five or six months. While helpless at birth, it requires a very limited time of nurturing by the mother; and in the case of cats and almost all other mammals *only* the mother. Mammalian fathers, with the exception of human beings, are little more than sperm donors. It is the human family of two parents that provides the child with years of nurture from both biological parents (with only occasional support from adoptive surrogates).

Human beings require genuinely long term nurturing, because the brain at birth is nowhere near final development. It couldn't be. To remain within the mother's womb until the brain was fully developed, the skull would be far too large to exit the birth canal. Humans compensate for this by rearing their children through a lengthy period during which the brain continues to grow in size and ability. A human child needs at least a decade of care before it is at all capable of self-sufficiency. In effect, human mothers give birth to a *fetus*, which has yet to complete its gestational period. All human births are in this sense *premature.*

It is for precisely this reason that *no list* of properties or characteristics can possibly distinguish between an unborn child, and a child after birth. It's a biological fact that they are not different. Nothing has happened "in the passage down the birth canal to make it OK to kill the foetus at one end of the birth canal but not at the other."

The earliest version of Warren's article seemed to have some sense of the problem without quite being willing to deal with it. In a 1982 postscript to her article (not always published with the early version) she makes an attempt.

She notes that

> *"A newborn infant is not a great deal more person like than a nine month fetus... Yet most people consider that infanticide is a form of murder, and thus never justified. While it is important to appreciate the emotional force of this objection, its logical force is far less than it may seem at first glance."*[265]

The phrase, "not a great deal more person like" is telling. Whether a day a week or a month apart, there are *no differences in kind* between a fetus and a newborn. She then makes a vague attempt (vague because relativistic) to reclaim the moral center by noting

> *"In this country, and in this period of history, the deliberate killing of viable newborns is virtually never justified."*[266]

Phrases like "in this country, and in this period of history" or "virtually never justified" are also telling. Is it really only in *our* society, country and historical period that infanticide is *in fact* wrong? This is the relativist position. Thus in Greco-Roman Society, infanticide was supposedly not wrong, contemporary Judeo-Christian disputes of the practice not withstanding? This can never be made into a coherent position, and that fact is made obvious a few lines further down.

---

[265] Warren.
[266] Ibid.

"It is a philosopher's task to criticize mistaken beliefs which stand in the way of moral understanding, even when-perhaps especially when-those beliefs are popular and widespread. The belief that moral strictures against killing should apply equally to all genetically human entities, and only to genetically human entities, is such an error. The overcoming of this error will undoubtedly require long and often painful struggle; but it must be done."[267]

Which is it? Is infanticide *in our culture* wrong, or is that belief a "popular and widespread" *error*? Isn't the fact of being popular and widespread precisely what's required to make something right or wrong for *our* society? This is the very point with cultural relativism. Widely accepted, even assumed sets of beliefs are a significant part of what makes up what we call a "culture". In medieval Japan the samurai had the authority to kill, if he chose, anyone who wasn't a samurai. Under traditional Islam a woman may not venture outside without male accompaniment. One could extend the list of examples indefinitely. For a relativist to be consistent she can only note that we, as cultural outsiders, can have no 0basis to pass judgment or condemn such practices. Some would even claim that we have no basis even to discuss or evaluate, in any way, another culture. However much these actions may repel westerners, the relativist position is that they are correct for medieval Japan and traditional Islam respectively. In our country and period in history it is never justified for a member of a dominant social class to kill someone of a lower class on a whim, nor is it permissible to imprison women in their homes until a male is willing to escort them outside. Our society's rules have the last say about what is right and wrong. So saith the relativist.

---

[267] Ibid.

So also, *"In this country, and in this period of history, the deliberate killing of viable newborns is virtually never justified."*[268] Doesn't this imply an end to the discussion for any relativist?

Here, at the end of the article, she drops the pretense of moral relativism that she used originally to make her seem a bit more "main stream". Here she says what she really thinks. If it's needed to make sense of the "right" to abortion, then she's perfectly OK with infanticide, even if *in our culture* it's "virtually never justified." Other "bio-ethicists" have given voice to the same idea, including John Harris, quoted above (he was trying to justify infanticide, not oppose abortion) and Princeton's Peter Singer.

> *"If a syllogism ended in a command to commit unspeakable evil, you did not doubt the premises or the argument but obeyed the command."*[269]

Warren claims that overcoming this "error" will "require long and often painful struggle". She doesn't specify what form the "struggle" should take. She must have known however, that the struggle won't be one of slowly persuading enough people of the rightness of her position thereby rationally building a societal consensus. It will come as all such things come, by court ordered mandate.

---

[268] Ibid.

[269] Theodore Dalrymple "Modernity's Uninvited Guest" *City Journal*, (Summer 2010, v. 20,# 3).

Obvious Murder
What Makes a Person

"One thinker has greater regard for sentience, another for cognition, another for self-awareness. One thinks the important thing is sociality, another the capacity to make plans. With each different criterion of personhood, a different set of beings is welcomed through the gates of others' regard. This writer says that higher mammals are persons, but human babies not. That one says that human babies are persons, but Grandma not. The one over there says that some human babies are persons, but only if their mothers think they are."[270]

J. Budziszewski

By about the thirty-second week of pregnancy a fetus will be able to hear, remember, and respond to its mother's voice. It will also remember her voice and be able to respond to it after it is born.[271] Elementary fetal memory begins well before birth as the child begins to learn about language, music and any other auditory signals that it can hear in the womb. It will remember and respond after birth to the theme song of a television show that the mother watched while she was pregnant.[272]

Its body, heartbeat, and brain have long since begun to develop and even when it is only about two inches long it already has the appearance of a miniature baby. As its brain, memory and learning ability develop, so inevitably do the rudiments of its personality.

---

[270] J. Budziszewski "The Second Tablet Project" *First Things* (June/July2002).

[271] Barbara Kisilevsky, M.D., et al, "Effects Of Experience On Fetal Voice Recognition", *Psychological Science* (Vol. 14, No. 3, May 2003).

[272] Hepper PG. "Fetal memory: Does it exist? What does it do?" *Acta Paediatrica* 1996; (Suppl 416:16-20), Stockholm.

Before the child is the size of a pea, its heart begins to beat at about 5 weeks. The next week, facial features begin to form and blood begins to circulate. By eight weeks it has a nose, arms, legs, fingers, and elementary lungs, even though it is only about a half inch in length and weighs only about a gram. By ten weeks, eyes, fingernails, toenails are formed and major organs, including the brain are functioning. By the end of the first trimester, the baby weighs about half an ounce and is around two inches long. It is then fully formed, looking like a small baby. It has thirty-two weeks to go before it is born, thirty-two more weeks before it can no longer be legally killed.

Before that time the baby will have facial expressions and suck its thumb (fourteen weeks). It can see light from outside the womb (fifteen weeks). Beginning at about eighteen weeks is the window (extending to about thirty weeks) when fetal surgery can be contemplated to correct bladder obstructions, heart valve problems, spina bifida, or other problems threatening the fetus. By nineteen weeks, it can hear its mother's heartbeat and voice, as well as other sounds from outside; it is capable of a startle reflex from a loud noise. Although it has been moving around for several weeks, it is only now that the motion is perceptible to the mother; this is what used to be called "quickening", and was, for millennia, the only accepted legal proof of pregnancy. Before the end of the second trimester, the baby has begun "breathing" the fluid it's living in, and its lungs will function if born prematurely; it can, therefore cry at that time; all it needs is air. It can live outside the womb (with help from a neonatal unit), but while inside, it still has little or no legal protection. If its mother decides to "un-want" it, she may do so, and legally it changes from being a baby to being a clump of cells.

Around the beginning of the third trimester, the baby will begin to dream. By the middle of the third trimester it is considered full term, although it usually takes several more weeks before normal labor begins.

The fetus begins to feel pain between 8 and 14 weeks. This is when the part of the brain known as the thalamus, the neural pathways and pain receptors being to function.

"Functioning neurological structures necessary for pain sensation are in place as early as 8 weeks, but certainly by 13-1/2 weeks...By 13-1/2 weeks, the entire sensory nervous system functions as a whole in all parts of the body (except in the skin or the back of the head)." [273]

After about 14 weeks, virtually all forms of abortion cause extreme pain in the victim. Saline abortion in particular causes striking reactions.

"It is well-known that the fetus reacts with aversive responses when saline is introduced into amniotic fluid. The aborting mother can feel her baby thrashing in the uterus..." [274]

The fact of fetal pain is, of course, why in all surgeries other than abortion both the mother and child are anesthetized. When an unborn child with spina bifida (like Samuel Armas) is operated on in utero, he is anesthetized. This is, after all, how we know that little Samuel wasn't "grasping" his doctor's hand in the famous 1999 surgery photo by Michael Clancy. Little Samuel was, like his mother, out cold.

It has become standard practice in neonatal units to provide analgesic to premature babies, even for simple procedures like the

---

[273] Vincent J. Collins, Steven R. Zielinski, and Thomas J. Marzen, "Fetal Pain and Abortion: The Medical Evidence", *Studies in Law and Medicine*, Chicago: American United for Life, Inc., (no. 18 1984), p.7.
[274] W. Edminson, "A Report on the Abortion Capital of the Country": *The New York Times Magazine*, (March 11, 1971).

pin-prick involved in taking blood. Sucrose (sugar) has been found to be effective.[275] These neonates are generally the same gestational age as "fetuses" subjected to late term abortions.[276]

Dr. Anthony Levatino, a former abortion doctor described for Congress what is involved with a simple and common abortion procedure known as a suction D&E (dilation and evacuation) on a 24 week fetus. This is well past the point where a baby in-utero can feel pain.

> *"With suction complete, look for your Sopher clamp ... This instrument is for grasping and crushing tissue. When it gets hold of something, it does not let go... Once you have grasped something inside, squeeze on the clamp to set the jaws and pull hard–really hard. You feel something let go and out pops a fully formed leg about six inches long. Reach in again and grasp whatever you can. Set the jaw and pull really hard once again and out pops an arm about the same length. Reach in again and again with that clamp and tear out the spine, intestines, heart and lungs...You can then extract the skull pieces. Many times a little face will come out and stare back at you.*
>
> *Congratulations!"*[277]

This type of late abortion, suction D&E is not the same as that which has typically been called partial birth abortion, or D&X. Since most abortions of either type, this late in term, require three days to complete, there is never a genuine health and safety reason to

---

[275] Murki S. and Subramanian S. "Sucrose for analgesia in newborn infants undergoing painful procedures: RHL commentary" (last revised: 1 June 2011). *The WHO Reproductive Health Library*; Geneva: World Health Organization.

[276] Jill L. Stanek, RN, Testimony on HR 1797, Pain-Capable Unborn Child Protection Act, May 23, 2013.

[277] Dr. Anthony Levatino, testimony before Congress, May 23, 2013.

prefer abortion at this stage. Immediately inducing labor and delivering a live baby is always quicker and safer for the mother than the three-day extensive procedure required for abortion after about 20 weeks.

When the late Mary Anne Warren wrote her essay "On the Moral and Legal Status of Abortion"[278] she listed six properties that any human must have to be considered a person. A person might still be a person, she reasoned, if lacking one or two, but no being lacking all six could be a person. The fetus, she said, thus lacked all six and was not a person. Let's look at them again.

Sentience
Ability to feel emotions
Ability to reason
Ability to communicate
Self-awareness
Moral agency or awareness

Interestingly, she lists sentience as separate from self-awareness. This is the ability to feel and respond to its environment, especially to feel pain, but also to hear, see, touch, and recoil from unpleasant stimuli (like an abortionists suction probe, a reaction you can see in ultrasound images of an abortion). Clearly modern embryology shows that the fetus is sentient in all these senses of the word well before birth.

The emotional capacity of the fetus may still be controversial, but a fetus will clearly respond to and remember music, the mother's voice, and according to some ultrasounds, smile. (Warren should certainly have included memory as one of her criteria.) In this sense, the fetus is capable of an at least rudimentary emotional capacity, perhaps more than rudimentary. To be sure,

---

[278] T.A. Mappes and D. DeGrazia, eds. *Biomedical Ethics*. 4th ed. (New York, NY: McGraw-Hill, Inc. 1996), pp. 434-440.

fetuses lack the ability to reason, but of course, so do children for several of the first years of their lives.

As for capacity to communicate, most mothers will tell you that the "quickened" fetus does indeed seem to be communicating something, and babies have no trouble communicating through crying from the moment of birth. In fact, as we've seen, babies are capable of crying the moment their lungs begin to function when they "breath" their amniotic fluid inside the womb. As *capacity* to communicate is a clear Warrenite property of personhood, an unborn baby has that capacity before it actually uses it to communicate its cries. Crying is also evidence of emotion. The rudimentary memory studied in fetuses includes, according to at least one researcher the beginnings of language learning.[279] Language, memory, learning, emotion, and communication are all part of the process of developing reason, which, while it takes many years is here present in embryonic form.

We can safely conclude that neither fetuses nor children up to a certain age are self-aware, and certainly not capable of moral agency. Just ask any parent with a toddler in the "terrible twos". Nevertheless, toddlers are indubitably people (at least until philosophers think they need to declare otherwise to keep their theory consistent).

Thus we have the beginnings of at least three of Warren's properties, and four when we add memory. Had she lived, even she might have been compelled to agree that a fetus becomes a person well before birth, even by her own criteria before the end of the first trimester. She might even have been persuaded to withdraw the following statement:

---

[279] Hepper PG ,"Fetal memory: Does it exist? What does it do?".

"It remains true that, on my view, neither abortion nor the killing of newborns is obviously a form of murder."[280]

Or not, since she also, *interestingly*, argued for abortion as a necessary means for population control. Abortion and population control are part of the inextricable and inter-related pantheon of modern liberal beliefs. Cutting them apart is like surgery on Siamese twins; one or both usually dies.

Warren's six criteria are dealt with more extensively elsewhere.[281] In the middle of her article, she snuck in the population argument, just to sort of seal the case.

> *"Furthermore, the world cannot afford the continued rapid population growth which is the inevitable consequence of prohibiting abortion...If fetuses were persons, then they would have rights that must be respected, even at great societal or personal cost."*[282]

Fortunately, Warren argued, fetuses are not people, so not to worry. Abortion philosophers seem to think that they've helped the world dodge a dangerous bullet. Without abortion we wouldn't be able to protect ourselves from the "bomb" of exploding humanity everywhere you look, more and more people.

Except that the world is *not* overpopulated. There has been adequate reason to know this since the 1960s. The world fertility rate is crashing. There is no need to promote abortion as a means to population control; unless, of course, you *want* abortion to be considered a woman's fundamental right and need yet another excuse to defend it. Depriving the unborn of personhood isn't enough for Warren; she needs the false ideology of population

---

[280] Warren.

[281] Ibid.

[282] Ibid.

control to convince people that only abortion in the hundreds of millions will save the world. The world doesn't need this kind of saving. In any case, sex selective abortions (the *inevitable* result of abortion for population control) can't be reliably done to "early fetuses", because fetal genitals can't be seen on an ultrasound image much before between twenty and twenty eight weeks. Currently a fetus is usually viable by about twenty weeks, but saving these fetuses voids the use of abortion as a means of population control. If depressing the birth rate is your thing, then nothing accomplishes that goal better than killing off lots of girls; it doesn't matter if it's via an abortion to a late term fetus, or if, as Olivia Vlahos has seen, after being born, *"she is drowned like a kitten."*[283] Selectively aborting girls is an effective force multiplier when using abortion for population control; too valuable to do without if, as Warren insists, "the world cannot afford the continued rapid population growth" which is the result of not killing more girls than boys.

In reality, the world doesn't need any of this. All human beings are persons, and the unjustified killing of an innocent person, is, always *obviously a form of murder*.

---

[283] Olivia Vlahos, "Sex and Consequences: An Anthropological View", *The Silent Subject*, Brad Stetson ed. (Santa Barbara, CA: Praeger Publishers, 1996), P.99. (*"It is sad, but not surprising, that in rural homes a bucket of water is placed beside the bed of a woman in labor. If the newborn turns out to be a girl, she is drowned like a kitten."*)

The Threshold of Infanticide
Intrauterine Cranial Decompression

"A voice was heard in Ramah, ... Rachel weeping for her children."
Jeremiah 31:15

In 1993 National Abortion Federation member, Dr. Abu Hayat, was sentenced to 9 to 27 years in prison by a New York judge. He had been charged with a variety of crimes, including injury to a baby (which was technically a fetus at the time of the injury) by means of an abortion begun but never completed. His patient, Rosa Rodriguez, ended up in the hospital giving birth to a normal baby girl; normal, that is but for the absence of her right arm. Many abortions are carried out by dismembering the baby in the uterus. In this case the doctor only got as far as removing the arm before stopping and telling the patient to come back the next day. In agonizing pain overnight and having changed her mind (despite Hayat telling her that it was impossible to stop) Rosa eventually ended up in the emergency ward of Jamaica Hospital Medical Center in Queens, New York.

The procedure used by Dr. Hayat on Rosa Rodriguez's baby Ana is known as a D&E (for dilation and evacuation). It involves dismembering the baby using forceps to rip body parts from the torso; rather like removing the leg of an over cooked turkey. This is how little Ana Rodriguez lost her arm. A cutting tool can also be used. While generally preceded by an ultrasound to determine the size of the baby, which lets the attending doctor know what he's getting into in advance, Dr. Hayat skipped this initial step. Thus, on encountering an unexpectedly late term pregnancy (in other words, an unexpectedly large baby) he decided he was in over his head and sent the patient home, with a still living (albeit partially dismembered) child in her womb. Rosa was not in the fourth month of her pregnancy, as she and Hayat believed, but well into her seventh. The ultrasound would have revealed this.

Earlier that same year, Dr. Hayat had, again without the benefit of ultrasound begun an abortion on a patient named Marie Moise, which again turned out to be further along than he expected. In this case, he stopped the procedure long enough to demand an extra $500 from her husband, David. Not having that amount of cash on his person at the time, the husband promised to get it. Instead Dr. Hayat refused to continue so the husband and his still sedated and bleeding wife found themselves on the street. Eventually the abortion was completed at St. Luke's Hospital. This earned Dr. Hayat an assault charge on Mrs. Moise, and, for this count alone, a fifteen-year prison sentence.[284] Dr. Hayat was ordered tried in a separate trial on a charge of sexually abusing another patient.

In any case Hayat was investigated by a medical hearing committee and found to have performed an excessive number of tests, failed to maintain accurate records, and abandoned several patients. So they found him guilty of gross negligence, fraudulent practice, being morally unfit to practice medicine and one illegal late term abortion. Hayat's license was revoked and the revocation was reaffirmed on appeal to the New York Senate appointed Administrative Review Board for Professional Medical Conduct in 1992.

It's true that in Roe v. Wade and Doe v. Bolton the Supreme Court struck down all restrictions on abortion, ruling that abortion was a basic right. Only after a clear understanding of a state's compelling interest in enforcing a law could a regulation limiting abortion be contemplated. Generally few restrictions passed this scrutiny standard before 1992.

---

[284] Orlando *Sentinel*, June 15, 1993.

In Casey v. Planned Parenthood (1992) the Court added substantial confusion to the mix by refusing to discard Roe's core ruling while at the same time replacing the strict scrutiny[285] standard with a vague standard of "undue burden". No portion of the decision had a majority behind it, so Justice O'Connor wrote a plurality decision regarding the meaning of undue burden.

In the aftermath of Casey, a few states did pass restrictions on abortion some of which limited the legality of the procedure to early trimesters. Some survived court scrutiny, others didn't.

As for Dr. Hayat, legal action from the courts followed hard on the heels of the medical board action, and Hayat was charged, in addition to the harm inflicted on the Rodriguez family, with abandoning a patient in the middle of an abortion because she couldn't come up with more cash. He was convicted of performing illegal abortions and assault on patients.

"In the weeks after his arrest, more than 30 women came forward to say that Dr. Hayat botched their abortions, and officials said that a 17-year-old girl died because he perforated her uterus during an abortion." [286]

Seventeen year old Sophie McCoy, died in September 1990 of septic shock after being seen at Hayat's National Abortion Federation clinic.[287] He was never charged with Sophie's death.

The D&E procedure is one that is generally carried out blind by the doctor. Until the advent of ultrasound it was a completely blind procedure. After dismembering most of the baby, the uterus is

---

[285] The Roe Court did not expressly mention "strict scrutiny" but subsequent lower court rulings did and Casey was responding to those.
[286] Richard Perez-Pena, "Doctor Said to Raise Price Mid-Abortion", *New York Times*, (January 30, 1993).
[287] Steven Lee Myers, "Doctor Describes Death of a Girl Who Suffered Botched Abortion", *New York Times*, (December 5, 1991).

sometimes vacuumed out by a powerful suction pump that dismembers the rest of the body by suctioning it through a tube into a bag. Also, the womb can simply be emptied by hand or by scraping with a curette. The contents of the bag are then examined by the physician to make sure that they represent enough tissue to constitute the entire body of the baby.

Some months earlier, in September of 1992, Dr. Martin Haskell had presented a paper to a medical risk management seminar sponsored by the same National Abortion Federation that Dr. Hayat was a member of. The paper described a type of abortion that, while not new, was increasingly finding favor among doctors who performed late term abortions, primarily late second and third trimester. The procedure that had come to be called "*intrauterine cranial decompression*" for the simple reason that the cranium, the skull, of the infant was collapsed with a suction device inserted into a hole in the skull produced by a pair of scissors.

Haskell called the procedure "dilation and extraction" (D&X) a less descriptive, but easier to remember name.[288] Traditional abortions had generally been accomplished by a procedure with the similar name of "dilation and evacuation" (D&E).

The D&X procedure outlined by Haskell suctions out only the contents of the skull, leaving the rest of the body relatively intact. The likelihood of an incomplete abortion, or of any part of the child being left behind is therefore reduced by the fact that the baby is delivered almost entirely before being killed. Only the head remains in the cervical canal when the scissors are inserted into the skull and

---

[288] Martin Haskell, M.D. "Dilation and Extraction for Late Second Trimester Abortion", Proceedings of the National Abortion Federation, *Second Trimester Abortion: From Every Angle*, (September 13-14, 1992), p. 28.

the brains vacuumed out. D&X is a procedure only useful for late term abortions when the fetus is capable of being a viable baby.

Haskell noted that D&E, itself a second trimester procedure, evolved as an alternative to instillation (injection of a solution into the abdomen) as well as artificially induced labor. Instillation fell out of favor due to the excessive risk to the mother from the various solutions used. Haskell wrote that "most surgeons find dismemberment at twenty weeks and beyond to be difficult due to the toughness of fetal tissues at this stage of development". Both "induce early fetal demise".[289]

Haskell describes the procedure, which involves two days of progressive dilation of the cervix, (between which the patient can go home) and a third day operation. With the aid of an ultrasound the doctor enters the uterus with forceps and grasps the baby's "lower extremities" i.e., its feet. The ultrasound allows the physician to be sure he has not grasped a part of the woman's uterus, and has only the baby in the forceps. The feet are then pulled through the vagina, and then the torso and shoulders, leaving only the head still lodged in the cervix, which has been carefully dilated only enough to allow the rest of the baby to protrude from the mother. The doctor grabs the child, with its spine up, with his hand by the shoulders.

> *"While maintaining this tension, lifting the cervix and applying traction to the shoulders with the fingers of the left hand, the surgeon takes a pair of blunt curved Metzenbaum scissors in the right hand ... the surgeon then forces the scissors into the base of the skull ... he spreads the scissors to enlarge the opening...and evacuates the skull contents."*[290]

---

[289] Haskell.
[290] *Ibid*, pp. 30-31.

Anesthesia of 1% lidocaine with epinephrine (for the mother, not the baby) is standard. As all such procedures are done on viable babies, the partially delivered child will tend to thrash about a bit before being killed. One of Haskell's nurses, Brenda Shafer, who witnessed him perform the procedure told the U. S. Congress in testimony.

> *"The baby's little fingers were clasping and unclasping, and his little feet were kicking. Then the doctor stuck the scissors in the back of his head, and the baby's arms jerked out, like a startle reaction, like a flinch, like a baby does when he thinks he is going to fall. The doctor opened up the scissors, stuck a high-powered suction tube into the opening, and sucked the baby's brains out. Now the baby went completely limp...*[291]

During the 1992 conference where Haskell presented his paper, artist Jenny Westberg obtained a copy of it and used Haskell's description to render a series of line drawings of the process. These were later turned into color illustrations of the procedure by medical artist Tanja Butler, which procedure by then had come to be called "partial birth abortion".

It became evident that the procedure of leaving only the head in the cervix was a legal fiction that allowed a form of infanticide to be called an "abortion". Haskell's paper noted the he had performed over 700 such procedures making it routine for any late term pregnancy.

The illustrations began to draw much unwanted attention to the procedure, and some doctors began to complain that it was only a

---

[291] Testimony Of Brenda Pratt Shafer, R.N. to the Committee on the Judiciary U.S. House of Representatives, March 21, 1996.

rare form of abortion useful in only a handful of cases. Haskell's admission of 700 by 1992 for his office alone, put the lie to all that.

The increasing controversy brought about congressional hearings like the ones that Nurse Shafer testified in, and a number of states began to look into legislation to ban the procedure in spite of Roe v. Wade. A Nevada law failed to pass scrutiny before the U.S. Supreme Court, when the Court ruled in the case of Stenberg v. Carhart in 2000. Citing both Roe and Planned Parenthood v. Casey the Court ruled that the Nevada law was unduly restrictive, even of this extreme form of abortion, posing an undue burden on the right to choose.

It had been the 1992 case of Planned Parenthood of Southeastern Pennsylvania v. Casey that some had thought might create some daylight in Roe v. Wade's armor. While the Court upheld Roe, it did state that some limitations on the right to abortion might be enacted by state legislatures. It upheld many portions of the Pennsylvania law, including the 24-hour waiting period, the strong informed consent provision, as well as parental consent for minors. These were ruled to be not undue burdens. The Court further stated that as medical science had improved a premature baby's chances of surviving outside the womb, a state could have some latitude in regulating abortions past the point where the fetus would be viable to survive on its own. Pennsylvania rewrote its abortion law to permit only first trimester abortions plus those necessary to save the life of the mother.

States other than Nevada passed their own versions of the ban on partial birth abortions. In 1997, the New Jersey state legislature passed its own version of a law prohibiting partial-birth abortion. It too was struck down, this time by the New Jersey Supreme Court, citing the Nevada Stenberg v. Carhart case decision in 2000 as well as Roe and Casey.

In this case of *New Jersey v. Farmer* the Court ruled in part that,

> "*Positing an 'unborn' versus 'partially born' distinction, the Legislature would have us accept, and the public believe, that during a 'partial-birth abortion' the fetus is in the process of being 'born' at the time of its demise. It is not. A woman seeking an abortion is plainly not seeking to give birth.*"[292]

While it is obvious that the woman is question is seeking an to terminate her pregnancy, the actual procedure in the case of D&X is identical to the act of giving birth, up until the point of the insertion of the Metzenbaum scissors. The distinction that the Court sought to make here, is therefore dependent on the woman's desires and intentions towards the fetus, rather that its obvious status as a baby.

Thus, the product of "abortion" in this case can be denied protection of the law based solely on the fact that its mother intends it to be killed. A September 2000 report from the House Committee on the Judiciary had this to say about that.

> "*The logical implications of Carhart and Farmer are both obvious and disturbing. Under the logic of these decisions, once a child is marked for abortion, it is wholly irrelevant whether that child emerges from the womb as a live baby. That child may still be treated as a non-entity, and would have not the slightest rights under the law—no right to receive medical care, to be sustained in life, or to receive any*

---

[292] U. S. Court of Appeals, Third Circuit, Planned Parenthood Of Central New Jersey V. Farmer.

care at all... The 'right to abortion,' under this logic, means nothing less than the right to a dead baby, no matter where the killing takes place."[293]

The Farmer Court accused the New Jersey legislature of engaging in semantics and "irrational line-drawing" ruling that the location of the baby had nothing to do with whether or not it was entitled to the protections of the Fourteenth Amendment. All that mattered to the New Jersey Court was the intention of the mother, whether to give birth or kill the child. Once that was decided in favor of abortion, the product of abortion could be killed anywhere by any means. This reading would have made everything discovered in the Philadelphia Gosnell clinic perfectly legal, *and* it constituted a serious broadening of the law, well beyond what the Roe and Casey Courts intended.

The effect of Farmer was *not* to provide a firm legal distinction between partial-birth abortion and infanticide, but rather to once again blur the distinction between abortion and the murder of a child. No court has yet had the moral courage to decide if this alleged distinction, on which Roe so vitally depends, might not itself be an illusion.

Instead the court decisions, in striking down any and all attempts to limit abortions, even in the most extreme cases, had the reverse effect of expanding the right to abortion to the region outside the womb. The inevitable progression from abortion to infanticide is therefore legitimated and encouraged.

Eventually in 2002 the U.S. Congress passed its own ban with a law carefully crafted to survive judicial scrutiny including

---

[293] Committee on the Judiciary Report to the House of Representatives, 106th Congress 2d session, Report 106-835.

177

Roe, Casey, Carhart, and Farmer. In April 2007 the Court ruled with its usual 5 to 4 decisiveness to uphold the federal ban on intrauterine cranial decompression, marking the first time since Roe that a line of demarcation between abortion and infanticide has been successfully litigated.

Abortion defenders were predictably outraged. There are those, after all, that even oppose laws at state and Federal level that protect the lives of infants born alive in failed abortion procedures. These infants are indisputably legal persons, even by the standards of Roe v. Wade and partial birth abortion. Here, no head is left inside the cervix; the child is completely delivered. This is the danger inherent in the induced labor form of abortion; a sufficiently late term child can survive induced labor (which is also performed on mothers who wish to keep their babies alive). It can produce a viable post-birth human being, who is thus legally a person.

Induced labor commonly produces a living baby (which in an abortion procedure, is not the intended outcome). This left abortion providers with a decision. Some hospitals and clinics performing abortions would just let the child die; or in the case of the Gosnell clinic "induce early fetal demise" by killing the baby. (Gosnell didn't invent that phrase, Haskell did.) Laws against this sort of thing were vigorously opposed by abortion advocates such as the National Abortion Rights Action League which has since removed the word "abortion" from its title and called itself just NARAL.

Note that this lacks even the legal fig leaf of leaving the head inside a dilated cervix before completing the abortion. Even by Roe standards an infant born alive (showing signs of life; heartbeat, breathing muscle movement), completely delivered and outside the mother's body is a legal person against which it is illegal to discriminate by depriving it of life without due process. It's not a restriction against abortion to require a doctor to save the life of any patient, even one that he's just unsuccessfully tried to kill. After all, by the time the baby has been completely delivered, it can no longer be reasonably asserted that this is a matter of a woman's control over *her own* body. Her body has becomes completely and physically separated from that other human body that has up until then been encased in her uterus. Even according to law, the fetus is now a baby, a completely separate unique human person entitled to the same protection of law as any other person.

One may wish to ask, Peter Singer, Michael Tooley, Mary Anne Warren, Bonnie Steinbock and other proponents of both abortion and infanticide, "What exactly *do* you people think has happened in the mere moments it takes for the baby to travel from one end of the birth canal to the other?" One can embrace one of two logical alternatives. Either it's legitimate to kill it in both places, or in neither. Some folks in the interest of preserving both abortion and their sense of logical consistency have agreed to permit the killing of babies outside the womb. There is no difference in the actual nature of that being we alternatively call a fetus and a baby. This is something that supporters and opponents of abortion now habitually agree on.

The only difference between them now is what *kind of choice* they think it compels. Some think that killing is still permissible, thereby extending the logic of death to gamely include those who within recent memory would have been considered by all to be sacrosanct living human persons. Others extend the right to life as far as the logic of life allows. Oddly we can see that the logic can be extended in either direction, to either life or death, and it's only a matter of choosing which is better. This is a test of character.

Since the early days of the debate, pro-life activists have insisted that the killing wouldn't be limited to the unborn. The irreducible logic of abortion justification would inevitably lead, they said, to killing other human beings, those who were not unborn; infants, children, the elderly, the handicapped and so forth. These arguments were initially dismissed as hysterical propaganda. Nevertheless, as knowledge of the in utero development progressed, and as ultrasound became more widely available to both parents and the general public via television specials such as *National Geographic's* "In the Womb" series, it became clear to most abortion proponents that something needed to be adjusted in their logic.

Justice Blackmun in writing the Court decision for Roe v. Wade stated baldly that,

> *"We need not resolve the difficult question of when life begins. When those trained in the respective disciplines of medicine, philosophy, and theology are unable to arrive at any consensus, the judiciary, at this point in the development of man's knowledge, is not in a position to speculate as to the answer."*[294]

Even at the time of Roe we knew better than that. It is well beyond speculation to state that life itself begins long before birth, and we now know that at the time of conception, the new life undergoes a radical and astonishing transformation. A zygote then embryo is an entirely different order of being from the sperm and egg from which it forms. While the embryo will continue to develop, it will never change completely into a wholly different kind of entity (the way sperm and egg do) until it dies. Even at the single cell stage, it is not a skin cell or a muscle cell, neither is it a part of another organism as skin and muscle cells are. It is a complete and individual organism, a self-directed entity, which develops and changes according to its own internal rules specific to its species.

---

[294] Roe v. Wade, 1993.

Its development constitutes a "series of quantifiable, noncontingent, scientifically verifiable and infinitely reproducible events that signifies the beginning of a new human life..."[295] The fact that a human life begins at conception is now recognized as being completely, conclusively, and scientifically demonstrated. The zygote/embryo/fetus is completely understood as a living human being, a member of the species homo sapiens. We need not wonder nor debate further as to when human life begins. It begins at the beginning. It begins at conception.

This is what necessitates the change in emphasis. The stoics may have believed that life begins only at birth, but a long and ancient chain of witnesses can claim the contrary with the full confidence that their faith is confirmed as scientific fact. Supporters of abortion have been forced irrevocably to change gears and shift to a new perspective, that of the "person". Various writers have made efforts to define the concept of the person as distinct from that of the human being. Not all have limited personhood to the human species. For the purposes of justifying abortion they have all denied personhood to unborn members of the human species. Invariably, this involves a list of properties involving sentience, the ability to feel pain, a sense of self-awareness and so forth. Giubilini and Minerva proposed this:

"We take 'person' to mean an individual who is capable of attributing to her own existence some (at least) basic value such that being deprived of this existence represents a loss to her. This means that many non- human animals and mentally retarded human individuals are persons, but that all the individuals who are not in the condition of attributing any value to their own existence are not

---

[295] Bernard Nathanson, *The Hand of God*, (Washington, DC:: Regnery Publishing, Inc., 1996), p. 137.

persons. Merely being human is not in itself a reason for ascribing someone a right to life."[296]

"This means that many … mentally retarded human individuals are persons." This would seem to imply that many, *but not all* mentally handicapped individuals are persons. They stopped short of saying this directly just as they stopped short of setting a deadline for infant termination. The reader is left to make the obvious deduction that some of the mentally handicapped are non-persons, and indeed that generally this may be extended to many other groups of human beings. "Mere" humanity is not enough.

The law adds its own set of complications. If a child is wanted it should be saved, and, depending on state law may be considered a murder victim. Physicians have commented on the difficult ethical predicament of trying, sometimes heroically, to save a newborn premature baby in one ward, while aborting a nearly identical healthy infant in the abortion ward on another floor.

While Mary Anne Warren's list of attributes is mercifully short at merely six, other writers have expanded the list to as many as a dozen or more. Inevitably the list will include a number of subjective mental states, including memory, desires and expectations, self awareness, desire to live, and awareness of time. Watch out when you're in the philosophy department and you wonder, "My, my, where has the time gone? You might be a non-person. If you can't remember what you had for breakfast, you might be a non-person. If you don't have expectations of future events (great expectations?) if you have an unusually high tolerance for pain, if you've done enough Buddhist meditation to no longer have an awareness of self, or if you're just asleep, *you might be* a non-person.

---

[296] Giubilini A, Minerva F. *J Med Ethics* (2012). doi:10.

If you think that the demonstrated conclusions of the pro-abortion league are absurd, so much the better. If an idea implies any obviously false or absurd statement, that constitutes proof of its falsehood. The original idea is reduced to an absurdity. The fact that your interlocutor doesn't admit the absurdity of his own conclusion is beside the point. If your abortion theory requires the killing of babies, then the theory is obviously wrong. So much the worse for anyone who denies it.

Reductio ad absurdum est quod erat demonstrandum.

The Right to a Dead Baby
Born Alive Infant Protection

"Suffer little children, and forbid them not, to come unto me: for of such is the kingdom of heaven."
Matthew 19:14

If the legal fiction of partial birth abortion weren't confusing enough, a number of abortion facilities that performed abortions by the induction method, artificially inducing labor to expel a presumably dead fetus, began to discover that not all the "products of abortion" were in fact dead. Normally the product of abortion, the tissue that remains outside the mother's body after being removed from the uterus contains no living entities. Indeed much of it is often dismembered and except for certain body parts (arms, legs, and the occasional facial expression) is unrecognizable as human. The usual purpose of an abortion, after all, is to terminate the pregnancy by killing the child.

The complication with the induction method, especially when performed late in the pregnancy, is that the baby is not necessarily killed by the procedure. Sometimes induced labor, like its natural counterpart, produces a living child outside the womb. If we are to use the moment of birth as a legally "bright" dividing line between a fetus which is legally killable, and a baby which is not, (the sometime interpretation of Roe v. Wade) a living child as product of conception immediately becomes the doctor's human patient with the same right to life as the rest of us.

Thus abortion clinics and hospitals performing abortions in this manner, who allowed these living "products" to die, were in fact committing homicide. It's no longer a matter of "ensuring *fetal* demise" if the baby is completely born and living outside its mother's body. Ensuring the demise of a human being, even a newborn baby isn't completing an abortion. Even under Roe, it's a form of murder.

After all, this is *exactly why* doctors engaged in partial birth abortions left the baby's head inside the cervix; to preserve at least an appearance of legality under the Roe decision.

Justice Blackmun declined to define an unborn infant as a "person". He noted that

> *"The Constitution does not define 'person' in so many words. Section 1 of the Fourteenth Amendment contains three references to 'person.' ... But in nearly all these instances, the use of the word is such that it has application only postnatally. None indicates, with any assurance, that it has any possible pre-natal application."*[297]

The words "pre-natal" and "postnatal" refer to the demarcation line of birth, such that "pre-natal" refers to the time before birth, and "postnatal" refers to the time after. Any product of abortion that has survived the procedure, and is living outside the mother's body is in a "postnatal" condition, and therefore is a person for the purposes of Justice Blackmun's reading of the Fourteenth Amendment. Any such person is covered under the Constitutions Fourteenth Amendment references to persons as citizens, and in reference to the "Due Process Clause and in the Equal Protection Clause".[298] Recall that it was at this postnatal point of Fourteenth Amendment coverage that Justice Blackman stipulated the right to abortion "collapses".

---

[297] Roe v. Wade, 1993, section IX.
[298] Ibid.

In theory, no additional law should be necessary for the protection of infants who have survived an attempted abortion. Nevertheless, the standard procedure in many, if not most abortion facilities appears to have necessitated just such a law.

So have some court decisions, as with the Farmer case, which places all its emphasis on the woman's intentions (leaving the child "marked for abortion") and none on the child's obvious postnatal condition. Testimony before Congress gave the distinct impression that at least some abortion providers were allowing postnatal products of abortion to die, or even a-la Gosnell, actively ensuring their demise.

Hadley Arkes, Edward Ney Professor of Jurisprudence and American Institution, Amherst College testified regarding recent court cases.

> *"With these steps, the Court has brought us to the threshold of outright infanticide, and it takes but the shortest step to cross that threshold."*[299]

This appears to have been the purpose of the Farmer Court's reasoning; to so fog the issue that infanticide will become accepted as an adjunct to abortion rights. Then there need be no effort to save the life of any product of abortion; the abortion can be carried out in the easiest fashion possible for the convenience of the abortionist with no complicating involvement of the emergency ward, the maternity ward, or the intensive care unit. The "precipitate" will die of its own accord whether from lack of oxygen, food, water, or

---

[299] Hearing before The Subcommittee On The Constitution of the Committee On The Judiciary House Of Representatives, 107th Congress, 1st session, p. 30.

186

simple exposure. How Roman. All that's required of the rest of us is to "pass by on the other side of the road". [300]

The fact that by expelling the fetus, alive or not, puts an end to the pregnancy (which is certainly what the patient *really* wanted in the first place) and removes the question of the woman's right to do as she pleases with "her own body". If what the woman intends is to terminate the pregnancy, that is accomplished by either the act of giving birth or abortion. Once the fetus becomes a baby by exiting the mother's body, no harm can come to the mother if at that time efforts are made to save the life of the living child. Indeed, as we've seen, immediately inducing labor and delivering a live baby is the fastest and safest procedure for the mother when her life is *genuinely* in danger from the pregnancy. Abortion procedures that involve the induction of labor generally take several days and include substantially greater risks as a result. The fantastical notion that by intending to terminate her pregnancy she intends only the death of the child, even when it's life is utterly and completely now independent of her own is what Jeremy Bentham once called "nonsense on stilts". Having thus used the concept of "abortion rights" to justify infanticide, no court upholding such an absurd decision could then reasonably claim that any daylight exists at all between abortion and the killing of children. They will, of course, have plenty of intellectual support from philosophers in bioethics departments world wide.

Arkes continued his testimony,

"But what seems to be at work... is a vibrant strand of opinion, holding that the logic of abortion rights entails that right to an 'effective abortion' or a dead child...the child has a claim to the protection of the law that cannot pivot on the

---

[300] *Luke* 10:31.

question of whether anyone 'wants' her. In that case, we would imply that the child has an intrinsic dignity, which must in turn be the source of rights of an intrinsic dignity, which cannot depend then on the interests or convenience of anyone else."[301]

This is exactly what is at work here. *Any effort* at saving life, no matter how inconsequential and harmless to the woman is to be seen as "chipping away" at her right to choose, even at the cost of embracing death as a good to be pursued for its own sake. This is how a "culture of death" works. It has the power to draw in otherwise rational beings into its matrix of sophistry, equivocation, and deception. This seduction produces what Arkes called "a momentum in principle to let the child die."

We might call this "target fixation". It's a common psychological effect noticed by fighter-bomber pilots engaged in attacking targets on the ground. The pilot becomes so concentrated on his goal of destroying the target that he forgets to avoid flying into it. It may even be that a "task oriented" character is part of the personality profile of a good pilot; maybe of a physician as well. It has been known to cause plane crashes, even of major jet liners.

In the Everglades crash of Eastern Airlines 401 in 1972, the entire cockpit crew, including both pilots became so focused on the failure of what turned out to be a faulty 59 cent nose gear indicator light that no one noticed the alarm that told them that the aircraft had slipped out of autopilot and was descending. Even after they realized their mistake a good 10 seconds elapsed before the aircraft hit the ground; more than enough time to take control and pull up. The voice cockpit black box of the crew conversations recorded the entire disaster as it unfolded. The recordings were used for years

---

[301] House Subcommittee hearing.

afterwards to train pilots to avoid the kind of fixation that made the crew of Flight 401 forget their primary duty, that of flying the plane.

The difference here is that no one is telling doctors to remember *their* primary duty to protect the life of *all* their patients. On the contrary, courts are encouraging them to continue on the initial path to abortion, even when it crosses the line into infanticide. When ethical lines are deliberately blurred by ideologically motivated activists and judges it can be a simple matter to fail to notice what lines have been crossed and when. It is, of course, at this point that it becomes imperative to begin drawing new and better lines; hence the Born-Alive Infants Protection Act.

Read the Court's decision in the Farmer case.

"It is shocking in the extreme that, whatever one may think of abortion...this wholesale mischaracterization of what is necessarily involved in the D&X procedure...is what has unquestionably, at least in large part, inflamed public opinion...

The Legislature's argument that Roe and Casey are inapplicable to "partial-birth" abortion procedures because such procedures are infanticide rather than abortion is based on semantic machinations, irrational line-drawing, and an obvious attempt to inflame public opinion instead of logic or medical evidence."[302]

"Whatever one may think of abortion?" It seems that it is the Court that is inflaming public opinion.

---

[302] U. S. Court of Appeals, Third Circuit, Planned Parenthood Of Central New Jersey V. Farmer.

"If there was ever a decision that embodied the very vices it was decrying, this must surely be it, for the argument here now was that it was all, in the end, a matter of perceptions, of 'semantics' and 'line-drawing': There were no objective facts—no birth, no "child" being killed at the point of birth, because the mother, you see, had elected an abortion. Once she had made that choice, there was no child to be killed, no birth to take place."[303]

After Arkes testified, the Committee took the testimony of Jill Stanek a registered nurse (R.N.) with the Labor & Delivery Department at (the staggeringly inappropriately named) *Christ Hospital* in Oak Lawn, Illinois. She related the nature of the common practice at her hospital and others of induced labor abortion. The procedure, at least to start, is the same as that of the Gosnell Clinic. The cervix is dilated and labor is artificially induced so as to use the natural birthing process of the mother's body to expel the fetus. The product of the procedure may or may not be a living baby. If the baby is alive but is sufficiently premature then its chances of surviving for very long are nil. If the baby is further along, its chances, if properly cared for, become progressively greater. Nurse Stanek noted,

"Up until recently, staff options were to hold the baby until death or put the baby in our Soiled Utility Room if we got busy or if the baby lingered too long. Indeed, it is not uncommon for one of these babies to live for an hour or two or even longer. Last year alone, of the 16 babies that Christ Hospital states were aborted, I am aware of four who were born alive. Each of these babies - two boys and two girls - lived between 1-1/2 and 3 hours. At Christ Hospital one of

---

[303] Hadley Arkes, Testimony before the Committee On The Judiciary House Of Representatives, p. 29.

*these babies once lived for almost an entire eight-hour shift.
At least two of the second-trimester babies who were aborted
last year at Christ Hospital were completely healthy.*"[304]

As medical science progresses, the threshold for "viability" will inevitably be pushed back, and more babies who might survive with proper care will, absent legal action, be allowed to die. As specified by the New Jersey Court, the policy at Christ Hospital is to defer to the mother's intention when deciding whether or not to care for a premature baby. One baby,

> "...*was completely healthy and had up to a 39 percent
> chance of survival according to the national stats, but the
> patient chose to abort. The baby was born alive. If the
> mother had wanted everything done for this baby, there
> would have been a neonatologist, a pediatric resident, a
> pediatric nurse, and a respiratory therapist present for this
> delivery and the baby would have been taken to our NICU
> for specialized care.*"[305]

However, in this case, the mother intended to abort, so only minimal "comfort care" was given. The 39 percent chance dropped to zero.

Nurse Stanek reported that Christ Hospital had recently opened up a "Comfort Room" where babies could be taken to die; or if their parents wanted, it provided

> "...*a First Foto machine in case parents want pictures of
> their aborted babies, baptismal supplies if parents would like
> their aborted babies baptized, and a foot printer and baby*

---

[304] House Subcommittee hearing, p. 43.
[305] Ibid.

bracelets if parents would like keepsakes of their aborted babies. There is also a wooden rocker to rock these babies to death."[306]

Birth photographs, souvenir bracelets and footprints, and baptismal supplies aren't things one normally associates with disposable beings. One does not baptize a tumor; only human beings are baptized. Human beings are the only sorts of things that can be the recipients of a sacrament. A clump of cells isn't baptized. Then again one doesn't normally associate the name of Christ with the killing of children. Do we really need a law to prevent that? Apparently.

This is truly astonishing. Anyone who wants a baby bracelet keepsake for a child they've decided to abort doesn't understand the concept of abortion: or parenthood for that matter.

Fortunately, the Born Alive Infants Protection Act was passed by Congress and signed into law in 2002. Unfortunately, that didn't end the media confusion. The Associated Press either couldn't or wouldn't get it straight. In an article about the legislation, it wrote that the law was meant to "define a fetus that is fully outside a woman's body as having been born alive, which would give the fetus legal protection". Fair enough: except of course, for the moronic confusion between a "fetus" and a baby. Note to AP: "fetus" inside; baby outside. Amendment to note: "outside a woman's body" means *not part* of what a woman has a right to when she's exercising her right to do as she pleases with her own body. The unsigned piece was published in, among other places, the *New York Times*.

Unfortunately, the AP continued with the article.

---

[306] Ibid.

"The Born Alive Infants Protection Act would amend the legal definitions of 'person,' 'human being,' 'child' and 'individual' to include a fetus that is either breathing or has a heartbeat once out of the womb as part of an abortion procedure."[307]

Was there no one at either the Times or the AP that understood Justice Blackmun's distinction between "pre-natal" and "postnatal"? To recap: "pre-natal" means "fetus". "Postnatal" means "baby", not to mention, "'person,' 'human being,' 'child' and 'individual'", *and not coincidentally*, entitled to all the protections of the Constitution, most particularly the Fourteenth Amendment; the very things that Blackmun in writing Roe denied to "pre-natal" entities.

Digging the journalistic hole even deeper the article goes on.

"The measure, which passed by voice vote, involves an abortion procedure whose opponents call partial birth,' in which a fetus is partly delivered before being destroyed."[308]

Actually, the form of abortion used here is generally induced labor abortion, *not* a type of "partial" birth abortion at all. One might even call it "complete-birth abortion". Nothing is left inside the mother before it is killed. The procedure mercifully does at least eliminate that legal fiction. *All the death involved* takes place (one more time) *outside* the womb.

One really begins to wonder if the "journalists" covering this story are purposely obfuscating the facts; without deliberation could

---

[307] "House Votes To Protect Aborted Fetus 'Born Alive'", New York *Times*, (March 13, 2002).
[308] Ibid.

anyone possibly be that obtuse? It is, of course possible that no one at the AP or the Times bothered to read the Act. That might be the most egregious example of journalistic laziness in recent memory. For the benefit of anyone wanting to cover the story in the future the Act isn't long. Here it is in its entirety.

Public Law 107-207
U.S. Code
Title 1, Chapter 1: Rules of Construction
Section 8.

"Person", "human being", "child", and "individual" as including born-alive infant

> (a) In determining the meaning of any Act of Congress, or of any ruling, regulation, or interpretation of the various administrative bureaus and agencies of the United States, the words "person", "human being", "child", and "individual", shall include every infant member of the species homo sapiens who is born alive at any stage of development. (b) As used in this section, the term "born alive", with respect to a member of the species homo sapiens, means the complete expulsion or extraction from his or her mother of that member, at any stage of development, who after such expulsion or extraction breathes or has a beating heart, pulsation of the umbilical cord, or definite movement of voluntary muscles, regardless of whether the umbilical cord has been cut, and regardless of whether the expulsion or extraction occurs as a result of natural or induced labor, cesarean section, or induced abortion. (c) Nothing in this section shall be construed to affirm, deny, expand, or contract any legal status or legal right applicable to any member of the species homo sapiens at any point prior to being "born alive" as defined in this section.

That's it. Easy peasy; even a Supreme Court Justice could understand it. Justice Blackmun seemed to have had no problem getting it. So what's with the AP and the *Times*?

Here's NARAL's take on it (dated two years earlier).

> *"The Act would effectively grant legal personhood to a pre-viable fetus -in direct conflict with Roe-... Roe v. Wade clearly states that women have the right to choose prior to fetal viability. After viability, Roe allows states to prohibit or restrict abortion as long as exceptions are made to protect the life and health of the woman. In proposing this bill, anti-choice lawmakers are seeking to ascribe rights to fetuses 'at any stage of development,' thereby directly contradicting one of Roe's basic tenets."*[309]

Strange, that's not what Justice Blackmun wrote, nor is it what the bill states. No rights to in utero "fetuses" were involved in the Act at all; only rights to post partum babies; and no rights were granted via Roe to "choose" anything with respect to infants outside the mother's body. If the individual is postnatal, it's covered by the Constitution and nothing in Roe violates its rights. Roe only allows the rights of pre-natal individuals to be violated.

NARAL's statement is even more obtuse than the AP's. That doesn't seem possible, but there you are. It does make it look like NARAL is where the AP got most of its information though; not exoneration by any stretch, but a plausible explanation.

---

[309] NARAL Press Release, "ROE V. WADE FACES RENEWED ASSAULT IN HOUSE" July 20, 2000.

This also has the effect of making the bill sponsor's point for him. If there's that much confusion being bandied about, then some clarification about who and what are covered by which law is in order. One wonders why all this became necessary in the first place; pre-natal and postnatal seemed clear enough in 1973.

In the end, of course, it wasn't that the pro-life folks were chipping away at abortion. It's the abortion lobby chipping away at our humanity. Is this the beginning of a long "slippery-slope" that can end only with the abolition of abortion?

Maybe that's not such a bad idea.

Demonic Demography
Half the Sky

"It is sad, but not surprising, that in rural homes a bucket of water is placed beside the bed of a woman in labor. If the newborn turns out to be a girl, she is drowned like a kitten."[310]
Olivia Vlahos

Mao Tse-Tung used to say that "Women hold up half the sky". Maybe that was true decades ago when Chairman Mao was around; now, not so much. In China and other parts of Asia, males are holding up about two thirds of the sky and the load is getting heavier. There is a distinct shortage of females, numbering in the hundreds of millions. Where have all these "missing" girls gone? Well, technically, they didn't go anywhere, because they were never there in the first place. In hospital wards where seventy percent of the births are boys, you can be sure that many of them are replacements for girls who were aborted. Amniocentesis and eventually ultrasound as well, have made prenatal testing cheap and routine around the world. In parts of the world where there is still a distinct preference for sons, couples now have an easy way to make sure that's what they get. What with dowries for girls costing upwards of 500,000 Rupies (about $13,000, USD) there's even a considerable financial incentive.

Author Mara Hvistendahl[311] notes various advertisements in the Indian press calling pre-natal testing "humane and beneficial".

"In developing countries like India as parents are encouraged to limit their family to two offspring, they will have a right to quality in these two." In case you were

---

[310] Olivia Vlahos, "Sex and Consequences: An Anthropological View", Stetson, *The Silent Subject*, p. 99.
[311] Mara Hvistendahl, *Unnatural Selection*, (New York, NY: Public Affairs books, 2011), p. 49.

wondering, the word "quality" in this context means "male".[312]

Our science hasn't quite proceeded to the state where we can manufacture in advance a child of either sex (although that's surely coming), so for the time being the method of selecting the sex of your child is to monitor (usually now via ultrasound, but also amniocentesis) the development of the child in the womb and when you see a girl, you kill it.

The sexual imbalance in Asia and elsewhere is demand driven. The moment amniocentesis became available demographers noticed a skewing of the ratio of boys to girls. This suggests a long standing pent up demand for a way to avoid having girls. This wasn't just among the poor who needed strong backs to work in the fields, or the middle class who wanted to avoid expensive dowries. Even Bollywood's rich and famous flocked to the abortion wards to weed out "undesirables". It's become a matter of entitlement, and given the ideology of the west where abortion is widely accepted, safe and legal (though far from rare) why wouldn't it be? As long as abortion is seen as a morally neutral act (and a right to boot) it can and will be done for any reason whatever. If people want to choose the sex of their baby, (or its eye color, hair color what have you) they'll use abortion to accomplish it until something easier and cheaper comes along.

Selecting females for the abortion mill is also an effective form of population control. When foundations and "experts" give aid to third world countries, they also call the shots. Not many third worlders like to have westerners explain that there are too many people like them, but when they're accepting aid money there's not much they can do about it. Population control's been a trendy topic for western elites for several decades, and it's often a condition of

---

[312] Ibid.

accepting assistance from western foundations and banks. The World Bank is one of the primary sources of spreading the population control ideology around the world, because it's one of the primary ways of spreading the money around, and eastern technocrats have learned that the best way to earn points is to go along with the ideology. So, the price of the new hospital may be to abort more than the usual number of girls.

A new medical student in India a few years back was astonished by the number of abortions and the careless way they were performed. The hospital neighborhood had large numbers of feral cats roaming the streets, and they sometimes made it inside the hospital. But he was surprised to see one carry off a piece of medical waste that looked suspiciously human.

> *"But then he worked up the nerve to approach the head nurse, Why had he seen a cat run off with what looked like fetal matter? And why had the fetus not been disposed of more carefully?... 'Because it was a girl' she said".*[313]

Just as ex-slave Frederick Douglass noted that a certain callousness comes with being a slave owner,[314] so callousness develops in hospital wards where abortions are routinely performed. Where sex selection is the purpose of abortion, the same attitude develops for girl fetuses and eventually for girls in general. The mind deadens and the heart hardens by constant repetition.

Thus, "conscience itself, darkened as it were by such widespread conditioning, is finding it increasingly difficult to

---

[313] Ibid., pp. 79-80.
[314] *Narrative Of The Life Of Frederick Douglass*, Chapter VI, (Boston, MA: The Anti-Slavery Office, No. 25 Cornhill), 1845.

distinguish between good and evil in what concerns the basic value of human life."[315]

While the strong cultural preference for sons is often part of eastern cultures no heavy imbalance in birth ratios could have been maintained over centuries, or India and China would have long since gone the way of the Romans. Safe abortion is a recent phenomenon, as is the ability to predict sex before birth. While population control has been a fashionable notion since the days of Malthus, it's only achieved worldwide popularity since the 1960's. One of the first methods advocated was that of sex selection.[316] If you don't make girls, you can't make babies. You can't make babies without males either, of course, but men can do prodigious duty with multiple partners in ways that women cannot.

An obvious problem with the strategy (aside from its odious moral quality) is that you get a temporary surplus of young men. Much has been written about the problem of young unattached (and usually fatherless) males in society, but when it's the result of a deliberately engineered policy it takes on a special urgency. Street gangs, drug use, and organized crime are the usual results. When the numbers get to a certain level a country may even resort to war to reduce their numbers. It is, as noted, a temporary problem. The population eventually declines, males and females, to an unsustainable level after which recovery is impossible. We see the results of this kind of policy all over Italy; Roman ruins. The late Roman Empire couldn't find enough males to recruit into their army, so they resorted to taking in outsiders, usually from the northern barbarian tribes. Those tribes were also their main adversaries, with the result that by the end of the fifth century Rome had been repeatedly sacked. The Romans gave up defending their own country

---

[315] Pope John Paul II *Evangelium Vitae*, March 25, 1995.
[316] Hvistendahl, p. 97.

because they didn't have the Roman men to do it and the foreigners they hired were a spectacularly inappropriate demographic.

Eugenics and population control have always been linked. In certain contexts they're the same thing. All eugenics seeks to control or eliminate certain "undesirable" populations, variously called "jukes"[317], "zeros", "Happy Hickories" "kallikaks"[318] or in this case, girls. Whether the eugenics is overt, as in the 1927 Buck v. Bell case, or subvert as in the more recent 1974 Relf v. Weinberger[319], the targets are those out of favor with cultural elites, rural "country folk" or as in the 1974 case rural, poor African Americans.

Eventually, of course, the population "bomb" turned out to be the population-control bomb in more ways than one. It imposed draconian methods to prevent a catastrophe that wasn't likely, and as a result killed millions in its wake. The agricultural revolution made population control irrelevant at the very time that it became such a fad. Activists moved on to other more trendy causes like DDT (which had all but eliminated malaria before its ban caused a massive resurgence in malaria deaths) or global warming (now mysteriously morphed into "climate change"). In each case draconian and unnecessary programs cause economic disaster and widespread death, mostly in the third world. More than one environmentalist has expressed satisfaction with these "side effects"

---

[317] Richard L. Dugdale, *The Jukes: A Study in Crime, Pauperism, Disease and Heredity*, (New York, NY: G.P. Putnam's Sons) 1877.

[318] Henry Herbert Goddard, *The Kallikak Family: A Study in the Heredity of Feeble-Mindedness*, (New York, NY: MacMillan), 1912.

[319] The Relf sisters (Minnie, 12 and Mary Alice 14) were sterilized without their consent in 1973. The Southern Poverty Law Center brought suit on their behalf and the case exposed widespread sterilization abuse by the Federal Government.

that reduce the number of people. "If they would rather die,...they had better do it, and decrease the surplus population."[320]

Former Planned Parenthood Director William Vogt wrote in 1948,

"One of the greatest national assets of China, perhaps the greatest asset, is its high death rate. China quite literally cannot feed more people...The greatest tragedy that China could suffer, at the present time, would be a reduction in her death rate...There can be no way out. These men and women, boys and girls must starve..."[321]

This kind of Malthusian eugenics is still standard fare among environmentalists.

Enthusiasm in the first world for population control was aimed primarily at the third world, although in America it was aimed at Native Americans as well.

"Constance Redbird Uri estimated that up to one-quarter of Indian women of childbearing age had been sterilized by 1977; in one hospital in Oklahoma, one-fourth of the women admitted (for any reason) left sterilized.... She also gathered evidence that all the pureblood women of the Kaw tribe in Oklahoma were sterilized in the 1970s-a truly genocidal process."[322]

---

[320] Charles Dickens, *A Christmas Carol*, Stave I, (London, UK: Chapman and Hall, 1843). Scrooge was nothing if not forward looking, even ahead of his time. The world's first true progressive and environmentalist.

[321] William Vogt, Stuart I. Freeman, *The Road to Survival*, (Neew York, NY: William Sloane Associates, 1948).

[322] Angela Franks, *Margaret Sanger's Eugenic Legacy: The Control of Female Fertility*, (Jefferson, NC: McFarland, 2005), p. 167.

The Johnson Administration's support for population control abroad was overseen by the United States Agency for International Development (USAID), often funneling its efforts through private groups, like the Ford Foundation, Planned Parenthood or the World Bank. It wouldn't be much of a stretch to call many of these groups a "front" for American foreign policy in the '60's and '70's. In the end it depended on coercion of foreign governments when they became dependent on American aid or needed a loan from the World Bank, run at the time by former U.S. Secretary of Defense, Robert McNamara. Little of USAID's money was spent directly. Most of it has been funneled through other agencies. It is in other words, "laundered" funding. This resulted in a remarkable degree of freedom from accountability.[323]

While female selective abortion is a largely modern phenomenon fueled by western technology and population control ideology, female infanticide has a very long and dismal history. British reports from the colonial era cite near unbelievable rates of baby girl killing.

The Bedi caste a sub-caste of the Khatri, was said by the Punjab administrative board to have killed all their female offspring for over 400 years. To replenish their ranks they took women from lower Khutri caste families.[324] While the British reports are too widespread and consistent to discount entirely, it appears that only the higher class families engaged in the extensive female murder, and forestalled extinction with the widespread traditional practice of hypergamy; men marrying women of lower social standing. The lower the caste, the less female infanticide is found. Absent such a

---

[323] Robert Zubrin, "The Population Control Holocaust", *The New Atlantis*, (Spring, 2012).
[324] L. S. Vishwanath, , "Efforts of Colonial State to Suppress Female Infanticide" *Economic and Political Weekly*, (33:19) May 9, 1998).

mechanism, India could never have become one of the most populous countries in the world.

Nevertheless, as recently as 1911, the "Census of the Bombay presidency, the proportion of females to 1,000 males in seven elite patidar villages under Baroda was 707 and 717 respectively, the other Hindus in these seven villages had 839 females and the entire population 813 females per thousand males."[325]

Hindu religion as expressed in its ancient sacred texts is strongly opposed to the killing of a fetus or a child regarding each as a form of murder punishable by many lifetimes of suffering. British efforts to discourage the custom began with citations of Hindu scripture. The custom was more related to high status and dowry avoidance (a modern motivation as well) than to anything specifically Hindu. Eventually, as religious persuasion yielded minimal results, the British Colonial masters resorted to force of law, often rigorously applied. Even here, the success was limited. After all, neglect is as deadly to a child as drowning, and harder to prove in court. That abortion of females is still widespread is testimony to the relative failure of the Colonial Government to reform the population.

Thus the preference for boys over girls has been a cultural preference in some countries for centuries.[326] While it was once enforced by infanticide (and often still is) the modern preference (reinforced by western feminism and population control ideology) is for abortion.

---

[325] Ibid., p. 4.
[326] Leela Visaria, "Deficit of Girls", *Sex-selective Abortion in India*, Tulsi Patel (ed.) (New Delhi/Washington, DC: Sage Publications Pvt. Ltd.), 2006 p. 76.

The situation is made more difficult by the fact that ultrasonography cannot determine the sex of a child much before 20 weeks. This makes for a wait and a relatively late term abortion. Doctors in many villages, eager to collect their fees, simply run the tests early, useless as they may be, and mark the results "female".[327] This results in abortions of both females and males, which causes endless consternation for the customers of the abortionist.

As in the west, when the results of the ultrasound are "unfavorable" the pressure on the mother to abort are sometimes extreme. In the west, including the United States a woman who has been informed by her doctor that the tests showed she's carrying a Down syndrome baby or one with achondroplasia ("dwarfism"), needs to be daring indeed if she wants to carry the child to term.[328] Often such babies are born without the conditions that were predicted for them. An abortion for them would have been as unnecessary was it is for male fetuses in India.

In India there have even been "cases of murder within the family when the young daughter-in-law refused to go for abortion after the very first conception".[329] It is not only in India that female selective abortion has found a receptive audience. There is also Communist China.

Dating from the late 1970s, China's policy, originating in the days of Mao himself, encouraged population reduction. The murder of several tens of millions of Chinese under Mao's reign did much to accomplish that goal. Even so, China's resilient culture and population managed to replenish much of what Mao destroyed, and the government resorted to forced population control, including forced abortions a few years after the U.S. lead the way with Roe v.

---

[327] Ashsh Bose, "Female Foeticide: A Civilizational Collapse", *Sex-selective Abortion in India*, Tulsi Patel (ed.) p. 83.
[328] Reist, *Defiant Birth: Women Who Resist Medical Eugenics*.
[329] *Bose/Patel*, p. 82.

Wade. After Mao's death and China "liberalized" a bit, China's own media began to report on the phenomenon.

> *"At present, the phenomena of butchering, drowning and leaving to die female infants and maltreating women who have given birth to female infants have been very serious. It has become a grave social problem."*[330]

In 1983, none of this did anything to dampen western liberal support for China's population control program. It was in this same year that the U.N. decided to give its United Nations Population Award to Communist China.[331]

While the figures from Asia are alarming enough (South Korea once had the highest abortion rate in the world: a staggering 2.75 abortions for every birth)[332] none of this explains similar patterns in Albania and Azerbaijan. In any event South Korea's population has largely recovered from the devastation of post-Korean War population control enthusiasts. What is clear is that from a world-wide perspective, wherever and whenever abortion flourishes, girls are at risk. They are at risk not just from abortion, but also "eve-teasing molestation and sexual harassment and, after marriage, exposed to the risk of bride burning and dowry death..."[333] As more Indians become increasingly prosperous, dowry becomes a minor factor. This is especially true since the greatest abuse of female abortion tends to be in the upper classes and highest earning of India's population.[334] They, of all people, don't really need the money. More insidious is son-preference, the widespread availability

---

[330] China *People's Daily* March 3, 1983.

[331] Steven W. Mosher, *Population Control: Real Costs, Illusory Benefits,* (Santa Barbara, CA: Transaction Publishers, 2008) p. 79.

[332] *Hvistendahl*, p. 133.

[333] *Bose/Patel*, p.87.

[334] Rainuka Dagar, "Rethinking Female Foeticide", *Sex-selective Abortion in India*, Tulsi Patel (ed.) p. 97.

of inexpensive western technology, the western attitude of guilt-free abortion and the false ideology of population control.

The fact that we're seeing these patterns not just in the far east, in India, China and South Korea, but also in Europe and the middle east; Albania and Azerbaijan, Georgia Armenia[335] points to a larger problem than just eastern traditional culture.

Part of the problem is in the modern west. Feminists don't like to talk about sex selective abortion. No one should be surprised. They haven't said much about female genital mutilation either; or the oppression of women under the Taliban in particular and in traditional (or radical) Islam in general.

> *"The new female activists mostly stayed silent, though... They neglected to stop sex selection for the memory of Roe v. Wade: they had cut their political teeth in the 1970s feminist movement, for which reproductive rights were paramount and any restrictions on abortion were a blow to women's freedom."*[336]

Feminists also don't say much about the other side effects of aborting lots of girls. Scarcity creates all kinds of markets, from sex trafficking in girls and women, to "bought brides" in every country where sex-selective abortion is popular.[337] Laws of supply and demand apply even here. When something is rare, men will pay more for it: sometimes a lot more. No one should want to see women and girls treated like a commodity, but the extreme gender imbalance in much of the world makes it inevitable.

It may not seem like an obvious implication, but if you want to abolish the sex trade, abolish abortion. In countries like Taiwan,

---

[335] *Hvistendahl*, p. 7.
[336] Ibid., p. 122
[337] Ibid., p. 163

about a third of all marriages are of local men to foreign women. For "foreign women" read arranged purchased marriages. In a traditional culture it's often the expected way for a daughter to help the family: find a rich husband from out of town.[338] Brokers will assist in this, much as they might for adoptions.

As there are fewer women, and fewer babies per woman, population declines, as the population controllers intended it to do. Over time, younger (and poorer) men have an increasingly difficult time finding wives. The wealthier men have fewer problems searching farther and farther afield, paying airfares and increased broker fees. None of this benefits women who are being bought and sold like cattle. Women may increase in monetary value because of their scarcity, but they're not the ones controlling the purse strings of value; it's only the husbands the brokers and the parents who sell their daughters who benefit from the "market". Market forces may be "crude" as Hvistendahl pints out,[339] but laws of supply and demand aren't there to benefit the items being bought and sold, only the buyers and sellers. When the object of the sale is a human being, we should look for ways to collapse the market. Here the best way is to remove the scarcity by abolishing the false ideology and the abortion practices that caused it in the first place.

This shouldn't be seen to imply that daughter's are *always* and *universally* despised in India. You might get that impression from leftist literature, of course, but that's an occupational hazard when you view everything in terms of victimology. The more harrowing the story, the more useful it is for political purposes.

"'Empowerment' in terms of higher access to education, health, income, decision-making, available more in the urban

---

[338] Ibid.
[339] Ibid., p. 172. Hvistendahl notes that some of the brokering even takes place on EBay.

areas has been the said panacea for discrimination against women.[340]

If "empowerment", were the solution we wouldn't be seeing higher levels of female abortion in the upper Indian classes among professionals, and higher educated groups. But that is what we do see. It is in precisely these advantaged groups where sex-selective abortion of females is most prevalent. How do we account for this?

Or, does it need accounting for? Should we be surprised that the groups of women most likely to be feminists are also the ones most likely to be aborting daughters? None of this can be analyzed in isolation, of course. It may simply be that upper class abortion is more visible and that the poorer classes resort to neglect of girl babies so as to favor their sons over their daughters: killing with neglect is still killing. This illustrates a fact that should be obvious by now: abortion and infanticide are the same thing.

It is useful and necessary to confront the cultural attitudes that lead to abortion and gender imbalance. There are many pro-life people in India and some have perhaps failed to completely overcome their preference for sons. They may express this not through abortion but through "visits to quacks, pilgrimages and pandits for evoking God's blessings for a male child".[341] While this may still exhibit a cultural preference for sons, the methodology is infinitely superior to the killing off of generations of girls. Indeed it illustrates the left's hollow insistence on the exclusive modification of cultural attitudes at the expense of legal enforcement. The left likes to see using the law as a cheap easy out, a panacea when their real goal is radical re-education.

That's no reason to avoid beginning with the "easier" action. In fact it points the way to a more comprehensive one. Rather than

---

[340] Dagar/Patel p. 114.
[341] Ibid., p. 119.

209

focusing just on sex-selective abortion of girls, it's would be far more effective to outlaw abortion itself. That too, requires addressing cultural norms, not all of which are peculiar to the east: re-education on a wide scale would be necessary to properly solve the problem. "Highlighting the power hierarchies"[342] isn't going to accomplish much. More practical is an inculcation of the idea that each conception and every child is a blessing (the real moral truth) regardless of gender, and we might add regardless of perceived defects like Down syndrome.

Patel does insist that if the first child is a daughter this is often seen as a joy, (while if it is a son they are "overjoyed"). The problem is the second (or third and fourth) daughters. Indeed Patel implies that testing and abortion are never used in a first pregnancy.[343] Perhaps. It is still true that "The majority of Indian women would be shattered to have only successive daughters."[344]

So many demographers working on the problem of the "missing girls" are mystified by the fact that although traditional ideas are deeply ingrained, modern ideology, that great destroyer of tradition, seems not to have fixed the problem. Why should the most westernized, highly educated, socially mobile, and prosperous be the ones who are even more interested in sex-selective abortion of girls than the poorer older more traditional villages? They needn't have wondered. Equating liberation of women to a "right" to abortion doesn't solve the problem.

It *is* the problem.

---

[342] Ibid., p. 120.

[343] Tulsi Patel, "Eliminating the Female Fetoetus" *Sex-selective Abortion in India*, p. 143.

[344] Ibid., p. 149.

Global Village of the Damned
Population Control

"It takes a village..."
Lemony Snicket[345]

S teven W. Mosher spent a year in Communist China studying anthropology. As a student he was an eye witness to the types of human rights abuse for which world communism has become infamous.

In Sandhead Village, He Kaifeng was a commune official overseeing, among other things, China's population control programs. Mosher witnessed his haranguing of pregnant women who had refused to abort their "over-quota" children.

> *"You who are eight or nine months pregnant should not think that you can hold out until you have your children naturally. When your time comes you will be taken to the clinic by commune order. All children must henceforth be born in the commune clinic. The safety of over-quota children born in the commune clinic is not guaranteed."* [346]

At the end of hours of heavy-handed indoctrination, the women were told they could go home now, if they would first agree to abort. One by one they were asked, "Who wants to go home?...Lin Xinlan do you want to go home...Su Shaobing do you want to go

---

[345] Lemony Snicket, (Daniel Handler), *A Series of Unfortunate Events #7: The Vile Village*, (New York, NY: Harper Childrens 2001), p. 15. (Also attributed to an African proverb, The Igbo Tribe, Toni Morrison, Jane Cowen-Fletcher, and others.)
[346] Steven W. Mosher "Forced Abortions and Infanticide in Communist China" *The Reach of Roe*, Ann Conlon (editor) (New York, NY: Human Life Foundation, 2012) p. 82.

home?"[347] Some went, knowing they had just "voluntarily" agreed to abort their child. Most others refused. In the end the results were the same; aborted fetuses and murdered babies.[348] Mosher has spent the rest of his life reporting on conditions in China. He notes that of the hundreds of millions of abortions in China many are carried out *during* birth, by injection, crushing of the skull, or strangulation. The Chinese Communist government doesn't see this as blurring the line between abortion and infanticide, because in under communism no one bothered to draw the line in the first place.

On China, as elsewhere, sons are prized, not merely because of "backward" bigotry against girls, but also because, as girls marry they move to their new husbands family. Only sons are left to care for elderly parents. In what is arguably the largest welfare state in the world, there are no government programs to take care of the rural peasants in old age or any other time. Welfare as it is understood in the west doesn't exist in China; all that remains is the totalitarian control that *always* accompanies the welfare state.

But population control does exist, and vast sums of money that might otherwise be spent on genuine public health programs is wasted destroying China's most important resource, her people.

After Mosher left China he was declared an "international spy" by Chinese security and Stanford University was told by the Communist Government to have nothing further to do with him. Stanford obligingly agreed to the Chinese demands and canceled the Ph.D. that Mosher had earned.

*****

Sometimes a single book can do a lot of damage. For some this will bring to mind *The Communist Manifesto* or *Mein Kampf.*

---

[347] Ibid.
[348] Ibid.

Rachel Carson's *Silent Spring*[349] did much to discourage and sabotage the eradication of malaria carrying mosquitoes, especially in the poorest reaches of the Third Word. The cost in unnecessary death by disease has run into the tens of millions. The world death rate from malaria had been brought under control after World War II due to the effective use of DDT. That's why Paul Hermann Müller was awarded the Nobel Prize in 1948 for discovering it. The National Academy of Sciences estimated that he saved around 500 million lives with his discovery. Malaria was nearly eradicated, but the Carson inspired ban on DDT sent the deaths from malaria and other insect born diseases skyward again. Few single books have caused so much damage.

In the seminal year of 1968 another best seller hit the bookstores, Paul Ehrlich's *The Population Bomb*[350]. Flashy and filled with descriptions of a dystopian future world, and the draconian measures that would be needed to save humanity (it began *"The battle to feed all of humanity is over…"*) it developed a cult following that has never completely dissipated. This is, despite the fact that it's terrifying predictions failed miserably to materialize. Ehrlich made a famous wager with Julian L. Simon about commodity prices that Ehrlich predicted would go up as a result of population-inflated demand; all prices declined and Ehrlich lost the bet. Nearly everything about the book has since been debunked.

Virtually all his predictions failed to come true, especially those related to a food crisis. The world population *has* more than doubled since the book first came out, but more people are being fed than ever before. Famine still exists, but is almost exclusively caused by political faction, revolution, and the use of hunger as a weapon by

---

[349] Rachel Carson, *Silent Spring* (New York, NY: Houghton Mifflin Harcourt, 1962).
[350] Paul Ehrlich *The Population Bomb,* (Cutchogue, NY: Buccaneer Books, 1968).

political and paramilitary groups that are nearly all Marxist. The warlord rule of failed states like Somalia is a classic case in point.

Ehrlich explained his emotional revulsion against expanding populations that he learned on a trip to New Delhi.

> *"The temperature was well over 100, and the air was a haze of dust and smoke. ...People eating, people washing, people sleeping. People visiting, arguing, and screaming. People thrusting their hands through the taxi window, begging. People defecating and urinating. People clinging to buses. People herding animals. People, people, people, people."[351]*

Later in the book he would refer to population as a "cancer" of which we were only treating the symptoms. The cancer itself must be cut out. The "cancer" was millions of people.

> *"The operation will demand many apparently brutal and heartless decisions. The pain will be intense. But the disease is so far advanced that only with radical surgery does the patient have a chance of survival."[352]*

There was nothing "apparent" about the brutality, the heartlessness or the pain. They were all too real. And they were unnecessary. The world's fertility rate had already begun to decline before the book was published. Today the primary continent in crisis is Africa, the most sparsely populated landmass in the world. Continent wide Marxist mismanagement of economies and resources, and war driven chaos are the real causes of Africa's poverty, not over population.

Another more humane solution was also already in progress. Since the end of the Second World War, scientists had been working

---

[351] Ibid., p. 1.
[352] Ibid., p. 152.

on increasing food production. In occupied Japan Cecil Salman noticed a species of mutant dwarf wheat the Japanese farmers had been successfully growing. He sent samples back to the U.S. Norman Borlaug, an American scientist working in Mexico, began in 1952 to cross this type of wheat with those he had been experimenting with under a Rockefeller grant. By 1963, five years before Ehrlich's book, the Mexican wheat harvest (95% Borlaug's genetically engineered hybrids) was six times what it had been less than two decades earlier.[353]

By 1968, Borlaug's wheat had made it to India and Pakistan, making the wheat harvests of both countries self-sufficient. India ran out of storage space for its sudden bounty. This, occurred "...in the very same year that Paul Ehrlich called for starving the 'hopeless' subcontinent whose people he founds so repellant..."[354] This series of scientific discoveries and innovations became known as the "Green Revolution", and it has saved over a billion lives; and counting.

The folks who still want to limit the population by "apparently brutal" means, are now (of course) adamantly opposed to genetically altered foods like Borlaug's wheat, just as they were to Müller's DDT. Another target of "green" radical population environmentalist wrath is carotene enriched "golden " rice, which holds the promise of eradicating vitamin A deficiency, and the blindness that it causes in millions of poor children world wide. As with the DDT ban, western liberals have succeeded in blocking much of the nutritious new foods from being distributed in third world countries. Some African governments have even refused to distribute American food aid in famine conditions, lest they offend

---

[353] Robert Zubrin, *Merchants of Despair: Radical Environmentalists, Criminal Pseudo-Scientists, and the Fatal Cult of Antihumanism*, (New York, NY: Encounter Books, 2012), p. 209.
[354] Ibid.

the green sensibilities of western liberals.[355] These followers of ZPG ideas would rather see the "teeming masses" starve.[356] There's more than a little racism here when white westerners are so eager to export their *apparently brutal and heartless decisions*" to brown peoples around the world whether those peoples want them or not.

Nevertheless, Zero Population Growth, has gained thousands of followers and admirers. ZPG has since changed its name to Population Connection (much like global warming is now known as "climate change"). There may be many theories as to why advocacy groups change their names. NARAL was once the National Abortion Rights Action League; some speculate that getting the word "abortion" out of the name must have been the motivation, but who knows. Population Connection sounds suitably vague and innocuous; who, ignorant of its provenance, would imagine that it used to be Zero Population Growth?

Ehrlich seems never to have repudiated his ideas. When population researcher Mara Hvistendhal[357] interviewed him she read him passages from his book and asked him if he wanted to rethink any of them. His response astonished her.

In a parry of masterfully skill, he denied remembering having written the passages. In a rambling series of thoughts he said that if he were to write the book over (he eventually did) he might restate some of his points. In the process of a few minutes he had replaced everything he had written with a slightly re-worded revision of the

---

[355] Ibid., *pp. 203-204.*

[356] "*It should be noted, first of all, that rich people are never called 'teeming masses,' no matter how many of them there are per square mile. Wealthy Park Avenue neighborhoods have concentrations of people that will compare with slums around the world.*"

Thomas Sowell, *The Economics and Politics of Race,* (New York, NY: William Morrow, 1983), pp. 209-210.

[357] Hvistendahl, p. 108-110.

original ideas, all while claiming not to have remembered having them or written them down.

> *"For it has apparently just occurred to Ehrlich that mass sterilization could be reworked to take advantage of the wide-spread preference for boys..."*[358]

Of course, nothing had to be reworked. The preference for boys was the force multiplier that population control needed, whether it came through sterilization, abortion or infanticide, and in general, for the liberal crowd there's never any difficulty sacrificing individuals to a larger cause.

Through repeated appearances on television, including the *Tonight Show with Johnny Carson*, Ehrlich promoted his theories creating a wide swath of followers. While the specifics of the book have been long forgotten, the central premise that the world is filled beyond capacity with too many people remains widely assumed as received wisdom. No one pays attention to the fact that it's devoid of substance to it. It's one of those ideas that everybody just "knows"; *of course we have to do something about population.* Much similar advocacy by many others would follow, although everyone involved *"decades later, pretended as if that advocacy never happened."*[359]

The Chinese didn't come up with the idea of radical population control on their own, although it was profoundly useful to the design of all communists - complete control over the society they govern. They got the original idea from the Club of Rome's publication *The Limits to Growth*.[360]

---

[358] Ibid.

[359] Ibid.

[360] Donella H. Meadows, Dennis L. Meadows, Jorgen Randers, William W. Behrens III, *The Limits to Growth: A Report for the Club of Rome's Project on the Predicament of Mankind*, (New York, NY: Signet, 1972).

It was eventually disclosed that the disaster predictions (which never happened) had been "exaggerated". The Club admitted in a subsequent volume that since countries can only be united by discovering a common enemy, "either a real one or else one invented for the purpose..."

"In searching for a new enemy to unite us, we came up with the idea that pollution, the threat of global warming, water shortages, famine and the like would fit the bill. All these dangers are caused by human intervention, and it is only through changed attitudes and behavior that they can be overcome. The real enemy then, is humanity itself."[361]

Hitler turned the Jews of Germany into an enemy to gain power. Stalin did the same with the Kulaks, so The Club of Rome (and eventually the entire environmental movement and the rest of liberalism with it) decided that humanity as a whole could do for them what the Jews had done for Hitler. Or something like that.

The Chinese never got the message that all the population explosion propaganda was just a stunt to get attention; they just took the original idea of making enemies out of all mankind and ran with it. On page 130 of *The Population Bomb* Ehrlich had recommended state enforced birth control something he called "compulsory birth regulation".[362] The idea was realized just over a decade later in a country that had apparently never heard of Paul Ehrlich or the Club of Rome.

The Club of Rome Report, *The Limits to Growth* had been widely disseminated in China by a Chinese missile scientist, Song

---

[361] Alexander King, Bertrand Schneider, *The First Global Revolution: A Report by the Council of Rome*, (New York, NY: Pantheon Books, 1991, p. 75.
[362] Paul Ehrlich *The Population Bomb*, Quoted in Robert Zubrin, *Merchants of Despair*, p. 184.

Jian, but not under the auspices of the Club of Rome. Song published the report as his own research and in the process became as famous inside China as Paul Ehrlich was elsewhere. The aging and isolated heads of China's ruling Politburo, especially its General Secretary, Deng Xiaoping, were favorably impressed by his presentation. Song told them that China had a "correct population" and that this figure was 300 million people *below the actual population* of the country. They would have to find a way to cull the Chinese herd. Murdering tens of millions of their own countrymen was something China's elite had done before, but 300 million would be a new stretch. Fortunately Song said he had a better answer; a one child per couple policy implemented *immediately*.

Once General Secretary Deng announced his support for the program, whatever opposition that might have materialized vanished. The Central Committee quickly assumed its *ex-cathedra* persona and declared infallibly that one child was the policy of China and "no further disagreements would be tolerated".[363]

For the Central Committee, it must have seemed like manna from Heaven, even for devout Marxists who didn't believe in Heaven. It was an offer too good to refuse. They were the custodians of the greatest political mismanagement disaster in human history, with some 80 million dead to be held account for. Here was a "genius" mouthing phrases completely new to them like "spaceship earth", with a Ph.D. from Moscow university, a boatload of computer generated numbers, a cultured accent, offering a get out of jail free card for the deaths of millions of Chinese who could now safely be put to rest in complete and permanent anonymity. The self-congratulations must have lasted a month.

Congratulations from the west also began to pour in; the 1983 United Nations Population Award, was only one. USAID

---

[363] Zubrin, p. 183.

funneled American cash through the U.N. and the International Planned Parenthood Foundation. A blind eye was turned to the atrocities that followed.

> *"Thus began the most forceful population control program since Nazi Germany...all women with one child were to have a stainless-steel IUD inserted, and to be inspected regularly...To remove the device would be deemed a criminal act. All parents with two or more children were to be sterilized...and all unauthorized pregnancies were to be aborted...Babies would be aborted right through the ninth month of pregnancy, with many crying as they were being stabbed to death at the moment of birth."*[364]

Few alarm bells went off in the west. Planned Parenthood's public relations officer, Penny Kane expressed concerns in an *internal* document from China.

> *"Very strong measures are being taken...including abortion up to eight months...forced family planning, murder of viable fetuses, parallels with India, etc.,... it is going to be very difficult to defend...We might find it extremely difficult to handle the press and the public if a there were a major fuss about the Chinese methods."*[365]

Planned Parenthood ignored the warning about a "fuss" and plowed ahead. Nevertheless, beginning in the early 1980's word began to leak out of something dreadful going on inside China. Stories by Michelle Vink in the *Wall Street Journal*[366], and

---

[364] Zubrin, p. 184.

[365] Quoted in Zubrin, p. 185.

[366] Michelle Vink, "Abortion and Birth Control in Canton, China" *Wall Street Journal*, November 30, 1981. Quoted in Zubrin, p. 185-186.

Christopher S. Wren writing for the *New York Times*[367] relayed harrowing tales of suffering and carnage from within China's gulag, which by then had become the entire country. Vink described transportation vans where "unauthorized" children were murdered en masse. Women were "handcuffed, tied with ropes, or placed in pig's baskets" as they were removed for forced abortion.[368]

In 1982 Christopher S. Wren in the *New York Times*, relayed reports of how

> "..*vigilantes abducted pregnant women on the streets and hauled them off, sometimes handcuffed or trussed, to abortion clinics. Other women, he said, were locked in detention cells or hauled before mass rallies and harangued into consenting to abortions. The reporter referred to 'aborted' babies which were actually crying when they were born.*'"[369]

Chinese Party leaders, of course dismiss these events as the product of over-zealous minor officials in remote provinces trying to deal with medieval feudal peasants "rather than to explicit directives from above".[370] The fact is that in a totalitarian country as rigidly centrally planned as Communist China, *nothing* happens without "explicit directives from above".

Not all of China's unauthorized children have been murdered; there are far too many for that. Chinese mothers often show the most remarkable courage in defending their children, before and after birth. Punishments can be severe; family members are arrested, and homes are demolished. After birth, those children

---

[367] Christopher S. Wren, "China's Birth Goals Meet Regional Resistance" Special to the *New York Times*, (May 15, 1982).
[368] Vink,. Quoted in Zubrin, p. 185-186.
[369] Wren, 1982.
[370] Ibid.

who somehow manage to elude the relentless Communist search parties and "vigilante" groups. If they survive into early childhood they are considered "black children". These are human beings who are not considered "persons" under Chinese law. They have no rights; not to education, not to health care (in a country where the state controls health care; called "single payer health care" in America) or even food. Those who do survive the hunting parties are caught and put into "dying rooms" where they are tied to a chair with a bucket underneath to collect their excrement and starved and neglected to death.[371]

"The Dying Rooms" became the title for a 1995 Peabody Award winning British television documentary. It was shot by Kate Blewett, Brian Woods and Peter Woolrich working undercover as employees in the "orphanages". There they witnessed the children (almost all girls) dying in agony over the course of days. The little ones struggle desperately in their chairs against the bonds holding them in; crying is constant. In one facility, (these places can't possibly be called "orphanages"; Charles Dickens' worst nightmare of an orphanage couldn't come close to these death camps) conditions were so extreme that the entire building was the "dying room". The lives that ended here "passed unnoticed and un-mourned" just like hundreds of other millions of victims of communism in China and throughout the world.

"The Dying Rooms" is available in four segments on YouTube.

It's strong stuff, almost too heartbreaking to watch. In at least one case, an infants' dying room, once emptied of babies, was used by the elderly for the same purpose. The film estimates a million

---

[371] Zubrin, p. 186.

children abandoned to their fate a year, that's over and above the 400 million already aborted or killed at the moment of birth (the two practices are indistinguishable) since the 1970s.

The workers in the death-camp-orphanages have largely turned into emotionless automata. As they are assigned and forced to work at their jobs, the responsibility for the loss of their own humanity should be laid primarily at the doorstep of the Chinese Communist Party; and any westerners still stupid enough to admire it.

Communist China wants to be seen as a civilized country so outright killing of children is technically against the law. Chinese dying rooms accomplish the same goal in as savage a manner as can be imagined, but in a way that is technically legal. The government of China has plenty of funds for all of its "orphanages", but these are spent on new dining halls and the like, rather than medical care for unwanted little girls.

The only saving grace of seeing what these producers have made available is a brief look into one of a tiny handful of private orphanages in China. These are supported almost entirely by charitable contributions from the Chinese people themselves. The views of happy children and their adoptive parent who live with them at the orphanage lighting candles for the Festival of Lanterns is a tonic to the unrelenting despair portrayed elsewhere in the film.

The happy interlude is all too brief. The documentary closes with footage of a baby girl who had been left alone in a room to die ten days before the film crew discovered her. The "orphanage" staff refused to enter and look at their handiwork, so they left an older child outside the room to alert them when the death agony had been finally consummated. What the film crew discovered was a still living, though skeletal baby in a condition too appalling to describe. The staff had named her Mei Ming, which means "No Name".

Though still able to cry, she died four days later; a total of two weeks after she was first placed in the room that the staff couldn't bother to enter. When the producers contacted the facility later, officials denied she had ever existed. The producers dedicated "The Dying Rooms" to Mei Ming.

The Chinese Government's gave a reply to the film a few days before it was released. The producers summarized it as follows:

> "The pernicious practice of abandoning female infants has not been entirely stamped out in some remote areas, but it is rare.

> "The welfare facilities in China provide orphans with adequate adopting, medical rehabilitation and educational services until they reach an adult age, when they are even helped with employment and marriage.

> "The living conditions of orphans have been improving continuously.

> "The so-called 'dying rooms' do not exist in China at all. Our investigations confirm that those reports are vicious fabrications out of ulterior motives. The contemptible lie about China's welfare work cannot but arouse the indignation of the Chinese people."

That the one child policy is possibly the most domestically unpopular policy ever decreed by the rulers of the PRC is testament to the general humanity and courage of the Chinese people. They deserve better, but for now, they will continue to be ruled by Chairman Deng's "Three Don't Be Afraids".

> "Don't be afraid of public opinion.
> Don't be afraid of foreign opinion.
> Don't be afraid of bloodshed."

For those who still think, "We just have to do *something* about population control" there is only this.

World population and fertility are declining, on their own, all over the planet. Moreover, most of the forced government efforts in this regard have done far more harm than good. They have resulted in widespread mass sterilizations, forced abortions and infanticide and, in societies that traditionally prize sons and where parents can only be cared for in their old age by a son, it has led to a gender imbalance unprecedented in human history.

"Missing" females the world-over are likely in the hundreds of millions. There is no agreement as to whether the correct figure is in the neighborhood of 100 million or is in the neighborhood of 200 million. In other words, the numbers are so vast that they cannot be reliably estimated even to the nearest *hundred million.*

The tripartite cluster of abortion, infanticide and population control is the largest crime against humanity ever perpetrated.

It is a simple fact. We don't have to do "something" about over population. What we might try instead is to *stop* the holocaust of abortion, infanticide and other brutalities that are being engineered in the name of population control and "choice".

And maybe the west might try and do something about controlling its liberals who are determined to export their agenda of death to the third world.

Peculiar Institution
The New Abolitionism

"He who sells my sister, for purposes of prostitution, stands forth as the pious advocate of purity. He who proclaims it a religious duty to read the Bible denies me the right of learning to read the name of the God who made me."[372]

Frederick Douglass

In 1857 the U.S. Supreme Court under the leadership of Chief Justice Roger B. Taney, rendered its decision in Scott v. Sandford. The decision was what is known as a "landmark". It was intended to settle the issue of slavery once and for all. It did the opposite. After the Dred Scot Decision, public passions became so inflamed over the matter of the ownership of human beings by other human beings, that it wasn't until 1865, in the wake of the Civil War that the issue was finally resolved for good. It took a constitutional amendment (the Thirteenth to the Constitution) to eliminate slavery. Justice Taney's dreams of being the man who would finally resolve the issue didn't survive the first printing of his Court proceedings.

Noted Civil War historian Shelby Foote once commented that one cause for the war was a failure of the great American genius for compromise. In an interview for the Ken Burns documentary *The Civil War* he noted:

> *"...we failed to do the thing we have a true genius for, compromise. Americans like to think of themselves as uncompromising but it's the basis of our democracy, our government is founded on it; it failed."*[373]

---

[372] Douglass, *Narrative*, 1845.
[373] Shelby Foote from Ken Burns' *The Civil War* episode One.

But, he also realized that

"There were issues that were so bitter between the abolitionists in New England and the fire-eaters in South Carolina and various other places in the South that I'm almost willing to believe that with all our genius for compromise, there still wasn't anyway to settle this thing except by fighting."[374]

Compromise was blocked by a simple fact. Human slavery was so monstrous an institution that no compromise with it could have endured. A number of compromises were tried; all failed in the end to prevent the ghastly casualties of 1861 to 1865, nor could they prevent the divisive legacy that followed in the war's wake. Justice Taney's "solution" to the slavery question was a delusion. If the final inability of compromise to work was a failure, the failure was inevitable. That was the pernicious nature of America's "peculiar institution". Whatever genius for compromise Americans had could never to be enough. Slavery was simply not an institution which permitted compromise.

A century and a half later we have our own "peculiar institution" which bears uncanny resemblance to that of 1860. In a column of August 23, 2012, Judge Andrew Napolitano drew the obvious conclusions.

"In a throwback to its infamous Dred Scott decision — in which a pre-Civil War Supreme Court declared that blacks are not persons and hence cannot claim the protections of the

---

[374] Shelby Foote Comments on *Booknotes* CSPAN, 1994.

Constitution — the court essentially said in Roe vs. Wade the same of fetuses in the womb."[375]

The parallels between Scott and Roe are striking. The Taney Court ruled that imported African slaves and their descendants, free or not, were of such an inferior order of being that they could never have been intended to be regarded as citizens. The Court cited both the Constitution and the Declaration of Independence as proof, specifically quoting the most famous Jeffersonian phrase, "All men are created equal."

As slavery was widespread at the time of the Founding, Taney reasoned, the Founders could not have meant, that "all men" really was intended to include blacks. The black race…

> "…*had for more than a century before been regarded as beings of an inferior order, and altogether unfit to associate with the white race either in social or political relations, and so far inferior that they had no rights which the white man was bound to respect, and that the negro might justly and lawfully be reduced to slavery…*"[376]

Moreover, Taney ruled, just to be certain that no resistance whatever could be mounted to the decision of the Court, that no U.S. state *had any authority whatever* to make any African descendant a citizen of that state and thereby a citizen of the U.S. The words of the Declaration, he ruled,

> "…*would seem to embrace the whole human family, and if they were used in a similar instrument at this day would be*

---

[375] Judge Andrew Napolitano "Abortion and Rape" *Town Hall*, August 23, 2012.
[376] Taney, C.J., Dred Scott v. Sandford, p. 407.

so understood. But it is too clear for dispute that the enslaved African race were not intended to be included..."[377]

It took Abraham Lincoln some years later to argue that the words of the Declaration meant exactly what they seemed to mean in simple language. The phrase "all men are created equal" meant, and was always intended to include, people of African decent. Lincoln saw both the Constitution and the Declaration as equal founding documents. He aptly described the Declaration as an "apple of gold" encased in a frame of silver, the Constitution.[378]

In 1854 in a speech in Peoria Illinois Lincoln stated baldy, "*If the negro is a man, why then my ancient faith teaches me that 'all men are created equal;' and that there can be no moral right in connection with one man's making a slave of another... What I do say is, that no man is good enough to govern another man, without that other's consent.*"[379] This, Lincoln argued was the plain meaning of the Declaration that Justice Taney would deny three years later.

Lincoln gave a speech in June of 1857, speaking specifically to Taney's unusual interpretation of "all men are created equal". Taney, he argued, was assuming that the status of the black man had improved since the time of the Revolution. On the contrary, said Lincoln, the reverse was the case. If the people of any era believed that the phrase "all men" was meant to include the black man, it was certainly more likely to be the generation of the founders rather than the "current" age of the 1850's.

---

[377] Ibid. p. 410.

[378] Abraham Lincoln "Fragment on the Constitution and Union", ca. 1861. ("*A word fitly spoken is like apples of gold in settings of silver.*" Proverbs 25:11)

[379] Abraham Lincoln, speech in Peoria, Illinois: October 16, 1854.

"Chief Justice Taney, in his opinion in the Dred Scott case, admits that the language of the Declaration is broad enough to include the whole human family, but he and Judge Douglas argue that the authors of that instrument did not intend to include negroes, by the fact that they did not at once, actually place them on an equality with the whites. Now this grave argument comes to just nothing at all, by the other fact, that they did not at once, or ever afterwards, actually place all white people on an equality with one or another. And this is the staple argument of both the Chief Justice and the Senator, for doing this obvious violence to the plain unmistakable language of the Declaration...They did not mean to assert the obvious untruth, that all were then actually enjoying that equality, nor yet, that they were about to confer it immediately upon them...The assertion that "all men are created equal" was of no practical use in effecting our separation from Great Britain; and it was placed in the Declaration, not for that, but for future use."[380]

Lincoln intended to appropriate that "future" use for his own day. We should contemplate its use in ours. The phrase "all men" means all human beings. It follows that dividing the human race into separate and unequal groups: master and slave; fetus and born; person and non-person cannot be contained in the "plain unmistakable language of the Declaration". Neither, then can it be contained in any of the intentions of the framers of the Constitution itself. The most we might say is that the Constitution itself is silent on the issue of abortion, although we must conclude that the Declaration is *not* silent at all. This is especially so given all that we have learned scientifically about the genesis of the human being from conception to death.

---

[380] Abraham Lincoln Speech on the Dred Scott Decision, June 26, 1857.

"...are human embryos human beings?
Indeed they are, and contemporary human embryology and
developmental biology leave no significant room for doubt
about it."[381]

Lincoln argued further, in November of 1863, in his most famous speech at Gettysburg, that the *founding of the country* had taken place *before* the Constitution was adopted. The date he refers to, 87 (fourscore and seven) years before is 1776. The new country was *then* "dedicated to the proposition that all men are created equal". This was the central founding moral principle on which the country was built. The Constitution was enacted to ensure, more than anything else, a guarantee to that moral first principle. This was the cause for which so many soldiers on the Gettysburg battlefield had "given the last full measure of devotion". This was the principle that all human beings were created equal and could not be divided into separate and unequal camps, as Taney did in Dred Scott v. Sandford and Blackmun did in Roe v. Wade. Any interpretation of the Constitution that enshrines something other than the central principle of the Declaration must be null and void.

Abolition in law via constitutional amendment wasn't quite enough to eliminate slavery and the same should be said for abortion. Abortion practices may well survive underground. In a way, that's what happened with slavery as well. Many of the oppressive aspect of slavery were maintained by the "Jim Crow" culture that lasted until the civil rights movement. The technical result of overturning Roe would be to declare the Constitution silent on the issue. This would turn the law back to the states. Perhaps from the standpoint of an avid federalist this is where it belongs, but the fact of abortion could be as omnipresent as ever. Some states would make it illegal, others wouldn't and women seeking to end

---

[381] Robert P. George, and Patrick Lee, "Acorns and Embryos", *The New Atlantis*, (Fall 2004 - Winter 2005).

their pregnancies would simply travel across state lines to find a clinic in a legal state. A constitutional amendment would send those same women to Canada.

It's not likely that any final compromise will settle the issue of abortion either, although the prospect of a civil war like the last one is far-fetched. Even so, as Hadley Arkes has written,

> *"That we are not at the threshold of a civil war at this moment is hardly a test of the proposition ... If the American people, in 1860, had made themselves so suggestible to slavery that they were no longer willing to resist in principle, there would have been no war. But there would have been a deep alteration in the character of the people. And there would have been a critical change in the nature of the democracy in America... So much may be said, in turn, about our own people...Times may be good, the mood may be buoyant, but ... there is a crisis nevertheless, a crisis every bit as grave, running to the core of the regime, and to the soul of our people."*[382]

The division on the issue of abortion may continue indefinitely. The likelihood of a permanent compromise settlement seems nil. Opposition to abortion will continue and grow as our imaging technology improves and our scientific knowledge about the womb improves. Already, mainstream media outlets like the National Geographic Channel have produced startling graphic images based on ultrasound, and a new Japanese company is now marketing, not just 3D images from the womb, but also 3D printing of the fetus[383] in the womb while the mother is still pregnant. (You

---

[382] Hadley Arkes *Natural Rights and the Right to Choose* (New York, NY: Cambridge University Press 2004), p. 71.

[383] 3D printing produces a three-dimensional model usually out of a composite type material. It's already being used to make replacement hips,

can get either a full sculpture of the womb and its contents, or a model of the infant's face.) How long will it be before a state legislature requires this version of ultrasound imaging before a woman can choose an abortion? After all, it's just an extension of fully informed consent that medical practice requires for even routine medical procedures; a number of states now require making an ultrasound image of the baby available to the mother before she chooses abortion.

The tools available to abortion abolitionists are expanding every day, while the only tool the pro-abortion movement has is censorship of inconvenient ideas it doesn't approve of. Our new abolitionists should exploit every new form of communication the moment it comes on line.

Two years before his death, John Adams wrote about the old days of the American Revolution.

> *"But what do we mean by the American Revolution? Do we mean the American war? The Revolution was effected before the war commenced. The Revolution was in the minds and hearts of the people; a change in their religious sentiments of their duties and obligations...The people of America had been educated in an habitual affection for England, as their mother country; and while they thought her a kind and tender parent, (erroneously enough, however, for she never was such a mother,) no affection could be more sincere. But when they found her a cruel beldam, willing like Lady Macbeth, to "dash their brains out," it is no wonder if their filial affections ceased, and were changed into indignation and horror. This radical change in the principles, opinions,*

---

dental implants and prosthetic limbs. There are even 3D copiers that can copy a tool, or a fetus in the womb. Coming soon to a mall near you.

sentiments, and affections of the people, was the real American Revolution."[384]

For abortion to be abolished completely, not just declared illegal, there needs to be another radical change in the principles, opinions, sentiments, and affections of the people.

---

[384] John Adams, "Letter to H. Niles" 1818.

Property Settlement
Can Human Beings be Property?

"My mother and I were separated when I was but an infant.... It is a common custom, in the part of Maryland from which I ran away, to part children from their mothers at a very early age."[385]
Frederick Douglass

In 1998 the New York Court of Appeals ruled in the case of Kass v. Kass that human embryos held in a custody dispute between a divorcing couple should be divided up according to the rules of the rest of the divorce settlement.[386] In other words, the status of certain immature human beings (and no American court has ever ruled that a zygote/embryo/fetus is anything other than a human being) can be determined according to the rules of ordinary contract law. That is to say, frozen embryos are property.

The rule of Roe decision applies only to pre-born human beings in the uterus, therefore to abortion. On the other hand, if the pre-born human being is not implanted in a uterus, then no one is pregnant, no pregnancy is to be terminated, no abortion is going to take place. *Those* human beings can be donated to science (as the Kass embryos were) or they can be bought and sold on any open market like any other sort of property. The New York Court specifically refrained from ruling that the embryos were not human; clearly that's exactly what they were. But it also ruled, for the first time since Dred Scott v. Sandford that these beings (that were so obviously human) could be treated as property, thus declaring them to be slaves. In theory, at least, they could be bought and sold on EBay.

---

[385] Douglass, Frederick, *Narrative of the life of Frederick Douglass.* (London: H.G. Collins, 1845).
[386] Maureen Kass, Appellant, v. Steven Kass, Respondent, 91 N.Y.2d 554, 696 N.E.2d 174, 673 N.Y.S.2d 350 May 7, 1998.

Just to be clear, EBay itself has strictly enforced rules against trafficking in anything human, which presumably includes unborn human beings. EBay notes that body parts, sperm or eggs are prohibited items. Fertilized eggs (zygotes or embryos) are not explicitly listed, but are almost certainly implied to be prohibited. But that's EBay policy, not a court ruling. The American court system does not rule out a market on embryos. The Kass ruling implies that neither Roe nor the Thirteenth and Fourteenth Amendments apply to embryos.

Briefly for a few months in 2006 and 2007 a Texas clinic did offer mail order babies to infertile couples. It gave up after a storm of protest from pro-life groups. There was a brief FDA investigation that only resulted in the FDA deciding that it had no jurisdiction or interest in pursuing the matter. In all likelihood, no babies (or embryos) were ever bought or sold, but who knows? A Texas daily suggested in 2007 that the whole thing was a scam.[387]

In any case, the Kass ruling in New York has opened up some disturbing legal questions. Former U.S. Civil Rights Commissioner Robert A. Destro is perhaps the most authoritative commentator on Kass as it relates to Roe. He notes that Steven Kass, the husband, viewed the disposition of the embryos as subject to the terms of the agreement that the couple drew up when the embryos were created. The agreement as quoted by the New York Court of Appeals in its ruling stipulated that "that they should be disposed of [in] the manner outlined in our consent form and that neither Maureen Kass[,] Steve Kass or anyone else will lay claim to custody of these pre-zygotes."[388]

---

[387]Craig Malisow, "Ringing up Baby", The Dallas *Observer*, (Thursday, June 7 2007).
[388] Kass v. Kass.

The wife, Maureen Kass, took a different view. She argued that, her previous agreement notwithstanding, she had exclusive right, according to the 1973 Supreme Court ruling in Roe v. Wade, to make determination as to their disposition. She was, after all, the mother in the case, and she claimed that the Roe Court had given her, by reason of her right to privacy (established in Griswold v. Connecticut, 1965) the right to be the only person consulted about her own reproductive freedom and rights, and that included the embryos (called "pre-zygotes" in this ruling).

Destro notes here, "In a stunning blow both to Mrs. Kass and to the broad 'reproductive autonomy' reading of Roe preferred by most abortion rights activists,"[389] the Court said "No". They made two points. A woman's abortion rights do not apply before implantation, in other words before she's actually pregnant. Thus, when parties have already agreed to the disposition of any unused embryos that agreement is what controls.[390]

The Court again quoted with comments what that agreement had stated.

> *"In the event of divorce, we understand that legal ownership of any stored pre-zygotes must be determined in a property settlement and will be released as directed by order of a court of competent jurisdiction.' Appellant would instead read that sentence: 'In the event of divorce, we understand that legal ownership of any stored pre-zygotes must be determined by a court of competent jurisdiction.' That is not, however, what the sentence says. Appellant's construction ignores the direction that ownership of the pre-zygotes 'must*

---

[389] Robert A. Destro, "Is Roe v. Wade Obsolete? 198, reprinted in *The Reach of Roe: Eugenics, Euthanasia, and Other Assaults on the Dignity of Human Life*, Anne Conlon Editor, (New York, NY: Human Life Foundation, 2013).
[390] Kass V. Kass.

be determined in a property settlement'-words that also must be given meaning, words that connote the parties' anticipated agreement as to disposition."[391]

The important and operative words here are "property settlement". The fertilized human eggs they call pre-zygotes, are here deemed *property* by the Court. The Court did note that by Roe v. Wade, the beings in question were not persons for purposes of the equal protection clause of the Fourteenth Amendment to the Constitution, but they also made no ruling to the effect that the beings in question were not human. "Any being that is human is a human being"[392], and in the case of these human beings the Court ruled that, just as Dred Scott[393] was property, so too are they *property*.

Destro again: "The literal words of *Roe v. Wade* cannot be read in any other way…" In other words, Roe …

> *"rests on an explicit balance struck by the Supreme Court between the interests of the* pregnant *woman and the right of the State of Texas to assert its sovereign power to protect the unborn from harm. Not only did this 'balance' affirm (at least in theory) a limited power to protect the unborn after viability, it simply* assumed *that unborn children capable of existing outside the womb of their mother were within the protective ambit of the State law.*"[394]

Nothing fits the definition of viable outside the womb more precisely than an in vitro fertilized embryo in cryogenic storage.

---

[391] Ibid.

[392] Arkes et al, "The Inhuman Use of Human Beings" A Statement on Embryo Research by the Ramsey Colloquium, *First Things* January 1995.

[393] Scott v. Stanford, 1857. Supreme Court Chief Justice Roger B. Taney infamously ruled that no black person could be a citizen and therefore had no rights any white person was bound to respect.

[394] Destro, *The Reach of Roe*, p. 181.

Such human beings can be the longest-lived people on the planet. They can survive *indefinitely* as long as they remain cryogenically frozen; a good deal less life support than is required in any neonatal unit for premature babies.

Eight babies were born from exactly such embryos stored in a freezer in a New Orleans hospital that was hit by Hurricane Katrina. A daring rescue in flat-bottomed boats saved the container before its freezing capability failed. The best known of these kids, Noah Markham, is now a healthy little boy.

Yet, according the New York Court of Appeals (the Supreme Court of the State of New York) earlier in his young life, Noah Markham was property that could have been bought and sold just as surely as Dred Scott.

The New York case was not the first to decide the fate of frozen embryos in a divorce case. In Davis v. Davis (Tennessee, 1992) the Tennessee Divorce Court ruled that embryos are *almost* children, so for the purposes of the divorce proceedings calling them "children" was close enough for government work. Since, as usual in divorce cases involving child custody, the original trial had awarded custody to the mother, the Tennessee Supreme Court had to re-decide what these strange beings were.

They ruled that "… any interest that Mary Sue Davis and Junior Davis have in the preembryos in this case is not a true property interest."[395]

Unlike in the Kass case, the Davis' had no written agreement with the clinic to refer to. The wife wanted to donate the embryos to an infertile couple, the husband didn't want "his" embryos to grow

---

[395] Davis v. Davis, 842 S.W.2d 588, 597 Supreme Court Of Tennessee, at Knoxville No. 34 1992.TN.1017 June 1, 1992 [at 63]

into children. The Tennessee Supreme Court eventually decided that the husband's right (protected by the Constitution, no less) not to have any more children, trumped her desire to give them away. Thus the Court instructed the clinic that had created the embryos in the first place to do whatever it was they normally do with unused human beings who happen to be embryos.[396]

The number of cases like this is still small. In general courts prefer to let whatever previous agreements between the parties stand with as little modification as possible, and intervening only where some ambiguity on the documented agreement surfaces.

Destro suggests that in the wake of Kass, it might be time for some brave lawyer to step up to the plate and tell some court, that it's time to fish or cut bait.[397] We've been debating the legal status of unborn children for decades and the only folks who can't make up their minds are court justices. The scientific, embryological and ontological nature of the zygote/embryo/fetus, implanted in a womb or not, has been known and widely if not universally agreed on for more than half a century. These beings are clearly human in nature, which is to say *they are human beings*.

Justices don't want to make the obvious inference that the unborn are also persons "in the whole sense". They *can* be murder victims, and are thus persons for purposes of criminal law. They can recover damages and thus are persons for purposes of tort law. They can inherit property and are therefore persons under inheritance law.

> "*Once the State recognizes, as it does, that an unborn child, or in some instances an unconceived child, has property*

---

[396] Ibid., at [114].
[397] Destro, *The Reach of Roe*, pp. 190-192.

rights, it is highly irrational to withhold the most valuable of all rights, which is life itself."[398]

In fact, the only law in which the unborn are arbitrarily held to be non-persons is abortion law, which says, however illogically, that here *and here alone*, an unborn child is a non-person, a piece of meat, clump of cells, or blob of tissue to be removed and killed at will for the convenience of the mother. Now we can add; this human being can also be bought and sold.

Consider the following from Joseph Dellapena:

"Today we find obstetricians referring to a conceptus as a 'baby' when the mother wants the child and as 'a product of conception' when the mother does not."[399]

And from Grace Olivares

"Human beings are not returnable items. Every individual has his/her rights, not the least of which is the right to life, whether born or unborn. Those with power in our society cannot be allowed to 'want' and 'unwant' people at will."[400]

Unless, you're a court judge, that is; most of them seem all too comfortable marking babies "return to sender".

Destro's article points out that while the Declaration of Independence said that all of us are "endowed with certain unalienable rights" and that these rights come to us merely by virtue of the fact that we are human beings: they come from "Nature and Nature's God", the courts now take a radically different view.

---

[398] Robert M. Byrn, v. New York City Health & Hospitals, Court of Appeals of New York, 1972, Judge Scileppi dissenting.
[399] Dellapenna, p. 926.
[400] Grace Olivares, dissenting from the report from the *Rockefeller Commission on Population Growth and the American Future*, 1972.

Almost all courts *"have accepted the proposition that the rights of human beings are conferred by the law. As a result, what (or who) counts as a human being does not (in the words of the New York Court of Appeals) 'necessarily correspond to the natural order.'"* This means that in "right to die" cases, for example, states are permitted *"to withdraw the protection of homicide law from the handicapped..."*[401]

These types of court rulings are more common than civilized people would like to admit. Courts rule all too often that *"some human beings are 'more equal' than others... In Dred Scott v. Sandford, the United States Supreme Court held that persons of African decent had no rights a white person or state was bound to respect."*[402]

Destro provides the *coup de grâce* as follows: *"All commentators agree that legal recognition of an 'ownership' interest in a human being is the functional equivalent of slavery."*[403] This is what the New York Court of Appeals did. They held that human beings are sometimes in an ownership interest relationship with other human beings.

The Thirteenth Amendment to the Constitution (passed by Congress January 31, 1865. Ratified December 6, 1865) has this on that. [404]

---

[401] Destro, *The Reach of Roe*, p. 188.

[402] Ibid.

[403] Ibid., p. 190.

[404] *Note:* A portion of Article IV, section 2, of the Constitution was superseded by the 13th amendment. "No Person held to Service or Labor in one State, under the Laws thereof, escaping into another, shall, in Consequence of any Law or Regulation therein, be discharged from such Service or Labor, but shall be delivered up on Claim of the Party to whom such Service or Labor may be due."

"AMENDMENT XIII

Section 1.

Neither slavery nor involuntary servitude, except as a punishment for crime whereof the party shall have been duly convicted, shall exist within the United States, or any place subject to their jurisdiction.

Section 2.

Congress shall have power to enforce this article by appropriate legislation."[405]

That's it. That's the whole Amendment. If human embryos, even frozen ones (which are if nothing else, *viable* outside the womb) are property, then they are slaves. That's against the law.

Isn't it?

Not so fast.

The courts have already been willing to "withdraw the protection of homicide law from the handicapped"[406]. This used to apply only to people like Terry Schiavo (who wasn't terminally ill, just severely handicapped when the court ordered her starved to death) it's a small expansion of authority to include folks who aren't quite exactly just as handicapped as she was. Your ninety-five year old mother and your eighty-five year old uncle aren't as quick as they used to be. When they become a burden to their families, it will

---

[405] *Constitution of the United States*, Amendment XIII.
[406] Destro, *The Reach of Roe*, p. 188.

be easier to remove them from the list of protected species. In other words, they become easier to kill.

Even your sixty-five year old brother-in-law may need medication for his prostate, high blood pressure, cholesterol, and erectile dysfunction. In a year or two he's going to start costing the health care system a bundle, if he isn't already. What's worse, he's a baby boomer. There were lots of little ones made back in the forties after the War and everybody felt like celebrating like there's no tomorrow. Nowadays, not so much. His generation of sixties idealists is still "passing like a great indigestible rock...through the national digestive tract".[407]

Remember what we learned about "population control". The world isn't over populated; the birth rate is crashing. It started going down in 1965,[408] and has never shown any sign of recovery. The population of the world is still increasing, of course, but that's only because we're living longer. Steven Mosher reminds us what that means. True the numbers of the population of the world doubled between 1960 and 2000, but that wasn't "because we suddenly started breeding like rabbits. They doubled because *we stopped dying like flies.*"[409]

This means that if the world population hasn't peaked yet, it soon will. The population of the planet stood at just over seven billion by late 2011 or early 2012. The United Nation expects the population to peak at around nine billion at mid-twenty-first century. The U.N. is usually optimistic about such things. Along with USAID and the World Bank, they've been ringing the population *explosion* alarm bells for a long time. If that number turns out to be (surprise)

---

[407] Chilton Williamson, Jr. "The Coming Inhumanity", *The Reach of Row*, p. 207.
[408] Steven W. Mosher, *Population Control*, (Santa Barbara, CA: Transaction Publishes, 2008), p. 5.
[409] Ibid., p. 4.

self-serving, then eight billion or seven and a half billion might be closer to the mark. In other words, we'd be at or near peak *now*.

Most developed countries have fertility rates between 1.1 and 1.6 per couple. Any country with a fertility rate of 1.1 will see each generation half the size of the previous. The effect accelerates as the fewer and fewer people who do want children can no longer find mates. This will be especially true if we've killed a lot of little girls in the womb. Below a certain point, no recovery is possible. This is true of Western Europe, but not only Europe. Mosher has Australia's fertility rate at 1.7, Canada's at 1.5, Iran, 1.79, South Korea, (which briefly had the highest abortion rate in the world at 2.75 abortions for every birth)[410] 1.2, Japan, 1.25, China 1.7. China's disaster is exacerbated by its cruel one child policy resulting in an epidemic of mass abortion, most of them girls.

Mosher comments on the advent of ultrasound in China:

"If the image of the screen reveals male genitalia, the family celebrates its good fortune. If the unfortunate fetus lacks that apparatus, however, her life is quickly extinguished...This means that over 10 percent of all girls conceived in China are killed in utero. *"[411]*

Add female infanticide to that by the way; and "dying rooms". Since only females get pregnant, the fertility rate (which is the rate of pregnant females) will not adequately predict the population collapse. Girls who were never there will never be measured.

The first obvious effect of all this is a graying of the population. As the bulk of the population gets older, more and more

---

[410] Hvistendahl, *Unnatural Selection*, p. 133. (This means that out of every child conceived, only about a quarter of them were allowed to live.)
[411] Mosher, p. 18.

retire, and more need additional medical assistance, prescriptions, walkers, retirement communities and nursing homes. With all of the developed world, and most of the developing world now having adopted the socialist model of caring for the elderly (all paid for by the state, which is to say, the still working younger taxpayers) this system can't continue. It can't continue because as there are fewer and fewer young working people in the population, there will eventually be not enough of them to sustain the growing population of needy elders. Medical science (dependent on an influx of socialist government funding) gets ever more expensive per patient. As patients become greater in their percentage of the population the system goes broke. It doesn't help if the system in question is already trillions (with a "*T*") in debt. Such a system will be bankrupt long before the medical bills come due for grandpa. What's a socialist bureaucrat to do?

They do the one thing socialist governments are better at than anything else. They "withdraw the protection of homicide law" from those they regard as "useless eaters". This is how one equalizes the generational imbalance between young (and productive) and old (and retired). It's what's already been done to fifty-three million human beings in the U.S. since January 22, 1973. We may have stopped dying like flies, but there's no reason a socialist government couldn't reintroduce that practice.

Socialist governments like the Chinese or Soviets have never had any problem with culling their population by hundreds of millions. The further left the politics, the more danger to the population.

"If your rulers start taking Marx seriously, run for your lives. Millions have done so, but survival is only to the swift."[412]

---

[412] Kenneth Minogue "The Goddess That Failed (Marxism and Feminism)" *National Review*, (Nov. 18, 1991 v43 n21 p. 46:3)

Santayana's Warning
Dreadful to Contemplate

"I have no words anymore." [413]
Elie Wiesel

To recap: The United States has aborted somewhere in the neighborhood of 55 million since 1973. The nature of these were living entities (actual, not potential) and having human DNA, human parents, they were human. "Any being that is human is a human being."[414] So far the facts and logic are inescapable, no matter the wishful thinking, rationalization, obfuscated language, lies and distortion. Unless we want to contemplate the killing of infants and children we must consider these aborted human beings as persons.

Even the simplest rules of morality and language require us to describe each of these abortions as the murder of an innocent human person, all 55 million of them. These are dreadful facts to contemplate.

"As much as some people resist the analogy, the question posed is essentially that posed by the Dred Scott decision of 1857...Even more strongly, some people resist the analogy with the Nazi doctrine of lebensunwertes Leben - lives that we deem unworthy of life...After all, we are not Nazis and we are not slaveholders...The differences between our circumstance and those other circumstances are very

[413] Elie Wiesel, "Some Questions That Remain Open", *Comprehending the Holocaust: Historical and Literary Research*, Asher Cohen, Joav Gelber, and Charlotte Wardi, ed., Strochlitz Institute of Holocaust Studies (New York, NY: Peter Lang International Academic Publishers, 1988), p. 13.

[414] Arkes, etal, "The Inhuman Use of Human Beings", 1995.

important, but so are the similarities important, and deeply troubling." [415]

This is a theme that runs through many of these chapters. If this is mass murder on such a scale, how do we avoid words like "holocaust"? Are we treating the unborn the way the Germans of the 1930s and 40s treated the Jews of Europe? Certainly our language disparages the unborn as un-human and sub-human.

We've seen phrases and words like "product of conception" or it's abbreviation "POC". Other dehumanizing rhetoric happens when the "unborn is labeled as "worm,' 'parasite,' 'glob of cells,' and 'cancer-like cells'." Thus the unborn are "dehumanized-even demonized". [416]

John Joseph Powell called the idea of a life not worth living (a popular enough concept in the US today) a "thinly disguised Nazi doctrine." [417] The phrase "life not worth living" is an exact English translation of the German lebensunwertes Leben. This isn't *"disguised"*. This *is* Nazi doctrine, although no one who espouses it today would agree to call it that. Of course, Binding and Hoche, who wrote the original tract and invented the phrase weren't Nazis either; but their ideas *were* adopted as official Nazi Party ideology and policy soon enough.

In order to select a population to be killed one must have their group dehumanized. The victims will be shown to be playing the part of the "villain", the ultimate danger to humanity. In the case of abortion ideology, that would be the mythology of "over-population". According to this scenario, there are too many people in

---

[415] Richard John Neuhaus, Forward to Stetson p. xiii.

[416] Michael McKenzie, "When Good Men do Nothing: Reflections From a Modern-Day Burgermeister", Stetson p. 158.

[417] John Joseph Powell, *Abortion, the Silent Holocaust*, (Allen, TX: Tabor Publishing, 1981), p. 63.

lifeboat Earth, and we need to find a way to start eliminating as many as possible.

Environmentalists like to work on the seniority method. They start by eliminating those who are just starting out. Ignore the fact that today's real population "crisis" is that in most developed countries, population is in the process of collapsing. Prosperous people tend to have fewer children, generally less that 2 per couple, which is a recipe for population decline not expansion. If population is a "bomb" it's an imploding one.

Spain has a reproduction rate of 1.15 children per couple. This is reflected in other European countries like Greece, Portugal, and Italy. The Organization for Economic Co-operation and Development (OECD) has reported that a long-term decline in fertility was briefly halted at the end of World War II.[418] This is the famous (or infamous) post-war baby boom. Since then the decline has resumed at an alarming rate. That these are countries experiencing general unrest and economic crisis is not a coincidence.

The preference for aborting girls can only add to the crisis, and is not likely to be reflected in fertility statistics, which, after all, only measure the fertility of *existing* couples or *existing* women. When a culture exhibits a gender imbalance unfavorable to females, the women aren't there and the couples never form in the first place. The fertility rate in India, for example of 3 children per woman[419] says nothing about the number of females that have been aborted thus preventing the birth of millions of girls who will never become women to be counted in fertility studies.

---

[418] Joëlle E. Sleebos "Low Fertility Rates in OECD Countries: Facts and Policy Responses" OECD Social, Employment and Migration Working Papers, (No. 15 October 7, 2003).
[419] Carl Haub, "India's Population Policy" *Berlin Institute Online-Handbook Demography.*

This isn't a population bomb it's a death spiral. None of this causes environmentalists to throttle back their calls for fewer people on Planet Earth. Their ideology does not respond well to evidence. Here's David Graber, for example.

> *"Human happiness, and certainly human fecundity, are not as important as a wild and healthy planet....[Nature has] intrinsic value, more value to me than another human body or a billion of them....Until such time as Homo Sapiens should decide to rejoin nature, some of us can only hope for the right virus to come along."[420]*

A virus, presumably to exterminate "a billion of them". Abortion has indeed exterminated about "a billion of them".

Environmentalists, rejoice. You have discovered the most effective way to avoid over population and all the alleged horrors your nightmares have conjured for it. Exterminate a class of human beings, the unborn (with special emphasis on females) and your hopes are realized. It turns out that *you are the virus* you've been waiting for.

Graber isn't the only environmentalist to call for human extermination as a solution to the horror of human population. Paul Taylor wrote, "[T]he total, absolute, and final disappearance of Homo Sapiens...would most likely be greeted with a hearty "Good riddance!"[421] Greeted by who, he does not explain. No doubt Graber and Taylor would appear shocked, shocked, if you called this "genocide" but what else is it?

---

[420] David M. Graber "Mother Nature as a Hothouse Flower" Los Angles *Times Book Review*, (October 29, 1989), p. 9

[421] Paul Taylor *Respect for Nature: A Theory of Environmental Ethics*, (Princeton, NJ: Princeton University Press, 1968), p. 115.

Walter Williams[422] has compiled a few more quotes of interest. All are in the same genocidal vein. The following are all from Williams' column. Alexander King, founder of the Club of Rome wrote that since DDT had in Guyana eliminated malaria in two years his objection to it was that in saving millions of lives "*it has greatly added to the population problem.*" Dr. Charles Wurster, former chief scientist Environmental Defense Fund wrote that since we need to "*get rid of some*" people "*(malaria) is as good a way as any.*" William Aiken decided that it is our "duty" to cause "*human diebacks*" so as "*to eliminate 90 percent of our numbers.*"

And this:

> "*This is a terrible thing to say. In order to stabilize world population, we must eliminate 350,000 people per day. It is a horrible thing to say, but it's just as bad not to say it.*"

> Jacques Cousteau in an interview with The UNESCO Courier, November 1991.

Studies of genocide talk about the "cloisterization" or we might say "ghettoization" of the murders. The killings are done behind high walls, or remote areas far from prying eyes. Abortions are done in clinics in "complete anonymity". Moreover, "it is valid to ask whether abortion would be as popular if all of us could see what the abortionists sees."[423]

Of course, even the abortionist doesn't always see everything. Bernard Nathanson had to request a videotape of the ultrasound of an abortion before he saw what caused him to stop. The doctor/videographer also never did another abortion after seeing the tape. The powerful impact of seeing an atrocity first hand can

---

[422] Walter Williams, "Understanding Liberal and Progressives" *TownHall*, June 5, 2013.
[423] Stetson, p. 160.

sway a lot of opinions. That was no doubt on Eisenhower's mind when he ordered both soldiers and German civilians alike to take a tour of the concentration camps.[424] He wanted to make sure that no room for "cynical doubt" would be left to posterity. Eisenhower noted in his cable to General Marshall, "The visual evidence and the verbal testimony of starvation, cruelty and bestiality were so overpowering as to leave me a bit sick."[425] This is also why pro-abortion advocates argue so vigorously against the kind of informational literature that the State of Pennsylvania had to argue twice before the Supreme Court to get permission to share, just as a part of their attempt to produce informed consent. This is why they get sympathetic judges to issue injunctions against distributing anti-abortion literature or videos. Laws that propose to require a potential abortion patient to view an ultrasound before consenting to the procedure meet howls of protest from pro-abortion advocates for the same reason. If the views of Ohrdruf concentration camp near the village of Gotha caused the battle-hardened and tough-as-mails General Patton[426] to gag, what might images of miniature arms and feet posed on a quarter do to the rest of us?

We know what we'll see, so we refuse to look. We want to protect our children from the violence of the images, even if we recognize that the images are just a representation of the violence in the real world. Many are willing to go to extreme lengths to avoid being forced to look. The vehemence of their response shows how deep a nerve has been struck. Take co-authors Sol Gordon and Craig Snyder.

---

[424] Dwight D. Eisenhower, *Crusade in Europe*, p.408.
[425] Dwight D. Eisenhower, letter to General George C. Marshall, April 15, 1945.
[426] Omar Bradley, *A Solder's Story*, (New York, NY: Henry Holt, 1951), p. 539.

"In our view, individuals who exhibit the least human dignity are those who compare the Holocaust, the mass murder of 6 million Jews, to abortion... [to] an individual woman's decision to terminate her pregnancy ..."[427]

The woman in question, of course, doesn't just decide to "terminate" her pregnancy; carrying to term would do that as well. She decides to kill her baby, and according to Gordon et al she has a right to do so, which generally means that, she has a right not to a terminated pregnancy, but to a dead baby. This alleged "right" has been exercised at least 55 million times since Roe, resulting in 55 million dead. That *ought* to be holocaust enough for anyone.

It turned out to be more than enough for Bernard Nathanson.

"I'm going to set it against my Jewish heritage and the Holocaust in Europe. The abortion holocaust is beyond the ordinary discourse of morality and rational condemnation. It is not enough to pronounce it absolutely evil. ... The abortion industry is a new event, severed from connections with traditional presuppositions of history, psychology, politics and morality. .... It trivializes itself to call itself merely a holocaust ... This is an evil torn free of its moorings in reason and causality, an ordinary secular corruption raised to unimaginable powers of magnification and limitless extremity."[428]

The etymological roots of "The English term "Holocaust" derives from the Greek holokauston, which means a fully burnt sacrifice,"[429] although its deeper roots are Hebrew. The modern

---

[427] Sol Gordon, Craig W. Snyder, *Personal Issues in Human Sexuality*, (Boston, MA: Allyn & Bacon, 1989), page 65.

[428] Dr. Bernard Nathanson, to an audience in California (date unknown).

[429] Peter Berger, "Misuses of the Holocaust" *The American Interest*, (February 20, 2012).

word still has a connotation of burning fire to it. Nuclear war has been called a nuclear holocaust for that reason. The victims of nuclear and thermonuclear blasts are incinerated. Still, the word with a capital "H" has rightly entered the lexicon as referring uniquely to the Nazi extermination of the Jews. By understanding the nature of this particular mass atrocity, "one becomes alert to all the other atrocities of which human beings are capable."[430]

Holocaust scholars (and survivors) rightly take offense at any comparison that appears to trivialize the full meaning and nature of the Nazi crimes against the Jews. There was a particularly Jewish aspect to the Holocaust; this is beyond dispute even while it is also true that many non-Jews suffered at the hands of the Nazis in the concentration camps; Gypsies, homosexuals, communists and other political opponents, even allied prisoners of war (both Jews and non-Jews) as well as numbers of Roman Catholic priests ended up in the camps.[431] The general estimate of 6 million Jews and 4 to 5 million others killed by the Nazis appears to stand as the best estimate.

Anthony Daniels (who often writes under the name Theodore Dalrymple) warns in a *City Journal* book review of Virginia Woolf's 1938 book *Three Guineas* how easy it is for some to make casual comparisons of whatever they dislike to the Nazis: "the British policeman and the Nazi storm trooper wore a uniform, [so] the British policeman was a brute." Woolf had written of the struggle for women's rights as follows: "you will agree that a battle that wastes time is as deadly as a battle that wastes blood." [432] Dalrymple can scarcely contain his disgust. "As deadly? *As deadly*? It is small

---

[430] Berger.

[431] See Jean Bernard, *Priestblock 25487: A Memoir of Dachau* (Bethesda, MD: Zaccheus Press, 2007).

[432] Theodore Dalrymple, "The Rage of Virginia Woolf" *City Journal*, (Summer 2002).

wonder that Mrs. Woolf finds it difficult to draw a distinction between the Church of England and the Nazi party."[433]

Nazism is the only universally agreed upon form of evil that all elements in society, red state, blue state, liberal, conservative, libertarian can join in condemning together. It is tempting to invoke the image of the Nazis whenever one wants to make a comparison between one form of evil, about which there is some disagreement, and *the* evil about which there is none. To suggest, for example that Camp Gitmo is just as bad as, say, al Qaida will only invite the quip that one man's terrorist is another man's freedom fighter, and maybe even that George Washington was worse than Osama bin Laden.

Modern descriptions of the Middle East are rife with malicious comparisons of the Israelis to the Nazis. The fact that it is the *Palestinians* who are behind the numerous deadly attacks against Israeli Jews, and that the Israelis have never put a gas chamber in Gaza is generally seen as beside the point. For elite liberals, Israeli Jews are Nazis and if you don't agree, you must be a Nazi too.

Then there are "art" works like the cans of Xyclon B (used in the death camps) adorned with Chanel labels as if the poison gas that was used to exterminate millions was nothing more than a sort of fashionable perfume. The "artist's" defense that "Fashion like fascism is about a loss of identity. Fashion is good when it helps you to look sexy, but it's bad when it makes you feel stupid or fat..."[434]

And then there's the miniature statue of Hitler "at prayer" set up in the heart of the Warsaw Ghetto, where thousands were murdered by Hitler's SS during the war. No doubt it's intended (like all modern "art") to be edgy, pushing the envelope of contemporary sensibilities and stereotypes and their relation to our awareness of

---

[433] Ibid.

[434] Deborah Solomon, "The Way We Live Now" The New York *Times Magazine*, (April 12, 2002).

the social construct of "evil" within the presumptions of modern oppressive society and "civilization". The museum merely noted that "There is no intention from the side of the artist or the centre to insult Jewish memory."[435]

Sure there is. No contemporary content provider (we needn't call him an "artist") puts up an installation so clearly designed to be "transgressive" without hoping to generate controversy. That means he *hopes* someone will be offended; the more offended the better. You can't buy that kind of publicity, not with a four page add in the *Times Sunday Magazine*. Trivializing the Holocaust in the middle of the Warsaw Ghetto is worth a whole string of articles in the L.A. *Times* and elsewhere; and it's all free.[436]

Certainly the Holocaust is trivialized when activists compare it to the slaughter of chickens. Yes, Chickens. So, if you eat KFC, or Hormel cans of chicken, or raise chickens for food as many did due to severe rationing during World War II, you're a Nazi. Apparently no one's decided if eating turkey or fish puts you in the Gestapo. You can't make this stuff up.[437]

Shimon Peres was once accused of trivializing the Holocaust when he compared the Islamic Republic of Iran with Nazi Germany. It's true that Iran doesn't have a swastika on its flag, but it has declared its intention (rather repeatedly) of "wiping Israel off the map", along with its population of six million Jews. These declarations have been made with sufficient frequency to be regarded as Iranian national policy. That's enough to merit a comparison. Sadly, being accused of trivializing the Holocaust has become a bit like being accused of racism. If everyone's a racist,

---

[435] Cass Jones, "Controversy over Adolf Hitler statue in Warsaw ghetto" The Guardian (UK), (December 28, 2012).

[436] David Ng, "Hitler statue...causes a stir" Los Angeles *Times*, (December 31, 2012).

[437] "Group blasts PETA 'Holocaust' project", CNN, (February 28, 2003).

then no one is. Accusations of trivializing the Holocaust have themselves been trivialized simply by the number of times they occur.

The wise Elie Wiesel once said,

"The "H" word has become so trivialized that I cannot use it anymore. First, because there are no words, and also because it has become so trivialized that I cannot use it anymore. Whatever mishap occurs now, they call it 'holocaust'... A commentator describing the defeat of a sports team, somewhere, called it a 'holocaust'... So, I have no words anymore."[438]

It was the Holocaust that inspired the phrase "Never again"[439]. To what does the word "again" refer? It surely refers to Iran's stated intention to exterminate the Israeli people with nuclear weapons. We might also include the killing fields of Cambodia, the Soviet Gulag, Mao's Cultural Revolution. None of these are trivial events. Each involves the murders of millions of individuals, in some cases, tens of millions; in the case of Communist China *hundreds of millions*. The pledge of "Never again" that the world made after the discovery of the horrors of Nazi Germany has been worthless. Mass murders in the millions *have* occurred again and again since 1945. The lesson we might have gleaned from the war has gone unlearned.

Santayana's warning that "Those who cannot remember the past are condemned to repeat it "[440] has gone unheeded. Perhaps this is why Wiesel calls his work a "literature of memory".

---

[438] Wiesel.

[439] The memorial at Dachau has the words on a plaque printed in five languages.

[440] George Santayana, *The Life of Reason, Vol. 1*, (Amherst, NY: Promethius books).

"I have tried to keep memory alive, I have tried to fight those who would forget. Because if we forget, we are guilty, we are accomplices... Human rights are being violated on every continent. More people are oppressed than free. How can one not be sensitive to their plight? Human suffering anywhere concerns men and women everywhere."[441]

Holocaust remembrance requires us to remain "alert to all the other atrocities of which human beings are capable."[442] The moment we accept the unborn as human beings we must "be sensitive to their plight". If we forget that there were tens of millions of them (perhaps over a billion world-wide) "we are accomplices".

---

[441] Elie Wiesel, Nobel Acceptance Speech, December 10, 1986.
[442] Berger, "Misuses of the Holocaust".

Uriah's Widow
What Everyone Really Knows

"Since the old ethic has not yet been fully displaced, it has been necessary to separate the idea of abortion from the idea of killing, which continues to be socially abhorrent. The result has been a curious avoidance of the scientific fact, which everyone really knows, that human life begins at conception and is continuous whether intra- or extra-uterine until death." [443]
California Medicine

If it's true that everyone knows that human life begins at conception, as the editors of *California Medicine* wrote in 1970, it's remarkably difficult to get very many people to admit that they know it. This is how rationalization works; also wishful thinking.

After they have their abortions (on occasion, even before) women have been known to reflect, "I hated myself. I felt abandoned and lost...I couldn't get it out of my head that I just killed a baby."[444] Sometimes there's an obvious reason for those things that we just can't get out of our heads. The tragedy of this knowledge is played out over the years for millions of women with Mothers Day depression, alcoholic addiction, thoughts of suicide, flashbacks, and anxiety attacks.[445] There is often a price to be paid for pretending to not know what we really do know. When we act on wishful thinking, the price can be high.

However, it's not surprising that among abortion defenders the emphasis has shifted away from embryology and towards personhood ideology. Ideology is easier to manipulate than facts,

---

[443] "A New Ethic for Medicine and Society" *California Medicine: The Western Journal of Medicine*, (113, no. 3, 1970), pp. 67-68.

[444] Linda Bird Franke, *The Ambivalence of Abortion*, Stetson, p. 138.

[445] David C. Reardon, "Women Who Abort" *Stetson*, p. 144.

especially a fact as obvious as the fact that life begins when life is conceived. That isn't just a fact for human beings; it's true for all species.

And yet, our ideologically motivated desires push us to claim that the beginning of life is an insoluble mystery. It isn't. Nevertheless, an extraordinary number of people *want* it to be. They want it so they can rationalize promiscuity without consequence. It's shouldn't be too surprising that people want sex, and sometimes the contraceptives don't work (although the pill is supposed to be 99% effective) and a baby results. It's so much easier to imagine that the embryo can be euphemized as mere "products of conception" or "just a clump of cells", or a parasitic growth, which can be removed and ignored. The baby has to be re-imagined as a thing of no more moral consequence than a hamburger in the stomach. It's astonishing the gymnastics people will put themselves through for "free love". Or maybe it's not.

In any case, a lot of people have convinced themselves that not only do *they* not know when life begins, but also that *nobody* knows; it's as if a simple obvious fact was a great and divine mystery. Mind you, it hasn't always been quite as obvious as it is today. Aristotle, to take one example from the ancient world, thought that the right testicle made boys and the left testicle made girls; if you wanted a son, you tied off the left ball. We can't very well blame the ancient Greeks for their ignorance, although it's hard to imagine how Aristotle decided which role the left played and which the right. Surely it could have been the other way round. We know more than the ancients did about such things; we even propose to teach them to children in sex education classes.

So, Nancy Pelosi claims that *nobody* knows when life begins, not even her own Roman Catholic Church, despite the fact that Church teaching have been remarkably consistent for 2,000 years.

The fact that life begins at conception was not repealed by Vatican II.

And Barack Obama claims that questions about abortion are "above my pay grade". Obama's a multi-millionaire, so that must be some pay grade. Perhaps he thought that like the identity of the Unknown Soldier, it's "known but to God". If God had a pay grade it presumably would be above that of the President. Sometimes pretending ignorance is just too useful a device for a politician to do without. How many times has a failing memory been invoked in testimony before Congress? What's useful to politicians and embezzlers isn't necessarily what's required for scientific "experts" and ordinary laymen.

That doesn't prevent panels of "experts" from claiming that decision of life and death are insurmountably difficult. After all, that's why we need "experts": to decide for us. Sometimes the decision is so difficult that a "Copernican revolution" in our ethical understanding is proposed. If the purpose is to deny the protection of law and morality to a large number of human beings, then a revolution in ethics is indeed required, although apart from its revolutionary status, there's no resemblance to anything published by Copernicus.

Revolutions are enthusiastic affairs in their beginning stages; it's easy for them to loose their way. Visitors to Germany in the 1930's were often struck by the shining faces and enthusiastic support for the sweeping reforms overtaking the country. It seemed to many that all these smiling Germans must be up to something good. This impression often lasted until they were taken aside and beaten bloody by a gang of brown shirts for failing to give the proper Nazi salute to a passing parade. More than one hapless American tourist found out the hard way that the new rules applied to him as much as to the ordinary German.[446] Revolutionary rules can be hard on ordinary folks.

If whole sets of human beings are now outside the protection of the normal rules of simple decency, you want to be sure that *you* are not among the excluded; this is harder than it looks. If everyone agrees that you are a human being, but thinks that you're not really a "person" your future will be bleak. It's a relatively simple matter to decide if someone is a human being. Even pro-abortion enthusiasts and scientists interested in embryonic research these days are willing to grant that the human being begins when it is conceived. This isn't rocket science, although it is science of some sort; it's obviously hard to deny what should be obvious.

> *"The embryo is a being; that is to say, it is an integral whole with actual existence. The being is human; it will not articulate itself into some other kind of animal. Any being that is human is a human being."*[447]

This may sound suspiciously like proclaiming that a "rose is a rose", and of course a rose *is* a rose; what else would it be? "Everything is what it is, and not another thing, unless it is another thing, and even then it is what it is."[448] It's amazing the amount of time philosophers spend discussing the obvious, but then, there are so many who deny the obvious. Confucius once said, "If names be not correct, language is not in accordance with the truth of things."[449] If "names" *are* correct, on the other hand, you can't get away with as much. That's why politicians like to obfuscate. Politics isn't the art of the possible;

---

[446] Erik Larson *In the Garden of the Beasts* (New York, NY: Crown Publishers, 2011) pp. 3-5/pp. 53 ff.

[447] Arkes, et al, "The Inhuman Use of Human Beings".

[448] W.K. Frankena, "The Naturalistic Fallacy" *Mind*, New Series, (Vol. 48, No. 192,1939), p 472.

[449] *Confucius, Analects, Book XIII, Chapter 3, verse 5, translated by James Legge.*

it's the art of pulling the wool over everyone's eyes. You may not be able to fool all the people all of the time, but 99% is close enough for government work. You can always buy off the rest with a little pork.

There are so many philosophers with a burning desire to be on the cutting edge of revolutionary thought, but it just isn't that often that we really need a "Copernican" revolution. Many of our philosophy texts date from about 2500 years ago. In your revolutionary zeal, you start to deny timeless moral truths and you end up responding to folks who think you're a moral monster. Maybe you are. You can care about that sort of thing or not. If you want to be a revolutionary, you don't want to be held back by moral squeamishness.

At least that's the fantasy of more than one philosophy professor. Philosophers get tired of being considered irrelevant. You don't get with the in crowd by translating the ancient Greeks. But bioethics on the other hand is a ticket to real influence. You just have to remember that nobody's going to pay you any attention if all you've got is the old outdated morality. The in crowd wants something new and flashy, something avant-garde, revolutionary, something to set old Lenin's beard on fire.

"After-birth abortion" is one way to go. Did we mention you need a flashy title to go with the revolutionary conceit? Maybe nobody wants to talk about killing babies, but fourth trimester abortion…what a concept. A certain gift for euphemism is necessary when you're selling ideas like this to the masses, which includes some government grant committees. Remind them that these are "technical terms". Try to describe the fetus as "a 'parasite'. Other terms favored after an abortion include the relatively bland terms 'tissue,' 'waste product,' or 'medical waste.' Perhaps the most extreme euphemism was a journalist's description of aborted children as 'just garbage.'"[450]

Or you might remind them that doctors have their own tech talk, and borrow some of it. Obstetricians often refer to "a conceptus as a 'baby' when the mother wants the child and as 'a product of conception' when the mother does not."[451]

"If language be not in accordance with the truth of things, affairs cannot be carried on to success."[452]

These kinds of verbal gymnastics and euphemistic jargon are designed to obscure from us what would otherwise be obvious. A being that is human is a human being[453] and that life begins at its beginning, when it is conceived. It's not impossible to know when life begins. On the contrary; everybody knows when life begins. It begins at the beginning. How hard is that? Politicians who are committed to defending the indefensible will resort to the most appalling doubletalk to cloud the issue. Consider the following:

"I would say that as an ardent, practicing Catholic, this is an issue that I have studied for a long time. And what I know is, over the centuries, the doctors of the church have not been able to make that definition."[454]

Any "ardent" Catholic knows that the Roman Catholic Church considers abortion to be a serious evil, and that any Catholic who procures, makes available, has or participates in an abortion will be automatically (*latae sententiae*) excommunicate. The Church

---

[450] Dellapenna p. 927.

[451] Ibid., p. 926.

[452] *Confucius, verse 5.*

[453] Arkes, et al,

[454] Congresswoman Nancy Pelosi on Meet the Press, August 24, 2008.

need make no pronouncement or perform any ceremony of excommunication; the excommunication is automatic. However "ardent" such an individual might be, after excommunication, her relationship with the Church is in jeopardy. She must refrain from Holy Communion until the sin of abortion is repented of, absolved and the excommunication is lifted. Certainly politicians who vote in favor of abortion rights are making it available.

> *"When affairs cannot be carried on to success, proprieties and music will not flourish. When proprieties and music do not flourish, punishments will not be properly awarded."*[455]

No doctor of the Church has ever had any problem declaring abortion a mortal sin. This doctrine has been in the Judeo-Christian tradition for millennia. Congresswoman Pelosi should consider that before making any more "ex-cathedra" pronouncements.

There has never been a time when abortion was permitted by the Catholic Church. The earliest Church incorporated the ancient Jewish abhorrence of child murder in all forms. The ancient prophets railed against child sacrifice among the Canaanite pagan cults, and the "gift" of children to pagan gods as a burnt offering. ("When you offer your gifts—the sacrifice of your children in the fire—you continue to defile yourselves with all your idols to this day.")[456]

None of this is hard; it's knowledge available to anyone who wants to know. Aristotle once said "All men by nature want to know". One has to wonder how true that is for many modern people who seem far more comfortable in their own ignorance than they ought to be. For such people, their system of beliefs is more like a form of brand loyalty, than a reasoned set of ideas. This is why they say "I feel that..." in place of "I believe ..." Feelings are subjective and therefore more legitimate than beliefs that lay claim to

---

[455] *Confucius*, verse 6.
[456] *Ezekliel* 20:31

knowledge. You can't be wrong if you like vanilla ice cream; some people try to claim that you can't be wrong if you like abortion. "Don't like abortion? Don't have one." Everybody knows that killing a child isn't a personal preference like a favorite flavor. That doesn't stop them from pretending otherwise. If you really, really want something, it's easy to pretend that it's OK to take it. This is the mentality of the shoplifter. With abortion available nationwide, it's a form of kleptomania writ large, only what's being stolen are human lives.

> *"When punishments are not properly awarded, the people do not know how to move hand or foot."*[457]

One suspects that's the idea.

Submit your best arguments are you're likely to be told, "I understand all that, but *I still feel* it's a choice." "I still feel…" is the ultimate trump card for any argument. It's a get out of moral responsibility free card for anyone who wants it. It lets you do anything you damn please and it's "judgmental" to say otherwise.

Physician Anthony Daniels wrote about one of his patients whom he had asked to describe herself. Her face beamed with a "beatific smile" as she said "non-judgmental". This, he concluded was the "ultimate term of self-praise".[458] We are never more judgmental than when we accuse someone else of being too judgmental. It is our most judgmental judgment. It places the accused in the same category as a lynch mob.

The only Bible verse most students in ethics classes are usually able to quote is "Judge not that ye be not judged", usually in grammatically correct Elizabethan English from the Authorized

---

[457] *Confucius*, verse 6.
[458] Theodore Dalrymple, *In Praise of Prejudice*, (New York, NY: Encounter Books, 2007) p. 120.

King James Version of 1611. Invariably they leave out the next critical verse. "For with what judgment ye judge, ye shall be judged".[459]

The Biblical book of *Second Samuel* Chapter 12 tells an interesting story that fills out the lesson. King David eagerly desires Uriah's wife Bathsheba and plots to have Uriah killed in action on the war front. He tells his general to put Uriah at the heaviest point of the fighting and then to have his men "stand down" (to coin a phrase) and let Uriah be killed. After Uriah is dead David takes Uriah's widow and thinks that's an end to it. Nathan the Prophet, having heard what David has done confronts the King with a parable about a rich man with great flocks of many sheep and a poor man with " one little ewe lamb, ... and lay in his bosom, and was unto him as a daughter."[460] The rich man steals the lamb for his own feast, leaving the poor man with nothing.

David, outraged at the injustice in Nathan's story answers the prophet back, "As the LORD liveth, the man that hath done this thing shall surely die". Nathan then tells the King, "You are the man". The point is simply made. No one is above the rules of conduct, not even (especially not even) the King. Everyone must be judged, and everyone must be judged by the same rules. David discovered that the judgment with which he judged was the judgment that must be applied to him. [461]

The study of ethics doesn't lead to "non-judgmentalism" but to rendering *correct* judgments. Correct judgments apply to everyone. Nothing is ever "right for me" (or you) and no one else. If it's right or wrong, it must be so for everyone.

---

[459] *Matthew* 7: 1-2.
[460] *II Samuel* 12:3.
[461] *II Samuel* 12: 1-15.

Nathan found a way to explain to the King something so simple that David already knew it. Overpowering the weak to feather your own nest and fulfill your own lust, or your own convenience, is an outrage. Nathan realized, as eventually David realized, that some moral "problems" are really very simple, and everyone knows how to deal with them, even when we want to do what we know we shouldn't. A great deal of rationalization, and corruption of language goes on, but it's all so we can get laid without consequence. If we have to kill a woman's husband or a woman's embryo, it's all in the service of old-fashioned promiscuity. Nothing more.

Try that out on an abortion defender next time and see what you get. It's all about getting laid. Sure, they'll say, "But what about if a woman gets raped?" It's a truism that hard cases make bad law, and that's definitely a hard case. However, punishment should go to the rapist not his child. Moreover, only about one percent of abortions are in the aftermath of rape. There's no need to base our policy on what happens to the one percent. Many pro-lifers might actually settle for allowing abortion after rape, if they could get the other ninety nine percent abolished.

As for the politician who thinks he's being clever when he claims that questions about abortion are above his pay grade, somebody should remind him that questions of national policy aren't above anyone's pay grade if they work in the Oval Office or Congress. That's what they are there to do; set policy. Thanks to the Supreme Court, abortion can't be above the President's pay grade. The POTUS gets paid around $400,000 a year plus $50,000 for expenses and retires at almost $200,000, so he should start boning up on questions of life and death, morality as well as "...the right to define one's own concept of existence, of meaning, of the universe, and of the mystery of human life."[462]

If you're President of the United States, you're supposed to know this stuff. If you want to be a cab driver, *then* you can claim it's above your pay grade. If you're President, try using that expense account, hire an ethicist (or maybe just a logician) to explain to you that life begins at the beginning, that a being that is human is a human being and other complicated exotica.

By the way, "the right to define one's own concept of existence" is *in the Constitution* (so says SCOTUS in Casey) and if you're a constitutional lawyer in addition to being President, you should know that too. We could save a lot of trouble of only the Court would extend this airy language to everyone, born and unborn. Knowledge of the Constitution really isn't above the pay grade of *anyone* who works in Washington. It gets difficult when the courts keep adding to it without going through the usual amendment process (Article V, Congress, the state legislatures and other arcana) but they do it so often it's become routine.

It's become common parlance to speak of Roe as something that was "passed" in 1973. Technically, courts don't pass laws, they interpret them and issue rulings. If Roe were to go away, it wouldn't be "repealed", but over ruled. On the other hand we should probably give up on this one. It's become so common to speak of Roe as a law that was passed that it's entered the common language and can't be expunged. Moreover, there's a large element of truth in the common parlance. The right to abortion wasn't in the Constitution before 1973; the Court put it there just as surely as if the country had amended the Constitution to include it. In a real sense the Court *did pass* Roe and Doe by a vote of seven to two, and made it a law by doing so. It's a law that Congress has no authority to repeal; only the

---

[462] Justice Anthony Kennedy, *Planned Parenthood v. Casey* (1992).

Court can do that. It wasn't always this way, but these days, laws are made both in Congress, and (more reliably) in the Supreme Court.

Merely reading the *actual* Constitution these days doesn't give you the slightest idea of what any judge will tell you is in it. For that you need to add on several legal encyclopedias worth of case law and court decisions. That's not something even lawyers and judges really have time to do; (they have law clerks for that). The living Constitution (as opposed to the small document of articles and amendments that you can read in an hour) looks a lot more like the Federal Tax Code than the pamphlet Senator Byrd used to carry around in his back pocket.

The living Constitution idea permits kicking up a lot of dust and then complaining that we can't see. Good luck getting lawyers and judges to put a to stop it. The status quo (in Latin *stare decisis*) gives them free reign to do whatever they want in court, and they're not about to give up the right to make law as they see fit.

It is unconstitutional for courts to make law. Legislatures are, by definition, and by the Constitution, the only bodies than can make new law, or change existing laws. If judges want new laws, or to change existing ones, they have the same right as everyone else to vote for members of the legislature that share their views. Progressives, liberals and other leftists don't like this cumbersome process; in fact they don't like any cumbersome impediments to their own agenda and personal opinions, but legislation is the only lawful way for them to proceed. Non-lawful ways are, of course, available, but they're …well…not lawful.

We have a Supreme Court majority opinion wherein the author went to the library to research the history of abortion and made reference to only one tract, by an attorney for the National Association for the Repeal of Abortion Laws. With this in hand he announced that abortion had not been against the law before the time of the Dred Scott decision, and proceeded to "resurrect" a right, phoenix like from the ash heap of history so as to give a mother the ability to legally murder her own child.

The corruptibility of power has a long and well-observed history. It enters the hospital ward and the courthouse by the same route as the slave plantation; by constant and common use. It deadens the soul to what should be obvious. It makes impossible any "peace with the modern-day slaughter of the innocents legislated for us by an intellectually bankrupt and morally corrupt Supreme Court."[463]

It's common for those with an interest in promoting abortion (or slavery) to resist attempts to re-awaken the soul's sensitivities by refusing to permit or see anything that would jar the senses. They will object vigorously to being shown images of dismembered fetuses, just as German citizens objected to being forced to tour the concentration camps. In 1945 as newsreels of the camps were being shown in movie theaters British moviegoers all over the country left the theaters rather than be confronted with grisly evidence of human inhumanity. In a number of these cases soldiers fresh from the front having been present where the films were taken barricaded the doors and forced people to "go back and face" the grisly images.[464]

The reason such facts are hard to face and such images are hard to look at is that they're showing us a level of depravity that everyone is repulsed by. It's for that reason that we punish murderers and child abusers; everyone knows instinctively that what they do is wrong. We're revolted by what we see in part because it is so obvious that we *ought to be* revolted. The revulsion is painful and we withdraw from it. All too often we need to be compelled to look

---

[463] Paul Rahe, *Soft Despotism, Democracy's Drift: Montesquieu, Rousseau, Tocqueville, and the Modern Prospect*, (New Haven, CT: Yale University Press) p. 279.
[464] Abzug, *Inside the Vicious Heart*, p. 172.

at it, to "go back and face it", simply because there are some things that we *may not* turn away from. We need to take a clear-eyed look at our darker selves to prevent them from taking over our lives; taking over our world.

There were ordinary Germans after the war who objected to being forcibly shown what had been going on under their noses and (what with the stench that emanated from the camps) *in spite of their noses* and they were not in any fundamental way different from the rest of us. It is astonishing the degree to which human beings are capable of denying what they know to be true in the face of the obvious evidence of their senses. Many who, in 1945, said they had never known about the extermination factories in their own towns probably believed what they were saying. Perhaps this is the meaning behind the mayor of Gotha's cryptic suicide note after seeing the Ohrdruf camp up close.

"We didn't know- But we knew."

"If thou sayest, Behold, we knew it not; doth not he that pondereth the heart consider it?"
Proverbs 24:12

Lucifer's Apostles
Legal Positivism in America

Here we may reign secure, and in my choice
to reign is worth ambition though in Hell:
Better to reign in Hell, than serve in Heaven. [465]
John Milton, *Paradise Lost*

Robert A. Destro says that almost all courts "have accepted the proposition that the rights of human beings are conferred by the law."[466] This is a legal doctrine known as "legal positivism". It isn't an American invention. Perhaps it was invented by the British Parliament in the years prior to the American Revolution; Parliament was an enthusiastic supporter of the idea that they and they alone could determine the nature of just law and the rights it conferred. A dedicated researcher might try to trace it back further, perhaps to the ancient Romans but they would find no support for it from at least one Roman.

Cicero wrote that if justice "were founded on the decrees of peoples, the edicts of princes, or the decisions of judges, then Justice would sanction robbery and adultery and forgery of wills..."[467] Cicero was arguing, as Plato had before him for a concept of natural law. Plato's Republic argues powerfully against the notion that justice is the "will of the strongest", which is the essential distillation of the legal positivist doctrine. The American founders clearly believed in a system of natural law, indeed in the "laws of nature and of nature's God"[468] a notion communicated to them from Plato,

---

[465] John Milton, *Paradise Lost*, (London, UK: Peter Parker printer, 1667).
[466] Destro, *The Reach of Roe*, p. 188.
[467] Marcus Tullius Cicero, *De Legibus*, trans. Clinton Walker Keyes, (Cambridge, MA: Loeb Classical Library), 1928.
[468] *When in the Course of human events, it becomes necessary for one people to dissolve the political bands which have connected them with*

Aristotle and Cicero via the works of Augustine, Thomas Aquinas, Hutcheson, Locke, Montesquieu and others. A legal positivist view holds that there is no natural order, no nature of mankind or human nature, and that all law is that which is promulgated by the state. Thus for the positivist,

> "Questions of right and wrong will therefore have to be resolved by the political process. If that process produces a Buchenwald or a Roe v. Wade, it cannot be said to be unjust. Describing Nazi Germany, Gustav Radbruch said that positivism 'disarmed the German jurists against law of an arbitrary or criminal content'."[469]

Positivism has been taught in the majority of law schools in the U.S. for over a century, which is why American jurists are now as intellectually disarmed as their German colleagues were before Hitler. Without a concept of natural law derived from a known human nature, there can be no human rights, and courts will decide what is legal whether or not it corresponds to the "natural order", even if, *especially if*, they want to decide that a fetus is not a person "in the whole sense".

---

another, and to assume among the powers of the earth, the separate and equal station to which the Laws of Nature and of Nature's God entitle them, a decent respect to the opinions of mankind requires that they should declare the causes which impel them to the separation.

We hold these truths to be self-evident, that all men are created equal, that they are endowed by their Creator with certain unalienable Rights, that among these are Life, Liberty and the pursuit of Happiness. That to secure these rights, Governments are instituted among Men, deriving their just powers from the consent of the governed, That whenever any Form of Government becomes destructive of these ends, it is the Right of the People to alter or to abolish it, and to institute new Government...
> Thomas Jefferson, 1776

[469] Charles E. Rice, *Beyond Abortion, The Theory and Practice of the Secular State*, Franciscan Herald Press, 1979, p. 9.

This has the exact same logic and effect as claiming that a dog has five legs. Lincoln once asked, "How many legs does a dog have if you call the tail a leg?" Lincoln said "Four. Calling a tail a leg doesn't make it a leg." The Blackmun Court might say "five" or perhaps that four-legged canines have never been considered dogs, "in the whole sense". The Kass Court in New York might have elaborated that what counts as a dog (with however many legs) need not *"necessarily correspond to the natural order"* wherein only natural dogs have four legs whether or not you count the tail as a leg.

Any court which fails to recognize the "natural order" of natural law will feel free to declare that for whatever purpose it arbitrarily chooses in any particular court session, a dog's legs may include the tail, ears, eyes and nostrils to create a virtual canine centipede, if the judge sitting on the bench is in the mood to declare it so. Lower courts risk being over-ruled by higher courts, but the Supreme Court of the United States doesn't have that problem. They claim that the Constitution is whatever they say it is, because, *they* say it is.

This is what Justice Blackmun decreed when he claimed that a fetus did not have the same right to life that other human beings did. The Court showed its positivist inclinations when it declared that it didn't need to decide when (human) life began, not because, they said, the beginning was already well known (which would have been scientifically correct), but because "philosophers" and others hadn't made up their own minds.

This is the meaning of the oft-quoted 1970 editorial in California Medicine that pointed out "the scientific fact, which everyone really knows, that human life begins at conception and is continuous whether intra- or extra-uterine until death."[470]

Medical doctors as well as obstetrics and reproductive science researchers had known for a long time when life begins, and all had since agreed that it began at conception.

Again, the now infamous passage from Roe reads,

"We need not resolve the difficult question of when life begins. When those trained in the respective disciplines of medicine, philosophy, and theology are unable to arrive at any consensus, the judiciary, at this point in the development of man's knowledge, is not in a position to speculate as to the answer."

If any of the Justices had bothered to actually read some of "those trained in the...[discipline] of medicine" they would have discovered that the question was not only not difficult, but also had already been answered by precisely the kind of "consensus" that they said didn't exist: no "speculation" required. If they had, the most appalling judicial ruling since the origin of Anglo-American Common Law might never have taken place.

But this is not what legal positivists do. Contrary to what you might imagine in reading that 1973 sentence by Justice Blackmun, the Court isn't about to defer to the opinions of "those trained in the respective disciplines of medicine, philosophy, and theology". The Court takes to *itself* the raw power to decide what it wants the words of the Constitution to mean. When they say, "We need not resolve..." that means that they have *already resolved* the issue before hearing the case. The Supreme Court "has become a

---

[470] "A New Ethic for Medicine and Society" *California Medicine: The Western Journal of Medicine*, 113, no. 3, (1970), pp. 67-68.

continuing constitutional convention".[471] This is obviously not what the framers of the Constitution ever intended, and takes the Court far beyond its own constitutional authority.

Of course, the Supreme Court has long since assumed itself to be the final arbiter of what constitutes constitutional authority. This amounts to the Court claiming that "Whatever we the court decide, we the court have authority to do. We have the authority, and have it solely by virtue of the fact that *we say* we have it". Such a court "*is thus marked by every act which may define a Tyrant,* [and] *is unfit to be the ruler of a free people.*"[472]

It was never intended that the courts be the sole arbiters of the Constitution. Were this not the case, no other officials would ever need to swear as their oath of office to "preserve, protect, and defend the Constitution of the United States". The President and all others on down could simply claim, "Hey man, that's not my job".

Lincoln famously ignored and resisted the Supreme Court's Dred Scott decision precisely because he refused to acknowledge the Court as the only constitutional authority. The President and Congress also take oaths to protect the Constitution and thus have similar authority to defend it. Lincoln by the time he took his oath of office as President of the United States had led a party and a movement that was in direct opposition to the Dred Scott decision of 1857. If he believed that the Dred Scott decision *was* the Constitution just because the Taney Court said it was, he could not have taken his oath of office. That would have been to swear to preserve protect and defend the institution of slavery that the Taney Court had upheld.[473] Lincoln had long since gone on record

[471] *Rice, p. 50.*

[472] Thomas Jefferson, et al *American Declaration of Independence*, 1776.

[473] Arkes, *Natural Rights and the Right to Choose*, p. 218.

opposing that idea; that's why he had been elected; that's why the Southern states seceded from the Union upon his election.

Chief Justice Marshall as long ago as 1803 explained in Marbury v. Madison that law is a hierarchical creation and that ordinary laws passed by legislatures are subsidiary to the higher law of the federal Constitution.[474] But the Constitution isn't self-creating. The founders could not have made it clearer 27 years earlier that all the just powers of human law are irrevocably rooted in a higher Law than anything humans can devise. Marshall noted,

> *"The distinction between a government with limited and unlimited powers, is abolished, if those limits do not confine the persons on whom they are imposed."* [Marshall makes it clear that it is established that there are] *"certain limits not to be transcended by* [its different] *departments."*[475]

The three branches of government, executive, legislative and judicial were always and are still intended by the Constitution to be separate and equal. The courts as much as any other branch are part of a government of limited powers; their authority is no less limited than that of the legislature. While it's true that Marbury has generally been seen as establishing a right of judicial review, judicial review is not the same as judicial supremacy. What Marshall did clearly hold is that,

> *"It is a proposition too plain to be contested, that the constitution controls any legislative act repugnant to it...then a legislative act contrary to the constitution is not law..."*[476]

However, this is true of any act by any branch of government. Marshall notes further that, "The constitution is ... a

---

[474] Ibid, pp. 216-217.
[475] Marbury v. Madison, 100 U.S. 1, 5 U.S. 137, 1803.
[476] Ibid.

superior, paramount law, unchangeable by ordinary means." Otherwise, "written constitutions are absurd attempts, on the part of the people, to limit a power in its own nature illimitable."[477]

Thus all human legal powers are and ought to be limitable. This holds for courts as well as for any other government entity. It follows that no court and no judge or justice, not even Chief Justice Marshall can rightly claim that the Constitution says something just because a court rules that it does. So, any court ruling contrary to the constitution is also not law.

Supreme Court Justice James Wilson (1743-1798), member of the Continental Congress, signer of the Declaration of Independence was also one of the six original members of the Court appointed by Washington. He was moreover, one of the chief original framers of the Constitution. Wilson, who could have given Marshall lessons in legal hierarchy, might have called legal positivism "another brat of dishonest parentage".[478] Wilson continued,

> *"If this view be a just view of things, then...man is not only made* for, *but made* by *the government: he is nothing but what the society frames: he can claim nothing but what the society provides."*[479]

Some original principles must be regarded as self-evident. Hadley Arkes has it that it would be an odd thing to suggest that one "believes in" the Pythagorean theorem.[480] Greek geometry, generally called Euclidean geometry, isn't about "Greek triangles". The truth of the theorem "is contained in the axioms and the reasons that bring

---

[477] Ibid.
[478] "Of the Natural Rights of Individuals", James Wilson, 1790.
[479] Ibid.
[480] The square of the length of the hypotenuse of a right triangle is equal to the sum of the squares of the other two sides.

it forth and no one seems to presume that those reasons and axioms are confined to Greece."[481] It's not just true for ancient Greeks or Greek culture, as if for some reason it might not be "true for" Japanese culture.

Plato's dialogue *Meno*, contains an interesting proof of the theorem, perhaps one of the most beautiful and profound passages in ancient Greek philosophy. In the dialogue, Socrates takes an illiterate slave boy, and by deft posing of several critical questions, elicits from him an understanding of the theorem's truth and validity. Even the uneducated child is capable of seeing for himself the rightness of the theorem. Moreover, this is precisely not because Socrates has him examine or measure a large number of triangles and thereby calculate that a high percentage of them fall within the parameters of the theorem, give or take a small error margin.

In fact, Socrates offers no evidence in the usual sense of the word at all; that is, he offers no *external* evidence. That $a^2 + b^2$ should equal c^2 has nothing to do with the measurements of actual triangles; it's true because that's the nature of all right triangles. The *evidential* nature of this theorem about triangles is contained in the thing it-*self.* It is *self-evident.*

It is self-evident for the ancient Greek boy slave, just as it would be for any samurai who might encounter Plato's Socrates, and listen to his critical questions.

This is exactly the sense of the words "self-evident" that the Founders held when they agreed that "we hold these truths to be self-evident: that all men are created equal." The phrase "all men" means *all human beings*, and "any being that is human is a human being".

"What is a human being cannot depend ... on whether any of us is inclined to impute 'value' to the life of any other human

---

[481] Arkes, pp. 46-47.

being."[482] In other words, if what constitutes a human being depends on the value judgments of other human beings, then "there is no objective truth or standing that attaches to a human being."[483] Lincoln, like the founders, knew that we could tell the difference between a man and a dog, and that such differences were "fixed in nature, in a way that we were obliged to accept, not in a way we were free to manipulate." Without *natural* rights (based in natural law) there can be no human rights, no rights at all, least of all a right to abortion.[484]

It is in precisely this fashion that the concept of abortion rights is self-refuting, the exact opposite of self-evident. This is also the same notion of natural law that the Kass court decided it was free to ignore when it decided that a human being could be property whether or not this "conformed to the natural order". In the natural order human beings are *not the kind of things* that can be property.

Lincoln formed the argument like this.

"If A. can prove, however conclusively, that he may, of right, enslave B.—why may not B snatch the same argument, and prove equally, that he may enslave A?—

You say A. is white, and B. is black. It is color, then; the lighter, having the right to enslave the darker? Take care. By this rule, you are to be slave to the first man you meet, with a fairer skin than your own.

You do not mean color exactly? You mean the whites are intellectually the superiors of the blacks, and, therefore have the right to enslave them? Take care again. By this rule, you

---

[482] Arkes, p. 32.
[483] Ibid.
[484] Ibid.

are to be slave to the first man you meet, with an intellect superior to your own.

But, say you, it is a question of interest; and, if you can make it your interest; you have the right to enslave another. Very well. And if he can make it his interest, he has the right to enslave you."[485]

We should return again to Mary Anne Warren. To divide humanity into groups, with different rights; master and slave, or woman with a right to kill and the fetus that has no right not to be killed, we need to say why. We recall Warren's conditions.

Sentience
Ability to feel emotions
Ability to reason
Ability to communicate
Self-awareness
Moral agency or awareness.

Lincoln might respond,

"You say A. is sentient, and B. is not. It is sentience, then; the more aware, having the right to kill the unconscious? Take care. By this rule, you are to be killed by the first one you meet, with a greater awareness than your own. If you are asleep or comatose, you may be killed without remorse."

"You do not mean sentience exactly? You mean the mothers are intellectually the superiors (with greater capacity for emotion and reason) of the fetus, and, therefore have the right to kill them? Take care again. By this rule, you are to be killed by the first one you meet, with greater capacity for reason, emotion, capacity to

---

[485] Abraham Lincoln, "Fragments on Slavery", April 01, 1854.

communicate than your own. Toddlers and the very old often have none of these. May we kill them too?"

Nathan the Prophet instructed King David in the matter of guilt for another man's death, "You are the man."[486]

In each case one standard of judgment must be applied to all concerned. Lincoln's comment, "take care" is good advice. Abortion-style killing will be (has in some cases already been) extended to people outside the human sub-group of the unborn. Recall that abortion is the progressive's ethical Swiss Army knife: it opens everything.

Is it OK to kill a newborn for the same (non) reason that justifies abortion? Peter Singer, Mary Anne Warren, and John Harris say "yes". Is it legal and proper to kill someone who is extremely handicapped? Pinellas County, Florida Judge George Greer said "absolutely" and ordered *"each and every and singular sheriff of the state of Florida"* to ensure the death of Terry Schiavo.[487]

"For with what judgment ye judge, ye shall be judged,"[488]

"Take care" says Mr. Lincoln. You may find yourself on the receiving end of your own reasoning. It's no simple matter to declare some sub-set of the human race to be inferior in life or rights without getting caught in your own logic.

It is impossible to limit the right to kill to just unborn human beings, as we've seen with Warren's conversion to infanticide derived from her own set of principles. Peter Singer and John Harris have likewise embraced the deadly logic, while trying to dodge it's implications for themselves.

---

[486] *II Samuel*, 12:7.

[487] Judge George Greer, Court order directing the feeding tube to be removed from Theresa Marie Schiavo ,March 24, 2005.

[488] *Matthew*, 7:2.

"Take care." Not so fortunate are the severely handicapped or aged. Anyone can be disabled by chance, and there's only one way to avoid ending up in the latter group; to die first. There's no telling where the expanding group of killable humans will be taken next by the "new" ethics.

"For with what judgment ye judge, ye shall be judged."

A wise man was once said to have remarked that he would "give the Devil benefit of the law for my own safety's sake."[489] We might think about giving the same benefit to our children: all of them.

---

[489] Robert Bolt, *A Man for All Seasons*, (New York, NY: Heinemann, 1960), Act 1

Epilogue

"The Mills of God grind slowly, yet they grind exceedingly small."[490]
Longfellow

This book has been a cursory effort to do a forced tour of our own version of the death camp, the abortion mill, as well as its coming analogues, the euthanasia mill, the infanticide mill, and the death panel.

Of course, it isn't really forced. We aren't occupied by Patton's Third Army. We don't have soldiers to shove us back into the theater to face reality. "We must be our own soldiers, constantly on the look out for subtle evasion."[491]

There is no camp to take a tour of. The bodies number in the millions but they are very small, and have already been mostly disposed of like so much trash, all too often *in* the trash.

The Germans soldiers fleeing Patton left behind piles of corpses, and thousands of near dead survivors. A few of these survivors have given voice to their memories of the conditions in the camps. Viktor Frankl, Elie Wiesel, Andrew Rosner and others have been witnesses to the horror from inside its belly. There are no survivors who can speak to the suffering of the innocents in our own dark Satanic mills. There are no piles of bodies, no films of bulldozers burying the dead in pits to turn the stomach. There are no chimneys, no columns of smoke rising from the nearby facility, no stench of death in the air smelled from miles away.

What *will* we tell our children and grandchildren when they ask what did we do in the age of abortion and infanticide when the

---

[490] Henry Wadsworth Longfellow, "Retribution" translating Friedrich von Logau, 1654.
[491] Abzug, *Inside the Vicious Heart*, p. 173.

285

culture of death was running the country and the world? We should start composing our answers now.

If we don't, we will find ourselves one day quoting the mayor of Gotha:

"We didn't know!- but we knew."

A Note on Sources and Readings

All of the Supreme Court Rulings are on line, in a variety of places. Various law schools, Cornell is just one example, have searchable websites containing court decisions.

Dred Scott v. Sandford
http://www.law.cornell.edu/supct/html/historics/USSC_CR_0060_0393_ZS.html

Buck v. Bell
http://www.law.cornell.edu/supct/html/historics/USSC_CR_0274_0200_ZO.html

City of Akron v. Akron Center for Reproductive Health
http://www.law.cornell.edu/supct/html/historics/USSC_CR_0462_0416_ZS.html

Roe v. Wade
http://www.law.cornell.edu/supct/html/historics/USSC_CR_0410_0113_ZS.html

Doe v. Bolton
http://www.law.cornell.edu/supct/html/historics/USSC_CR_0410_0179_ZS.html

Casey v. Planned Parenthood
http://www.law.cornell.edu/supct/html/91-744.ZS.html

Thornburgh v. American College of Obstetricians & Gynecologists
http://www.law.cornell.edu/supct/html/historics/USSC_CR_0476_0747_ZO.html

Davis v. Davis
http://biotech.law.lsu.edu/cases/cloning/davis_v_davis.htm

Kass v. Kass
http://caselaw.findlaw.com/ny-court-of-appeals/1146864.html

U.S. v. Vuitch
http://caselaw.lp.findlaw.com/scripts/getcase.pl?court=US&vol=402
&invol=62

Ankrom v. Alabama (amicus brief)
http://www.liberty.edu/media/9980/attachments/brief_amicus_curiae
_al_akrom_032712.pdf

Planned Parenthood Of Central New Jersey V. Farmer
http://caselaw.findlaw.com/nj-supreme-court/1090635.html

McDonald v. Chicago
http://www.law.cornell.edu/supct/cert/08-1521

Heller v. District of Columbia
http://www.law.cornell.edu/supct/html/07-290.ZS.html

Younger v. Harris
http://www.law.cornell.edu/supct/html/historics/USSC_CR_0401_0
037_ZS.html

Cano v. Baker
http://caselaw.findlaw.com/us-11th-circuit/1095945.html

In addition, the grand jury report on the Kermit Gosnell run
Women's Medical Society, which runs close to 300 pages is also on
line. It makes for fascinating and compulsory reading.

http://www.phila.gov/districtattorney/PDFs/GrandJuryWomensMedi
cal.pdf

For those who have the ability to sit through "The Dying Rooms", its
four segments can be found on YouTube here:
1. http://www.youtube.com/watch?v=AE-U_Pq80OA
2. http://www.youtube.com/watch?v=W6gwjJrea9U
3. http://www.youtube.com/watch?v=WcRJnG44j6M
4. http://www.youtube.com/watch?v=98gAkzDSzvg

Essential readings include (but are certainly not limited to)

Joseph W. Dellapena *Dispelling the Myths of Abortion History*, Durham, NC: Carolina Academic Press, 2006.

Philip K. Dick, "The Pre-persons" *Fantasy and Science Fiction*, October 1974.

Robert P. George and Christopher Tollefsen, *Embryo*, New York, NY: Doubleday, 2008.

Alberto Giubilini and Francesca Minerva: "After-Birth Abortion" *Journal of Medical Ethics* 23 February 2012.

Michael J. Gorman, *Abortion and the Early Church*, Eugene, OR: Wipf & Stock Publishers, 1998.

Mara Hvistendahl, *Unnatural Selection*, New York, NY: PublicAffairs, 2011.

Christopher Kaczor *The Ethics of Abortion: Women's Rights, Human Life, and the Question of Justice*, New York, NY: Routledge, 2010.

Bernard Nathanson, *Aborting America*, New York, NY: Pinnacle Books, 1981.

John Joseph Powell, *Abortion the Silent Holocaust*, Allen, TX: Tabor Publishing, 1981.

Melinda Tankard Reist *Defiant Birth: Women Who Resist Medical Eugenics*, N. Melbourne, Vic. Australia: Spinifex Press, 2006.

Dale Evans Rogers, *Angel Unaware*, Grand Rapids, MI: Fleming H. Revell Company, 1953.

Roger Scruton *Modern Culture*, New York, NY: Continuum, 2006.

Rodney Stark, *The Rise of Christianity*,(1996) *The Triumph of Christianity*, (2011) New York, NY: Harper.

Brad Stetson, (ed.) *The Silent Subject: Reflections on the Unborn in American Culture*, Santa Barbera, CA: Praeger Publishers, 1996.

On the shoulders…

Much has been written in greater detail than could be covered here.

The analysis of the Supreme Court's faulty history in Roe has been explored in detail by a number of writers. Dellapena's mammoth book is mentioned above. Philip Rafferty has done yeoman work in detailing the flaws of the Court's reasoning.

His *Roe v. Wade: Unraveling the Fabric of America*, is a revised version of his *What's Really Going On With Pro-Roe v. Wade Catholic Politicians*. Both can be had on Amazon. Rafferty covers similar material in an online PDF, "Roe v. Wade A Scandal Upon The Court".
(http://lawandreligion.com/sites/lawandreligion.com/files/Rafferty.pdf)

Both Rafferty and Robert Cetrulo criticize Justice Blackmun's failure to recognize the fetus as a human person, particularly his a-historical comment that "the unborn have never been recognized in the law as persons in the whole sense."

There is copious history that demonstrates the contrary, and both Rafferty and Cetrulo demolish Blackmun's pretended ignorance of the subject. Both appear to argue that a Roe overturn could plausibly involve a revised interpretation of the Fourteenth Amendment to include unborn human beings as persons under the Constitution. This would obviate the need tor a constitutional Amendment declaring the unborn as such.

Recently Republican Kentucky Senator Rand Paul has introduced to Congress a law (S. 583) requiring exactly that. He's called it "The Life at Conception Act". The Fourteenth Amendment contains the clause, "The Congress shall have power to enforce, by appropriate legislation, the provisions of this article." Senator Paul describes the act as follows: *"The Life at Conception Act legislatively declares what most Americans believe and what science has long known- that human life begins at the moment of conception, and therefore is entitled to legal protection from that point forward. The right to life is guaranteed to all Americans in the Declaration of Independence and ensuring this is upheld is the constitutional duty of all Members of Congress."*

Senator Paul reminds us again that the courts aren't the only source of interpretation of the Constitution. Congress also has its duties.

More on line

Daniel J. Castellano's "Legal Issues of Roe v. Wade" is at the *Repository of Arcane Knowledge*,
http://www.arcaneknowledge.org/histpoli/roe.htm

Gregory J. Roden's "Unborn Persons, Incrementalism & the Silence of the Lambs" (Human Life Review, Fall 2007) is on line at
http://www.humanlifereview.com/index.php/archives/40-2007-fall/81-unborn-persons-incrementalism-a-the-silence-of-the-lambs

Also see Robert C. Cetrulo's "Constitutional Personhood of the Unborn Child" is from *University Faculty for Life's Life and Learning Conference XVIII*
http://www.uffl.org/pdfs/vol18/Cetrulo_08.pdf

Samuel W. Calhoun's "'Partial-Birth Abortion' Is Not Abortion: Carhart II's Fundamental Misapplication of Roe" at
http://www.uffl.org/pdfs/vol18/Calhoun_08.pdf.
The entire proceedings of the conference are at
http://www.uffl.org/lifelearningxviii.html

O.W. Bartley's *A Treatise on Forensic Medicine* from 1815 is a Google book and has interesting if early chapters on the twin phenomena of abortion and infanticide.
http://books.google.com/books/about/A_Treatise_on_Forensic_Medi cine.html?id=E6I3YgEACAAJ

Arkes et al, "The Inhuman Use of Human Beings" A Statement on Embryo Research by the Ramsey Colloquium, *First Things* January 1995.
http://www.firstthings.com/article/2008/08/001-the-inhuman-use-of-human-beings-23

FILM: *It's a Girl*
TAG LINE: The three deadliest words in the world today "It's a Girl".

It's a Girl! Documentary Film – Official Website

http://www.itsagirlmovie.com/

Appendix A
Early Cases and Sources

Ancient Law and Attitudes

"If men strive, and hurt a woman with child, so that her fruit depart from her, and yet no mischief follow: he shall be surely punished, according as the woman's husband will lay upon him; and he shall pay as the judges determine. And if any mischief follow, then thou shalt give life for life, Eye for eye, tooth for tooth, hand for hand, foot for foot, Burning for burning, wound for wound, stripe for stripe."

Exodus 21: 22-25

"I call heaven and earth to record this day against you, that I have set before you life and death, blessing and cursing: therefore choose life, that both thou and thy seed may live."
Deuteronomy 30:19

"For thou hast possessed my reins: thou hast covered me in my mother's womb."
Psalm 139:13

"I will not give deadly medicine to any even if asked, nor suggest any such; also I will not offer any woman a pessary to produce abortion."
Hippocratic Oath

"Who can be greater haters of their own people than those who are the determined and savage enemies of their own children?"
Philo Judaeus of Alexandria (died c. 50) *The Special Laws* III

"The law, moreover requires us to bring up all our children, and forbids women to abort what is conceived, or to destroy it later; if

any woman appears to have done so, she is a murderer of her own child, by killing a living creature, and diminishing mankind."
> Jewish Historian Flavius Josephus (37- c. 100)

"Slay not the child by abortion, nor kill what is conceived."
> *Didache* (First or second century)

"Thou shalt not kill the child by abortion; nor destroy it after it is born."
> *Epistle of Barnabas* (written between 70 and138)

"A person is an individual with a rational nature."
> Boethius, (480-525) *De duabus naturis*, sec. 3

"In our case, murder is for everyone forbidden, we are not allowed to destroy even the fetus in the womb... To hinder a birth is merely speedier than killing; and it matters not whether you take a life that is born, or destroy one that is coming to the birth. That is a human being which is going to be one; the fruit is found already in the seed."
> Tertullian (160-225)- *Apologia* 9.6

Common Law Through the 18th Century

"One who strikes a pregnant woman or gives her pessary to procure an abortion, if the fetus is formed or quickened, especially if it is quickened, he commits homicide."
> Henry de Bracton 1260

Robert Byrn has this on medieval law.

"Anglo-Saxon law before the Norman Conquest penalized abortion civilly in the form of heavy fines, and ecclesiastically in the form of penances. In the thirteenth century, abortion of a fetus 'formed [or] animated, and particularly if it be animated,' was condemned as homicide by Bracton and, later in the same century by the anonymous legal writer, Fleta, although Fleta used the term 'formed and animated.'"[492]

"The principal reason I go upon in the question is, that the plaintiff was in ventre sa mere at the time of her brother's death, and consequently a person in rerum natura, so that both by the rules of the common and civil law, she was, to all intents and purposes, a child, as much as if born in the father's life-time."
Lord Chancellor Hardwicke *Wallis v. Hodson,* 1740

"Life is the immediate gift of God, a right inherent by nature in every individual; and it begins in contemplation of law as soon as an infant is able to stir in the mother's womb. For if a woman is quick with child, and by a potion or otherwise, killeth it in her womb; or if any one beat her, whereby the child dieth in her body, and she is delivered of a dead child; this, though not murder, was by the ancient law homicide or manslaughter. But the modern law doth not look upon this offence in quite so atrocious a light but merely as a heinous misdemeanor."
William Blackstone *Commentaries on the Laws of England* (1765-1769)

---

[492] Robert Byrn, "An American Tragedy: The Supreme Court on Abortion" Fordham Law Review, Vol. 41, 1973

"No sooner is the female ovum thus set in motion, and the fetus formed, then its capacity of life is supported."
Benjamin Rush, *Medical Inquiries & Observations* (1809)

The Nineteenth Century

"To extinguish the first spark of life is a crime of the same nature, both against our Maker and society, as to destroy an infant, a child, or a man...."
Thomas Percival, *Works, Literary, Moral, And Medical*, J. Johnson, St. Paul's Church-yard London, 1807.

"person: an individual human being consisting of body and soul. We apply the word to living beings only, possessed of a rational value; the body when dead is not called a person. It is applied alike to man, woman, or child."
Webster's *Dictionary* 1828

"man: an individual of the human race; a human being, a person.*"*
Webster's *Dictionary*, 1865

[Abortion is]*"The slaughter of countless children; no mere misdemeanor or no mere attempt upon the life of the mother, but the wanton and murderous destruction of her child; such unwarrantable destruction of human life."*
AMA Position on Abortion 1859

"It is a flagrant crime at common law to attempt to procure the miscarriage or abortion of the woman because it interferes with and violates the mysteries of nature in the process by which the human race is propagated and continued. ...It is not the murder of a living child which constitutes the offence, but the destruction of gestation by wicked means and against nature. The moment the womb is

instinct with embryo life and gestation has begun, the crime may be perpetrated."

Supreme Court of Pennsylvania in *Mills v. Commonwealth*, (1850).

"The common law is distinguished, and is to be commended, for its all-embracing and salutary solicitude for the sacredness of human life and the personal safety of every human being. This protecting, paternal care, enveloping every individual like the air he breathes, not only extends to persons actually born, but, for some purposes, to infants in ventre sa mere.... The right to life and to personal safety is not only sacred in the estimation of the common law, but it is inalienable."

Iowa Supreme Court *State v. Moore*, 25 Iowa 128, 136 (1868)

Twentieth Century

"When a virile spermatozoon unites with a fertile ovum in the uterus, conception is accomplished. Pregnancy at once ensues, and under normal circumstances continues until parturition. During all this time the woman is 'pregnant with a child' within the meaning of the statute. She cannot be pregnant with anything else than a child. From the moment of conception a new life has begun, and is protected by the enactment. The product of conception during its entire course is imbued with life, and is capable of being destroyed as contemplated by the law. By such destruction the death of a child is produced and often that of its mother as well."

Oregon Supreme Court, *State v. Ausplund*, 1917

"We hold that the anti-abortion statutes in Oklahoma were enacted and designed for the protection of the unborn child and through it society."

Oklahoma Supreme Court *Bowlan v. Lunsford* 1936

"Medical authority has long recognized that an unborn child is in existence from the moment of conception.... All writers who have discussed the problem have joined in condemning the total no-duty rule and agree that the unborn child in the path of an automobile is as much a person in the street as its mother, and should be equally protected under the law...."

Prosser and Keaton on Torts, 2nd ed. (1955)

"The child, by reason of his physical and mental immaturity, needs special safeguards and care, including appropriate legal protection, before as well as after birth."

U.N. Declaration of the Rights of the Child, 1959

"Biologically speaking, the life of a human being begins at the moment of conception in the mother's womb, and as a general rule of construction in the law, a legal personality is imputed to an unborn child for all purposes which would be beneficial to the infant after its birth.... A child unborn at the time of the death of its parent has also been considered a 'child' of the decedent in determining beneficiaries of an award in a wrongful death action or in a workman's compensation case."

American Jurisprudence *Encyclopedia of United States Law* 2nd Ed. (1962)

"We are satisfied that the unborn child is entitled to the law's protection and that an appropriate order should be made to insure blood transfusions to the mother in the event that they are necessary in the opinion of the physician in charge at the time."

New Jersey Supreme Court in Ruling that the unborn child's right to life preempts even his mother's religious (Jehovah's Witness) beliefs. *Raleigh Fitkin-Paul Morgan Memorial Hospital v. Anderson*, 42 N.J. 421, 201 A.2d 537, 377 U.S. 985 (1964)

"Once human life has commenced, the constitutional protections found in the Fifth and Fourteenth Amendments impose upon the state the duty of safeguarding it."

U.S. District Court, Ohio, *Steinberg v. Brown*, 321 F.Supp. 741, 1970.

"If the mother can die and the fetus live, or the fetus die and the mother live, how can it be said that there is only one life? ...The phenomenon of birth is not the beginning of life; it is merely a change in the form of life. The principal feature of that change is the fact of respiration.... A baby fully born and conceded by all to be "alive" is no more able to survive unaided than the infant en ventre sa mere. In fact, the babe in arms is less self-sufficient—more dependent—than his unborn counterpart.... The fact of life is not to be denied. Neither is the wisdom of the public policy which regards unborn persons as being entitled to the protection of law."

Michigan Supreme Court *O'Neill v. Morse*, 188 N.W.2d 785 (Mich., 1971).

"If the deliberate extinguishment of human life has any effect at all, it more likely tends to lower our respect for life and brutalize our values."

Supreme Court Justice William Brennan *Furman v. Georgia*, 1972

"Inanimate objects are sometimes parties in litigation. A ship has a legal personality, a fiction found useful for maritime purposes. The corporation sole - a creature of ecclesiastical law - is an acceptable adversary and large fortunes ride on its cases. The ordinary corporation is a 'person' for purposes of the adjudicatory processes, whether it represents proprietary, spiritual, aesthetic, or charitable causes.

"So it should be as respects valleys, alpine meadows, rivers, lakes, estuaries, beaches, ridges, groves of trees, swampland, or even air that feels the destructive pressures of modern technology and modern life. ...The voice of the inanimate object, therefore, should not be stilled."

> Justice William O. Douglas dissenting in *Sierra Club v. Morton*, 1972

"The Court chooses to conclude its opinion with a footnote reference to De Tocqueville. In this environmental context I personally prefer the older and particularly pertinent observation and warning of John Donne."[493]

> Roe author Justice Harry Blackmun dissenting in *Sierra Club v. Morton*, 1972

"...due to the pervading public purpose of our wrongful death statute, which is to prevent homicide through punishment of the culpable party and the determination of damages by reference to the quality of the tortious act, we are again extending out judicial prerogative as was done in Huskey and Wolfe to hold that the parents of an eight and one-half month old stillborn fetus are entitled to maintain an action for the wrongful death of the child."

> Supreme Court Of Alabama, *Charlotte Eich V. Town Gulf Shores* 1974

"The notion that the Constitution of the United States, designed, among other things, 'to establish Justice, insure domestic Tranquility, ... and secure the Blessings of Liberty to ourselves and our Posterity,' prohibits the States from simply banning this visibly brutal means of eliminating our half-born posterity is quite simply absurd."

---

[493] "No man is an Iland, intire of itselfe; ... any man's death diminishes me, because I am involved in Mankinde;", John Dunne Devotions XVII, 1624.

Antonin Scalia – on partial-birth abortion, dissenting in *Stenberg v. Carhart* 2000.

Twenty-first Century

"Likewise, in the present case, we do not see any reason to hold that a viable fetus is not included in the term 'child,' as that term is used in § 26-15-3.2, Ala. Code 1975. Not only have the courts of this State interpreted the term 'child' to include a viable fetus in other contexts, the dictionary definition of the term 'child' explicitly includes an unborn person or a fetus."
Court of Criminal Appeals *Ankrom v. Alabama* 2011

"Today, this Court reaffirms that the lives of unborn children are protected by Alabama's wrongful-death statute, regardless of viability... with regard to the law of wrongful death, Roe's viability standard should be universally abandoned."
Alabama Supreme Court, *Hamilton v. Scott*, 2012

"The decision of this Court today is in keeping with the widespread legal recognition that unborn children are persons with rights that should be protected by law."
Alabama Supreme Court upholding conviction in *Ankrom v. Alabama* 2013

****

"The appellee and certain amici argue that the fetus is a 'person' within the language and meaning of the Fourteenth Amendment....If this suggestion of personhood is established, the appellant's case, of course, collapses, for the fetus' right to life would then be guaranteed specifically by the Amendment."
Justice Harry Blackmun in Roe v. Wade 1973

Appendix B
Embryology and Human Beings

"Among the most glaring indications that we are in exile is the necessity of contending for the most basic truth of the dignity of the human person. If we don't get that right, we are unlikely to get right many other questions of great moral and political moment."[494]

"...Human development begins at fertilization, when a male gamete or sperm unites with a female gamete or ovum to form a single cell called a zygote (Gr. zygotos, yoked together). This cell marked the beginnings of each of us as a unique individual."[495]

"If we took a movie of everyone alive and ran it backward, we would see that we are continuous with our embryonic beginnings..., we can rationally infer that the child and the infant--and before that the fetus and the embryo--are continuously us."[496]

"An abortion kills the life of a baby after it has begun...Abortion is dangerous to your life and health. It may make you sterile, so that when you want a child you cannot have it ... Birth control merely postpones the beginning of life."[497]

"Human beings are not returnable items. Every individual has his/her rights, not the least of which is the right to life, whether born

---

[494] Richard John Neuhaus, *American Babylon:Notes of a Christian Exile*, (Philadelphia PA: Basic Books, 2009), p. 4.

[495] Moore KL, Persaud TVN. *The Developing Human: Clinically Oriented Embryology* (Philadelphia, PA: W.B. Saunders Company, 1998).

[496] Sidney Callahan "The First Stage of Life is Life" L.A. *Times* June 19, 1991, p. B7

[497] *Plan Your Children* (Planned Parenthood, 1963).

or unborn. Those with power in our society cannot be allowed to "want" and "unwant" people at will. " [498]

Grace Olivares

"Everyone of the higher animals starts life as a single cell the fertilized ovum... The union of two such sex cells (male germ cell and female germ cell) to form a zygote constitutes the process of fertilization and initiates the life of a new individual." [499]

---

[498] Grace Olivares, In Dissent from *The Report of the Rockefeller Commission on Population Growth and the American Future,* 1972.

[499] Bradley M. Patten, *Foundations of Embryology* (New York: McGraw-Hill, 1964), p. 2.

Appendix C
Final quotes and Reminders

"Forgetting extermination is part of extermination, because it is also the extermination of memory, of history, of the social, etc. This forgetting is as essential as the event," [500]

"I am beginning to think that when God goes, all goes."[501]

"Once you permit the killing of the unborn child, there will be no stopping. There will be no age limit. You are setting off a chain reaction that will eventually make you the victim."[502]

"It was left to the Nazi dictatorship to make medical science into an instrument of political power—a formidable, essential tool in the complete and effective manipulation of totalitarian control. ... Whatever proportions these crimes finally assumed, it became evident to all who investigated them that they had started from small beginnings... It is the first seemingly innocent step away from principle that frequently decides a career of crime. Corrosion begins in microscopic proportions. "[503]

[500] Jean Baudrillard *Simulacra and Simulations* - III. Holocaust, (Ann Arbor, MI: University of Michigan Press, 1995).

[501] Dorothy Thompson "The Lesson of Dachau", *Ladies Home Journal,* September 1945

[502] R.A Gallop, M.D. quoted in John Waddey, *Euthanasia:"Good Death" or Selective Killing*? 1978.

[503] Leo Alexander, M.D., "Medical Science Under Dictatorship" *The New England Journal of Medicine* July, 1949.

"I call heaven and earth to record this day against you, that I have set before you life and death, blessing and cursing: therefore choose life, that both thou and thy seed may live."

Deuteronomy 30:19

Bibliography

Abzug, Robert H., *Inside the Vicious Heart*, New York, NY: Oxford University Press, 1987.

Adams. John, "Letter to H. Niles" 1818.

Aiken, Jonathan, *John Newton,* Wheaton, IL: Crossway Books, 2007.

Alan Guttmacher Institute Report, "Facts on Induced Abortion Worldwide".

Albee, Edward, *Who's Afraid of Virginian Woolf?*, (New York, NY: Penguin/Mass Market, 1985.

Alcorn, Randy *Pro-life Answers to Pro-Choice Arguments,* Colorado Springs, CO: Multnomah Publishers, 2000.

Alexander, Leo, M.D., "Medical Science Under Dictatorship," *The New England Journal of Medicine,* July, 1949.

Alter, Robert, *The Five Books of Moses: A Translation with Commentary*, New York, NY: W. W. Norton & Company, 2008.

AMA Report on Criminal Abortion, 1859.

Angier, Natalie, "Ultrasound and Fury: One Mother's Ordeal," *The New York Times*, November 26, 1996.

Andrusko, Dave, "Editorial on the 30th anniversary of Roe v. Wade and Doe v. Bolton," National Right to Life, http://www.nrlc.org/news/2003/NRL01/editb.html

Aristotle, *Politics*, H. Rackham, tr. Cambridge, MA: Harvard University Press, 1944.

Arkes, Hadley, *Natural Rights and the Right to Choose,* New York, NY: Cambridge University Press, 2004.

Arkes, Hadley, Testimony before the Committee On The Judiciary House Of Representatives, 107th Congress, 1st session.

Arnold, Robert M. and Stuart J. Youngner, "The Dead Donor Rule: Should We Stretch It, Bend It, or Abandon It?", *Kennedy Institute of Ethics Journal,* Volume 3, Number 2, June 1993.

Akron Beacon Journal, April 24, 2013, "Abortion provider in Cuyahoga Falls being shut down".

Bachiochi, Erika, ed., *The Cost of Choice: Women Evaluate the Impact of Abortion*, New York, NY: Encounter Books, 2004.

Bartley, O.W., *A Treatise on Forensic Medicine*, Whitefish, MT: Kessinger Publishing, 1815.

Basil the Great, "Letter to Amphilochius, Bishop of Iconium," (Letter #188) *First Canonical Epistle*.

Bakke, O. M., Brian McNeil *When Children Became People: The Birth of Childhood in Early Christianity*, Minneapolis, MN: Augsburg Fortress Publishers, 2005

Barnabas, Epistle, (Epistle of St. Barnabas) tr., Roberts/Donaldson.

Baudrillard, Jean, *Simulacra and Simulations*, Ann Arbor, MI: University of Michigan Press, 1995.

Bauman, Michael, "Beware of Feminist Euphemisms," *Life Advocate*, May/June, 1999 Volume XIII Number 6.

Beckwith, Francis J., Gregory Koukl, *Relativism: Feet Firmly Planted in Mid-Air*, Grand Rapids, MI: Baker Books, 1998.

Beckwith, Francis J., *Defending Life: A Moral and Legal Case Against Abortion Choice*, New York, NY: Cambridge University Press, 2007.

Beckwith, Francis J., *Politically Correct Death: Answering the Arguments for Abortion Rights,* Grand Rapids, MI: Baker Book House, 1993.

Berlinski, David, *The Deniable Darwin and Other Essays*, Discovery Institute Press, 2010.

Berlinski, David, *The Devil's Delusion: Atheism and its Scientific Pretensions*, New York, NY: Basic Books, 2009.

Bernard, Fr. Jean, *Priestblock 25487: A Memoir of Dachau*, Bethesda, MD: Zaccheus Press, 2007.

Berger, Peter, "Misuses of the Holocaust," *The American Interest*, February 20, 2012.

Besançon, Alain, *A Century of Horrors*, Wilmington, DE: Intercollegiate Studies Institute, 2007.

Binding, Karl and Alfred Hoche *Permitting the Destruction of Life Unworthy of Life*, 1920.

Bolt, Robert, *A Man for All Seasons*, New York, NY: Heinemann, 1960.

Bose, Ashsh, "Female Foeticide: A Civilizational Collapse", *Sex-selective Abortion in India*, Tulsi Patel (ed.)

Bracton, Henri de, *The Laws and Customs of England*, III, ii, 4.

Brady, Jeff, "Pennsylvania Tightens Abortion Rules Following Clinic Deaths," *NPR* "All Things Considered," March 28, 2013.

Bradley, Omar, *A Solder's Story*, New York, NY: Henry Holt, 1951.

Brennan, William, *The Abortion Holocaust: Today's Final Solution*, St Louis: Landmark Press, 1983.

Budziszewski, J., "The Second Tablet Project," *First Things,* June/July, 2002.

Butler, J. Douglas, David F. Walbert, *Abortion, Medicine and the Law*, New York, NY: Facts on File, 1992.

Robert Byrn, "An American Tragedy: The Supreme Court on Abortion", *Fordham Law Review* May 1973.

Calderone, Mary Steichen. M.D., "Illegal Abortion as a Public Health Problem," *American Journal of Public Health*, VOL. 50. NO. 7, 1960.

Calhoun, Samuel W., "'Partial-Birth Abortion' Is Not Abortion: Carhart II's Fundamental Misapplication of Roe", http://www.uffl.org/pdfs/vol18/Calhoun_08.pdf.

Callahan, Sidney, "The First Stage of Life is Life" *LA Times* June 19, 1991.

Carson, Rachel, *The Silent Spring*, New York, NY: Houghton Mifflin Harcourt, 1962.

Chambers, Whittaker *Witness*, Washington, DC: Regnery Publishing, 1980.

California Medicine: The Western Journal of Medicine, "A New Ethic for Medicine and Society", 113, no. 3, 1970.

Castellano, Daniel J., "Legal Issues of Roe v. Wade," *Repository of Arcane Knowledge*, http://www.arcaneknowledge.org/histpoli/roe.htm

Celsus, Aulas Cornelius, *De Medicina.*

Centers for Disease Control, "Abortion Surveillance Annual Summary" 1972.

Centers for Disease Control, "Morbidity and Mortality Weekly Report", ce Summaries, 9/4/92.

Cetrulo, Robert C. "Constitutional Personhood of the Unborn Child," *University Faculty for Life's Life and Learning Conference XVIII.*

China *People's Daily,* March 3, 1983.

Cicero, Marcus Tullius, *De Legibus*, trans. Clinton Walker Keyes, Cambridge, MA: Loeb Classical Library, 1928.

Cleaver, Cathleen A. and Edward Grant, "Lessons From History's Most Calamitous Experience", *Assisted Suicide & Euthanasia, Past & Present*, by J.C. Willke, M.D., et al, Cincinati, OH: Hayes Publishing Company, 1998.

CNN, "Nebraska lawmakers vote to limit safe-haven law", November 22, 2008.

Cohen Asher, ed., *Comprehending the Holocaust: Historical and Literary Research*, New York, NY: Peter Lang International Academic Publishers, Strochlitz Institute of Holocaust Studies.

Cohen, Shawn, "Coroner: Woman bled to death after late-term abortion," The (Westchester County, N.Y.) *Journal News*, February 21, 2013.

Collins, Vincent J., Steven R. Zielinski, and Thomas J. Marzen, "Fetal Pain and Abortion: The Medical Evidence", *Studies in Law and Medicine*, no. 18, Chicago: American United for Life, Inc., 1984.

Confucius, Analects, Book XIII, trans., James Legge.

Conlon, Anne Editor, *The Reach of Roe: Eugenics, Euthanasia, and Other Assaults on the Dignity of Human Life*, New York, NY: Human Life Foundation, 2013.

Dale, Maryclaire, "Dr. Kermit Gosnell's employees saw few options, three have plead guilty to third-degree murder", Associated Press, WPTV 04/12/2013.

Daniels, Anthony, (Writing as Theodore Dalrymple), "Modernity's Uninvited Guest," *City Journal,* Summer 2010.

Daniels, Anthony, (Theodore Dalrymple), "The Rage of Virginia Woolf," *City Journal*, Summer 2002.

Daniels, Anthony, (Theodore Dalrymple), "Trivializing the Holocaust II: Auschwitz Isn't a Metaphor," *City Journal*, April 12, 2002.

Daniels, Anthony, (Theodore Dalrymple), *In Praise of Prejudice*, New York, NY: Encounter Books, 2007.

Dann, Sam, ed., *Dachau 29 April 1945: The Rainbow Liberation Memoirs*, Lubbock, TX: Texas Tech University Press, 1988.

Dagar, Rainuka, "Rethinking Female Foeticide", *Sex-selective Abortion in India*, Tulsi Patel (ed.)

Darwin, Charles, *On the Origin of Species,* London, UK: John Murray publishers, 1859.

Darwin, Charles, *The Decent of Man,* London, UK: John Murray publishers, 1871.

Darwin, Erasmus, *Zoonomia, Or, the Laws of Organic Life,* London, UK: J. Johnson, 1796.

Darwin, Erasmus, *The Temple of Nature,* London, UK: J. Johnson, 1803.

Dellapenna, Joseph W., *Dispelling the Myths of Abortion History*, Durham, NC: Carolina Academic Press, 2006.

Demarco, Donald, and Benjamin D. Wike, *Architects of the Culture of Death*, San Francisco, CA: Ignatius Press, 2004.

DeNoon, Daniel, "A History of Birth Control," WebMD Feature, August 6, 2001.

Destro, Robert A., "Is Roe v. Wade Obsolete?" *The Reach of Roe Eugenics, Euthanasia, and Other Assaults on the Dignity of Human Life*, New York, NY: Human Life Foundation, Anne Conlon Editor, 2013.

Deveruex, George, *A Study of Abortion in Primitive Societies*, New York, NY: Julian Press, 1955.

Dick, Philip K., "The Pre-persons" *Fantasy and Science Fiction,* October 1974.

Dickens, Charles, *A Christmas Carol*, London, UK: Chapman and Hall, 1843.

Didache, tr., Donaldson Roberts.

Douglass, Frederick, *Narrative of the Life of Frederick Douglass An American Slave*, Boston, MA: The Anti-Slavery Office, 1845.

Dugdale, Richard L., *The Jukes: A Study in Crime, Pauperism, Disease and Heredity*, New York, NY: G.P. Putnam's Sons, 1877.

Dunne, John, *Devotions upon Emergent Occasions*, 1624.

Dyer, Justin, "Fictional Abortion History" National Review Online, December 24, 2012.

Edminson, W., "A Report on the Abortion Capital of the Country", *The New York Times Magazine*, March 11, 1971.

Ehrlich, Paul, *The Population Bomb*, New York, NY: Ballantine Books, 1968.

Eisenhower, Dwight D., *Crusade in Europe*, New York, NY: Doubleday, New York, 1948.

Eisenhower, Dwight D. "Letter to General George C. Marshall", April 15, 1945.

Ellis, Havelock, "Birth Control and Sterilization", *Birth Control Review*, Vol. XVII No. 4, April 1933.

Elsakkers, M.J., *Reading between the lines: Old Germanic and early Christian views on Abortion*, (Thesis, University of Amsterdam) 2010.

Ertelt, Steven, "Medical Examiner Still Refuses Proper Burial for Babies Kermit Gosnell Killed", *Life News*, July 15, 2013.

Ezekiel J. Emanuel, M.D., PhD., "Depression, Euthanasia, and Improving End-of-Life Care", *Journal of Clinical Oncology*, 2005.

Emanuel LL, von Gunten CF, Ferris FD. "Physician-Assisted Suicide", The Project to Educate Physicians on End-of-life Care, The Robert Wood Johnson Foundation, 1999.

Epictetus *Discourses*, Chapter XXIII, "Against Epicurus," tr. P.E Matheson.

Estrich, Susan, "Laci Peterson's unborn child becomes pawn in abortion debate", *USA Today*, April 29, 2003.

Feldstein, Mark, "Investigation of Dr. Milan Vuitch," WDVM-TV, Washington, D.C., 1984.

Flesh, George, M.D., "Why I No Longer Do Abortions," L.A. *Times* Sept. 12, 1991.

Finley, Kimyette, "New Exhibit Tells the Story of Human Struggles to Control Fertility" *The Daily: digital news of Case Western Reserve University,* (http://blog.case.edu/case-news/2009/09/14/dittrickexhibit), September 14, 2009.

First Things, January 1995, "The Inhuman Use of Human Beings" A Statement on Embryo Research by the Ramsey Colloquium.

Foote, Shelby, Comments on *Booknotes,* CSPAN, 1994.

Forsythe, Clarke D., *Abuse of Discretion*, New York, NY: Encounter Books, 2013.

Forsythe, Clarke D., et al, "Constitutional Law and Abortion Primer," Advocates for Life, 2011.

Forsythe, Clarke D., "The Supreme Court's Back Alley Runs Through Philadelphia," *The Weekly Standard*, January 24, 2011.

Franke, Linda Bird, *The Ambivalence of Abortion,* New York, NY: Random House, 1978.

Franke-Rutam, Garance, "Kermit Gosnell and Intelligence Failures," *The Atlantic*, April 17 2013.

Frankena, W.K., "The Naturalistic Fallacy," *Mind*, New Series, Vol. 48, No. 192,1939.

Frankl, Victor, *Man's Search for Meaning,* Boston, MA: Beacon Press, 2006.

Franklin, Benjamin, "An Address to the Public", 1789.

Franks, Angela, *Margaret Sanger's Eugenic Legacy: The Control of Female Fertility,* Jefferson, NC: McFarland, 2005.

Garrow, David J., *Liberty and Sexuality, the Right to Privacy and the Making of Roe v. Wade,* New York, NY: Scribner, 1994.

George, Robert P., Patrick Lee, "Acorns and Embryos", *The New Atlantis,* Number 35, Spring 2011.

George, Robert P., Christopher Tollefsen, *Embryo: A Defense of Human Life,* New York, NY: Doubleday, 2008.

Geisel, Theodor Seuss, (Dr. Seuss), *Horton Hears a Who!,* Random House, 1954.

Gerdtz, John, "Disability and Euthanasia: The Case of Helen Keller and the Bollinger Baby" University Faculty for Life, Vol. 16. http://www.uffl.org/vol16/gerdtz06.pdf.

Gilberson Karl, *Saving Darwin,* New York, NY: HarperOne, 2009.

Giubilini, Alberto and Francesca Minerva: "After-Birth Abortion, Why Should the Baby Live?" *Journal of Medical Ethics* 23 February 2012.

Goddard, Henry Herbert, *The Kallikak Family: A Study in the Heredity of Feeble-Mindedness,* New York, NY: MacMillan, 1912.

Goodman, Ellen, "Not just a march on Washington," Boston *Globe,* April 25, 2004.

Gordon, Sol, and Craig W. Snyder, *Personal Issues in Human Sexuality,* Boston, MA: Allyn & Bacon, 1989.

Gorman, Michael J., *Abortion & the Early Church,* Eugene, OR: Wipf and Sock Publishers, 1982.

Gould, Stephen Jay, "Carrie Buck's Daughter" *Natural History* Magazine, July 1984.

Grant, Madison, *The Passing of The Great Race,* New York, NY: Charles Scribner's Sons, 1916.

Graber, David M. "Mother Nature as a Hothouse Flower," L.A. *Times Book Review*, October 29, 1989.

Gregory of Nyssa, "On the Making of Man," in *Nicene and Post - Nicene Fathers,* V, eds. Schaff and Wace Grand Rapids: Eerdmans, 1979.

Guttmacher, Alan, *Birth Control and Love: the Complete Guide to Contraception and Fertility,* New York, NY: Collier-Macmillan 1969.

Guttmacher Alan, "The Shrinking Non-Psychiatric Indications for Therapeutic Abortions," Harold Rosen, *Abortion in America: Medical, Psychiatric, Legal, Anthropological, and Religious Considerations*, Boston, MA: Beacon Press, 1967.

Hart, David Bentley, *Atheist Delusions*, New Haven, CT: Yale University Press, 2009.

Haub, Carl, "India's Population Policy," *Berlin Institute Online-Handbook Demography*.

Hanson, Victor Davis, *The Soul of Battle*, New York, NY: Anchor Books, 2001.

Haskell, Martin, M.D., "Dilation and Extraction for Late Second Trimester Abortion", Proceedings of the National Abortion Federation, *Second Trimester Abortion: From Every Angle*, September 13-14, 1992.

Hepper, PG., "Fetal memory: Does it exist? What does it do?" *Acta Paediatrica* 1996; Suppl 416:16-20. Stockholm.

Hirsh, Michael, *The Liberators: America's Witnesses to the Holocaust*, New York, NY: Bantam 2010.

Hitler, Adolph, *Mein Kampf,* Volume Two: The National Socialist Movement, 1926.

Holt, Jim, "Euthanasia for Babies?" *New York Times*, July 10, 2005.

Hutton, James, *Theory of the Earth*, Royal Society of Edinburgh, 1788.

Hsu, Kenneth J., *The Great Dying*, New York, NY: Ballantine Books, 1989.

The Huffington Post, July 12, 2013, "Texas State Troopers Confiscate Suspected Feces, Urine, Other Items Ahead Of Abortion Bill Vote".

Hvistendahl, Mara, *Unnatural Selection*, (New York, NY: Public Affairs Books, 2011.

Janssen-Jurreit, Marielouise, *Sexism-The Male Monopoly of History and Thought*, New York, NY: Farrar, Strauss and Giroux, 1976.

James, Susan Donaldson, "Down Syndrome Births Are Down in U.S.," ABC News, November 2, 2009.

Jastrow, Robert, *God and the Astronomers*, New York, NY: W. W. Norton & Co., 1980.

Jennings, David, the *Houston Chronicle*, "Will Houston's version of Kermit Gosnell be investigated and charged?", May 15, 2013.

Pope John Paul II, *Evangelium Vitae*, March 25, 1995.

Johnson, Phillip E., *Darwin on Trial*, Downers Grove, IL: Intervarsity Press, 2010.

Jones, Cass, "Controversy over Adolf Hitler statue in Warsaw ghetto," The *Guardian* (UK), December 28, 2012.

Judiciary Committee Report to the House of Representatives, 106th Congress 2d session, Report 106-835.

Judiciary Committee Hearing: Hearing before The Subcommittee On The Constitution of the Committee On The Judiciary House Of Representatives, 107th Congress, 1st session.

Justinian, (Lavius Petrus Sabbatius Justinianus Augustus), *Enactments*, (Code of Justinian).

Kaczor, Christopher, *The Ethics of Abortion: Women's Rights, Human Life, and the Question of Justice*, New York, NY: Routledge, 2010.

Kaplan, Laura, *The Story of Jane: The Legendary Underground Feminist Abortion Service*, New York, NY: Pantheon Books, 1995.

Kasun, Jacqueline, *The War Against Population: The Economics and Ideology of World Population Control*, San Francisco, CA: Ignatius Press, 1999.

Keller, Helen, letter to *The New Republic*, Dec. 18, 1915, "Physicians' juries for defective babies".

King, Alexander and Bertrand Schneider, *The First Global Revolution: A Report by the Council of Rome*, New York, NY: Simon & Schuster Ltd., 1992.

Kisilevsky, Barbara, M.D., et al, "Effects Of Experience On Fetal Voice Recognition", *Psychological Science,* Vol. 14, No. 3, May 2003.

Laughlin, Harry H., "Eugenical Aspects of Legal Sterilization", *Birth Control Review*, Vol. XVII No. 4, April 1933.

Langman, Jan, *Medical Embryology*. 3rd ed. Baltimore, MD: Williams and Wilkins, 1975.

Larson, Erik, *In the Garden of Beasts: Love, Terror, and an American Family in Hitler's Berlin*, New York, NY: Crown Publishing, 2011.

Lazarus, Edward, *Closed Chambers: The Rise, Fall, and Future of the Modern Supreme Court*, New York, NY: Penguin Books, 1999.

Lebak, Jane, "Dealing With The Clueless", *Carrying to Term Pages*, http://www.janelebak.com/ctt/tips-clueless.html.

Levatino, Dr. Anthony, testimony before Congress, May 23, 2013.

Levi, Primo, *Survival in Auschwitz*, Stuart Woolf, trans., New York, NY: Touchstone, 1987.

Lifton, R. J. *The Nazi Doctors: Medical Killing and the Psychology of Genocide,* New York, NY: Basic Books, 1988.

Linacre Centre for Healthcare Ethics, "On the place of the human embryo within the Christian tradition", Submitted to the House of Lords by The Linacre Centre, 2001.

Lincoln, Abraham, "Fragment on the Constitution and Union", ca. 1861.

Lincoln, Abraham, "Fragments on Slavery", April 01, 1854.

Lincoln, Abraham, "Speech on the Dred Scott Decision", June 26, 1857.

Lindsay, Jack, *The Ancient World: Manners and Morals,* New York, NY: G.P. Putnam's Sons, 1968.

Linton, Paul Benjamin, "Planned Parenthood V. Casey: The Flight From Reason In The Supreme Court," *Saint Louis University Public Law Review,* [Vol. 13:1] 1993.

Longfellow, Henry Wadsworth, "Retribution".

Loudon, Irvine, *The Tragedy of Childbed Fever*, Oxford University Press, 2000.

Malinowski, Bronislaw, *The Sexual Life of Savages in North-Western Melanesia*, New York, NY: Eugenics Publishing, 1929.

Malisow, Craig, "Ringing up Baby", Dallas *Observer*, Thursday, June 7, 2007.

Malthus, Thomas Robert, "An Essay on the Principle of Population," London, UK: Joseph Johnson Publisher, 1798.

Madison, James, *Federalist* No. 46, *New York Packet,* 1788.

Mappes, T.A. and D. DeGrazia, eds., *Biomedical Ethics*, 4th ed. New York, NY: McGraw-Hill, Inc. 1996.

McClary, Susan, *Minnesota Composers Forum Newsletter*, January 1987.

McCormick, C. 0., M. D. "Defective Families", *Birth Control Review*, Vol. XVII No. 4, April 1933.

McLendon, Kelly, "50 rally for reinstatement of UTMC transfer agreements with abortion clinics," *Toledo Blade*, April 19, 2013.

McKenzie, Michael, "When Good Men do Nothing: Reflections From a Modern-Day Burgermeister", Brad Stetson, ed., *The Silent Subject*, Santa Barbara, CA: Praeger Publishers, 1996.

McSherry, Bernadette, "The Return of the Raging Hormones Theory: Premenstrual Syndrome, Postpartum Disorders and Criminal Responsibility," *Sydney Law Review,* 15 Sydney L. Rev. 1993.

Meadows, Donella H., Dennis L. Meadows, Jorgen Randers, William W. Behrens III, *The Limits to Growth: A Report for the*

Club of Rome's Project on the Predicament of Mankind, New York, NY: Signet, 1972.

Means, Cyril "The Phoenix of Abortional Freedom", 17 N.Y.L.F. 335, 1971.

Means, Cyril, "The Law of New York Concerning Abortion and the Status of the Foetus," 1664-1968, 14 N.Y.L.F. 411, 1968.

Meehan, Mary, "Justice Blackmun and the Little People," *Human Life Review*, Summer 2004.

Melchior, Jillian Kay, "Abortion's Underside (Kermit Gosnell is not the only seedy backroom abortionist operating in the age of Roe v. Wade)" *National Review Online*, May 8, 2013.

Milton, John, *Paradise Lost,* London, UK: Peter Parker printer, 1667.

Minogue, Kenneth, "The Goddess That Failed (Marxism and Feminism)," *National Review*, Nov. 18, 1991 v43 n21.

Moore, Keith L. and Persaud, T.V.N., *Before We Are Born: Essentials of Embryology and Birth Defects*, 4th edition. Philadelphia, PA: W.B. Saunders Company, 1993.

Moore, Keith L., and Persaud T.V.N., *The Developing Human: Clinically Oriented Embryology,* Philadelphia, PA: W.B. Saunders Company, 1998.

Moore, Keith L., *Essentials of Human Embryology*, Toronto: B.C. Decker Inc., 1988.

Mosher, Steven W. "Forced Abortions and Infanticide in Communist China," *The Reach of Roe*, Ann Conlon (editor) published by New York, NY: *Human Life Review*, 2012.

Mosher, Steven W., *Population Control: Real Costs, Illusory Benefits*, Transaction Publishers, 2008.

Murki, S, and Subramanian, S., "Sucrose for analgesia in newborn infants undergoing painful procedures: RHL commentary" (last revised: 1 June, 2011). *The WHO Reproductive Health Library*; Geneva: World Health Organization.

Murray, Frank J., "Daschle bill may not ban anything; Abortionists could use own judgment," *Washington Times*, May 15, 1997.

Myers, Steven Lee, "Doctor Describes Death of a Girl Who Suffered Botched Abortion", *New York Times*, December 5, 1991.

Napolitano, Judge Andrew, "Abortion and Rape" *Town Hall*, August 23, 2012.

National Geographic, *"The Biology of Prenatal Development,"* 2006.

National Review, Editors, "Gosnell Is Not an Aberration," May 13, 2013.

NARAL Press Release, "Roe V. Wade Faces Renewed Assault In House," July 20, 2000.

Nathanson, Bernard, *Aborting America*, New York, NY: Doubleday, 1981.

Nathanson, Bernard, *The Hand of God*, Washington, DC: Regnery Publishing, Inc., 1996.

Nuland, Sherwin B., *The Doctors' Plague: Germs, Childbed Fever, and the Strange Story of Ignaz Semmelweis*, New York, NY: W. W. Norton & Company, 2004.

Neuhaus, Richard John, *American Babylon: Notes of a Christian Exile*, New York, NY: Basic Books, 2009.

Neuhaus, Richard John, "The Return of Eugenics", *Commentary*, April, 1988.

Neuhaus, Richard John, Forward to Stetson, Brad, ed., *The Silent Subject*, Santa Barbara, CA: Praeger Publishers, 1996.

Newton, John Rector of St. Mary Woolnoth, "Thoughts Upon the African Slave Trade," 1788.

Newman, Richard, *Alma Rosé, Vienna to Auschwitz*, Cambridge, UK: Amadeus Press, 2003.

Nietzsche, Friedrich, *Beyond Good and Evil*, Leipzig: 1886.

Ng, David, "Hitler statue...causes a stir," Los Angeles *Times*, December 31, 2012.

Notice from Ohio Department of Health to Capital Care Network re: license number 0763AS, April 4, 2012.

"House Votes To Protect Aborted Fetus 'Born Alive,'" *New York Times*, March 13, 2002.

Olasky, Marvin, *Abortion Rites: A Social History of Abortion in America*, Wheaton, IL: Crossway, 1992.

Olasky, Marvin, "The Most Influential Philosopher Alive," Townhall.com, December 2, 2004.

Olivares Grace, dissent from the report of the *Rockefeller Commission on Population Growth and the American Future*, 1972.

O'Rahilly, Ronan and Fabiola Müller, *Human Embryology & Teratology*, 2nd ed., New York, NY: Wiley-Liss, 1996.

"Abortion Doctor Blamed For 1-armed Girl Sentenced", Orlando *Sentinel*, June 15, 1993.

Oveyssi, Natalie, "The Short Life and Eugenic Death of Baby John Bollinger" *Psychology Today*, Oct. 12, 2015.

Paley, Willam, *Natural Theology, or Evidences of the Existence and Attributes of the Deity collected from the Appearances of Nature*, Philadelphia, PA: John Morgan, 1802.

Papyri Oxyrhynchus IV, 744.

Patten, Bradley M., *Foundations of Embryology*, New York, NY: McGraw-Hill, 1964.

Parker, Theodore, "The New Crime Against Humanity", a sermon preached at the Music Hall in Boston, on Sunday, June 4, 1854, *The Collected Works of Theodore Parker*, (Discourses of Slavery, Vol. 2), London, UK: Trubner & Co., 1864.

Patel, Tulsi, *Sex-selective Abortion in India*, New Delhi/Washington, DC: Sage Publications Pvt. Ltd., 2006.

Patel, Tulsi, "Eliminating the Female Foetus" *Sex-selective Abortion in India*, New Delhi/Washington, DC: Sage Publications Pvt. Ltd., 2006.

Percival, Thomas, *Works, Literary, Moral, And Medical*, London, UK: J. Johnson, St. Paul's Church-yard, 1807.

Perez-Pena, Richard, "Doctor Said to Raise Price Mid-Abortion", *New York Times*, January 30, 1993.

Pernick, Martin S., *The Black Stork: Eugenics and the Death of "Defective" Babies in American Medicine and Motion Pictures since 1915*, London, UK: Oxford University Press, 1999.

Philo Judeaus *Special Laws* translated by Charles Duke Yonge.

Planned Parenthood *Publication, Plan Your Children,* 1963.

Plato, *Republic,* translated by Paul Shorey, Cambridge, MA: Harvard University Press, 1969.

Podhoretz, Norman, *The Prophets: Who They Were, What They Are*, New York, NY: Free Press, 2010.

Popenoe, Paul, "Eugenic Sterilization", *Birth Control Review*, Vol. XVII No. 4, April 1933.

Popenoe, Paul & Roswell Hill Johnson, *Applied Eugenics,* New York, NY: Macmillan, 1918.

Ponnuru, Ramesh, *The Party of Death: The Democrats, the Media, the Courts, and the Disregard for Human Life*, Washington, DC: Regnery Publishing, 2006.

Powell, John Joseph, *Abortion, the Silent Holocaust*, Allen, TX: Tabor Publishing, 1981.

ProLiving - a Disability perspective on euthanasia and physician-assisted suicide, November 8, 2011, http://proliving.blogspot.com

Prosser, William L., *Handbook of the Law of Torts*, St. Paul, MN: West Academic Publishing, 1971.

Prosser, William L., Page Keeton, *Prosser and Keeton on Torts*, St. Paul, MN: West Academic Publishing, 1955.

Quinn, William W., Colonel, G.S.C., forward to Ray Merriam, *Dachau*, Bennington, VT: Merriam Press, 1988.

Rachels James, "Egoism and Moral Skepticism" *A New Introduction to Philosophy*, Steven M. Cahn, ed. New York, NY: Harper & Row, 1971.

Rahe, Paul Anthony, *Soft Despotism, Democracy's Drift: Montesquieu, Rousseau, Tocqueville, and the Modern Prospect*, New Haven, CT: Yale University Press, 2000.

Rafferty, Philip, *Roe v. Wade: Unraveling the Fabric of America*, Mustang, OK: Tate Publishing, 2013.

Rafferty, Philip, *What's Really Going On With Pro-Roe v. Wade Catholic Politicians*, Mustang, OK: Tate Publishing, 2011.

Ramsey Colloquium, "The Inhuman Use of Human Beings," *A Statement on Embryo Research, First Things*, January, 1995.

David C. Reardon, "Women Who Abort" Stetson, *The Silent Subject*, Santa Barbara, CA: Praeger Publishers, 1996.

Reist, Melinda Tankard, *Defiant Birth: Women who Resist Medical Eugenics,* N. Melbourne, Vic. Australia: Spinifex Press, 2006.

Report of County Investigating Grand Jury XXIII, First Judicial District Of Pennsylvania Criminal Trial Division, (Kermit Gosnell Grand Jury Report), R. Seth Williams, District Attorney, January, 2011.

Rice, Charles E., *Beyond Abortion: The Theory and Practice of the Secular State*, Franciscan Herald Press, 1979.

Riddle, John, *Contraception and Abortion from the Ancient World to the Renaissance*, Cambridge, MA: Harvard University Press, 1994.

Robie, Theodore Russell, M.D., "Towards Race Betterment," *Birth Control Review*, Vol. XVII No. 4, April 1933.

Roden, Gregory J., "Unborn Persons, Incrementalism & the Silence of the Lambs," (*Human Life Review*, Fall 2007).

Rogers, Dale Evans, *Angel Unaware*, Grand Rapids, MI: Fleming H. Revell Company, 1953.

Rose, Mark, "Ashkelon's Dead Babies", *Archeology,* Newsbriefs, Archaeological Institute of America, Volume 50, Number 2, March/April 1997.

Rosner, Andrew, Remarks to the 89th Infantry Division on April 23, 1995.

Rüdin, Ernst, M.D., "Eugenic Sterilization: An Urgent Need", *Birth Control Review*, Vol. XVII No. 4, April 1933.

Rüdin, Ernst, M.D., "Aufgaben and Ziele der Deutschen Gesellschaft fur Rassenhygiene," *Archiv Fur Rassen- und Gesellschafts- biologie* 28 (1934): 228-29).

Russell, Josiah Cox, *Late Ancient and Medieval Population*, Philadelphia PA: American Philosophical Society, 1958.

Saltzman,Wendy, "Delaware abortion clinic facing charges of unsafe and unsanitary conditions," 6ABC Action News Philadelphia, PA. April 10, 2013

Sanger, Margaret, "A Plan for Peace", *Birth Control Review*, April, 1932.

Sanger, Margaret, *The Pivot of Civilization*, New York, NY: Brentanos, 1922.

Sanger, Margaret, *Margaret Sanger: An Autobiography*, New York, NY: W.W. Norton and Company, 1938.

Santayana, George, *The Life of Reason, Vol. 1*, Amherst, NY: Promethius Books.

Scammell, Michael, "The Price of an Idea: Where, when, and why 85 million people died," *The New Republic*; 12/20/99, Vol. 221 Issue 25, p. 32.

Scruton, Roger, *Modern Culture*, New York, NY: Continuum Press, 2006.

Senate Committee on the Judiciary, Testimony of Sandra Cano (The former Doe of Doe v. Bolton), June 23, 2005.

Semmelweis, Ignatz, *The Aetiology, the Concept, and the Prophylaxis of Childbed Fever*, 1861.

Sexton, Anne, "The Abortion" *The Complete Poems: Anne Sexton*, New York, NY: First Mariner Books, 1999.

Shafer, Brenda Pratt, R.N., testimony to the Committee on the Judiciary, U.S. House of Representatives, March 21, 1996.

Sibylline Oracles, tr. Milton S. Terry.

Singer, Peter, "Making Our Own Competency Should Be Paramount Decisions about Death", Free Inquiry, August/September 2005.

Singer, Peter, interview with *The Independent*, September 11, 2006.

Singer, Peter, "The Sanctity of Life," *Foreign Policy*, August 30, 2005.

Singer, Peter, *Practical Ethics*, 2nd ed. New York, NY: Cambridge University Press, 1993.

Sleebos, Joëlle E., "Low Fertility Rates in OECD Countries: Facts and Policy Responses," OECD Social, Employment and Migration Working Papers, No. 15 October 7, 2003.

Slobodzian, Joseph A., "Gosnell guilty of three murder counts" *The Philadelphia Inquirer*, May 13, 2013.

Smith, Marcus J., *Dachau, The Harrowing of Hell,* Albany, NY: State University of New York Press, 1995.

Smith, Wesley J., *The Culture of Death: The Assault on Medical Ethics in America*, New York, NY: Encounter Books, 2000.

Snicket, Lemony, (Daniel Handler) *A Series of Unfortunate Events #7: The Vile Village*, New York, NY: Harper Collins, 2001.

Snopes.com, April 12, 2013.

Snyder, Timothy, *Bloodlands: Europe Between Hitler and Stalin*, New York, NY: Basic Books, 2010.

Soames, Christopher, "Tired and Weary, He Battled On", A Speech To The Sir Winston S. Churchill Society Of Edmonton, Alberta, 1979.

Solomon, Deborah, "The Way We Live Now," The New York *Times Magazine*, April 12, 2002.

Somashekhar, Sandhya, Lena H. Sun, and Alice Crites, "Antiabortion group releases videos of clinic workers discussing live births", *Washington Post*, April 29, 2013.

Soranus, *Gynecology,* tr., Owsei Temkin, Baltimore, MD: Johns Hopkins University Press, 1991.

Sowell, Thomas, *The Economics and Politics of Race,* (New York, NY: William Morrow, 1983, 1985.

Stanek, Jill L., R.N., Testimony on HR 1797, Pain-Capable Unborn Child Protection Act, May 23, 2013.

Stark, Rodney *The Triumph of Christianity*, New York, NY: Harper Collins, 2011.

Stark, Rodney, *The Rise of Christianity*, New York, NY: Harper Collins, 1997.

Steinhauer, Jennifer, "House Rejects Bill to Ban Sex-Selective Abortions," *The New York Times*, May 31, 2012.

Steyn, Mark, "Fourth-Trimester Abortion," National Review Online September 13, 2011.

Steyn, Mark "The Collapsing of the American Skull" *National Review Online*, April 26, 2013.

Staff Report, "Abortion provider in Cuyahoga Falls being shut down", *Akron Beacon Journal*, April 24, 2013.

Stetson, Brad, ed., *The Silent Subject*, Santa Barbara, CA: Praeger Publishers, 1996.

Stove, David, *Darwinian Fairytales: Selfish Genes, Errors of Heredity and Other Fables of Evolution*, New York, NY: Encounter Books, 2007.

Tacitus, Publius Cornelius, *The Histories*, (tr. Church and Brodribb, 1864).

Taylor, Paul, *Respect for Nature: A Theory of Environmental Ethics*, Princeton, NJ: Princeton University Press, 1968.

Tertullianus, Quintus Septimius Florens, A *Treatise on the Soul.*

Thompson, Dorothy, "The Lesson of Dachau," *Ladies Home Journal*, September 1945.

Tone, Andrea, *Devices and Desires: A History of Contraceptives in America*, New York, NY: Hill and Wang, 2002.

Tismaneanu, Vladimir, *The Devil in History: Communism, Fascism, and Some Lessons of the Twentieth Century*, Berkeley, CA: University of California Press, 2012.

United Nations Convention on the Rights of the Child, 1989.

UPI, "Judge rules Mississippi's only abortion clinic stays open for now" UPI.com, April 16, 2013.

U.S. Congress, Hearing before The Subcommittee On The Constitution of the Committee On The Judiciary House Of Representatives, 107th Congress, 1st session.

Van Wagenen, Bleeker, "Preliminary Report of the Committee of the Eugenic Section of the American Breeder's Association to Study and to Report on the Best Practical Means for Cutting Off the Defective Germ-Plasm in the Human Population," Eugenics Education Society, London, 1912. *College of Law Faculty Publications*, Georgia State University Archive, Paper 74.

van der Lee, Marije L. Johanna G. van der Bom, Nikkie B. Swarte, A. Peter M. Heintz, Alexander de Graeff and Jan van den Bout, "Euthanasia and Depression: A Prospective Cohort Study Among Terminally Ill Cancer Patients," *Journal of Clinical Oncology*, September 20, 2005.

Verhagen, E., Sol JJ, Brouwer OF, and Sauer PJ. "Deliberate termination of life in newborns in The Netherlands; review of all 22 reported cases between 1997 and 2004," Academisch Ziekenhuis, Beatrix Kinderkliniek, Postbus 30.001, 9700 RB Groningen. e.verhagen@bkk.azg.nl.

Eduard Verhagen, M.D., J.D., and Pieter J.J. Sauer, M.D., Ph.D., "The Groningen Protocol — Euthanasia in Severely Ill Newborns" The *New England Journal of Medicine*, March 10, 2005.

Vink, Michelle, "Abortion and Birth Control in Canton, China" *Wall Street Journal*, November 30, 1981.

Vishwanath, L.S., "Efforts of Colonial State to Suppress Female Infanticide" *Economic and Political Weekly*, 33, (19) May 9, 1998.

Vlahos, Olivia, "Sex and Consequences: An Anthropological View," *The Silent Subject*, Brad Stetson ed. Santa Barbara, CA: Praeger Publishers, 1996.

Visaria, Leela, "Deficit of Girls", *Sex-selective Abortion in India*, Tulsi Patel (ed.)

Vogt William, Stuart I. Freeman, *The Road to Survival*, William Sloane Associates, 1948.

von Logau, Friedrich, "Retribution", *Deutscher Sinngedichte drei Tausend*, 1654.

von Frank, Albert J., *The Trials of Anthony Burns*, Cambridge, MA: Harvard University Press, 1999.

Waddey, John, *Euthanasia: "Good Death" or Selective Killing?*, 1978.

Warren, Mary Anne, "On the Moral and Legal Status of Abortion", 1982, Postscript on Infanticide, *Biomedical Ethics*, 4th ed. T.A. Mappes and D. DeGrazia, eds. New York: McGraw-Hill, Inc. 1996.

White, Justice Byron V., "Dissent: Roe v. wade and Doe v. Bolton" January 22, 1973.

Whitney, E.A., M.D., "Selective Sterilization" *Birth Control Review*, Vol. XVII No. 4, April 1933.

Wiesel, Elie, *From The Kingdom of Memory: Reminiscences*, Summit Books, 1990.

Wiesel, Elie, *Comprehending the Holocaust: Historical and Literary Research*, Asher Cohen, Joav Gelber, and Charlotte Wardi, eds., Strochlitz Institute of Holocaust Studies.

Wiesel, Elie, Nobel Acceptance Speech, December 10, 1986.

Willke, Barbara, Willke, Jack, *Handbook on Abortion*, Hayes Publishing, 1979.

Williams, Walter, "Understanding Liberals and Progressives" *TownHall*, June 5, 2013.

Williamson, Chilton, Jr., "The Coming Inhumanity," *The Reach of Row*, New York, NY: Human Life Foundation, 2013.

Wilson, James, "Of the Natural Rights of Individuals," 1790.

Wren, Christopher S., "China's Birth Goals Meet Regional Resistance," Special to the *New York Times*, May 15, 1982.

Zubrin, Robert, "The Population Control Holocaust", *The New Atlantis*, Spring 2012.

Zubrin, Robert, *Merchants of Despair: Radical Environmentalists, Criminal Pseudo-Scientists, and the Fatal Cult of Antihumanism*, Encounter Books, 2012.

Index

www.ingramcontent.com/pod-product-compliance
Lightning Source LLC
Chambersburg PA
CBHW072033280526
45788CB00006B/2096